The Politics of Corruption in Contemporary China

The Politics of Corruption in Contemporary China

An Analysis of Policy Outcomes

TING GONG

PRAEGER

Westport, Connecticut
London

Library of Congress Cataloging-in-Publication Data

Kung, T' ing.
The politics of corruption in contemporary China : an analysis of policy outcomes / Ting Gong.
p. cm.
Includes bibliographical references and index.
ISBN 0-275-94689-4 (alk. paper)
1. Political corruption—China. 2. China—Economic conditions—1976- 3. China—Social conditions—1976- I. Title.
JQ1509.5.C6K8 1994
320.951—dc20 93-24829

British Library Cataloguing in Publication Data is available.

Library of Congress Catalog Card Number: 93-24829
ISBN: 0-275-94689-4

First published in 1994

Praeger Publishers, 88 Post Road West, Westport, CT 06881
An imprint of Greenwood Publishing Group, Inc.

Printed in the United States of America

The paper used in this book complies with the Permanent Paper Standard issued by the National Information Standards Organization (Z39.48-1984).

10 9 8 7 6 5 4 3

To my parents

Contents

Tables and Figures

TABLES

FIGURES

Preface

When I returned to China in the summer of 1990 for the first time since I left the country four years before, I was amazed by the economic changes taking place there: brisk markets with unstable prices, people freely talking about making money, and the prevalence of "gray incomes" associated with second vocations. However, complaints continued to emerge at the interface of these changes. I was told numerous stories in vivid tones about how reform measures enabled government officials to obtain personal gain. It appeared puzzling to me why people were on the one hand enjoying the fruits of reform while, on the other hand, blaming reform for corruption. This stimulated my interest in understanding corruption.

Returning to the campus, I started to survey literature on corruption in general and on China's corruption in particular. I was quite disappointed to find that there was a general shortage of studies on corruption in socialist countries—not a single book, in English or Chinese, dealt exclusively with China's corruption, while the existing corruption literature lost much of its insight when applied to China. I therefore saw the need for a chronological account of what had happened in China in terms of corruption, and also felt the necessity to develop a new approach beyond those conventional ones to analyze China's corruption issue.

From this unhappy discovery emerged my original plan to write something on this topic, which eventually led to this book. For the same reason, this book project has set forth as its dual goals to (1) present fresh source materials on China's corruption based on corruption cases and related statistics from China which may not be accessible to English-language scholars; and to (2) provide explanations for China's corruption problem from a new perspective.

To my good fortune, when I embarked on this book project, China was undertaking one of the largest anti-corruption campaigns in its post-1949 history, the Economic Rectification. A great number of fresh cases accordingly became available. I was therefore able to incorporate into this volume previously undiscovered or underexplored primary evidence published in Chinese, the language I read most easily.

This book results from several years of research, interviews, and discussions. It would never have taken shape without the generous support and guidance of numerous individuals. My most fundamental scholarly debt is to John D. Nagle and Lily H. M. Ling. They encouraged me to think about the nearly "unthinkable" project of writing a book on corruption at the earliest stage of my research. They also provided detailed and provocative comments throughout the whole writing process. I am also especially grateful to David Rosenbloom, Andrew Nathan, Ben Stavis, Michael Johnston, Marwyn Samuels, Edwin Bock, Kristi Andersen, Naeem Inayatullah, Mab Huang, and Freddie Robles, Jr. This book would have been much weaker without their suggestions at different stages of this project. I owe special thanks to my Chinese friends who provided valuable insights and materials about China's corruption: Wang Huning, Yang Shuying, Chen Baoping, Yang Xiaoxun, and many others who choose to retain their anonymity.

Colleagues and students at Ramapo College of New Jersey, where I teach, helped in different ways to facilitate and stimulate my progress on the book. Without the patience and efficiency of the staff of the library at Ramapo College, it would have been impossible for me to do research during the busy teaching years. I would like to express my heartfelt appreciation to Mr. Charles Jorgensen and Mr. William Briggs, who edited some sections of the manuscript. I also thank James Dunton, Jude Grant, and David Baker at Greenwood Publishing Group, Inc. for their help in seeing the book through publication. Finally, an immeasurable degree of thanks goes to Feng Chen, who has provided me with excellent comments and the greatest support. This work is a reflection of our close intellectual and personal partnership.

The American Association of University Women (AAUW) and the Roscoe Martin Fund of the Maxwell School, Syracuse University, provided me with grants which defrayed some of my research expenses.

I alone, of course, bear responsibility for any errors and shortcomings that may be contained herein.

The book is dedicated to my parents, who supported me in my studies abroad and instilled in me a love of my country.

Abbreviations

APCs	Agricultural production cooperatives
BKWZ	*Baokan Wenzhai* (Shanghai)
CCP	Chinese Communist Party
CD	*China Daily* (Beijing)
CPPC	Chinese People's Political Consultative Conference
CR	Cultural Revolution
CTW	*China Times Weekly* (Taiwan)
CW	Collected Works
DBRB	*Dongbei Ribao* (Northeast China)
FBIS	ForeignBroadcastingInformationService-DailyReport-China
FYP	Five Years Plan
FZRB	*Fazhi Ribao* (Beijing)
GLF	Great Leap Forward
GMRB	*Guangming Ribao* (Beijing)
JFRB	*Jiefang Ribao* (Shanghai)
KMT	Kuomintang
LHRB	*Lianhe Ribao* (Taiwan)
LW	*Liao Wang* (Beijing)
MB	*Ming Bao* (Hong Kong)
MOS	Ministry of Supervision
NFRB	*Nanfang Ribao* (Guangzhou)
OM	*Open Magazine* (Hong Kong)
PLA	People's Liberation Army
PRC	People's Republic of China
QS	*Qiushi* (Beijing)
RMRB	*People's Daily*
RMSC	*Renmin Shouche* (Beijing)
SCMP	*Survey of the China Mainland Press* (U.S. Consulate-General, Hong Kong)

SPC	Supreme People's Court
SPP	Supreme People's Procuratorate
SW	Selected Works
SYRB	*Shuiyuan Ribao* (Northeast China)
TJRB	*Tianjin Ribao* (Tianjin)
WEH	*World Economic Herald* (Shanghai)
WHB	*Wenhui Bao* (Shanghai)
XCGZTX	*Xuanchuan Gongzuo Tongxun* (Shanghai)
XHYB	*Xinhua Yuebao* (Beijing)
XMWB	*Xinmin Wanbao* (Shanghai)
XX	*Xuexi* (Beijing)
ZM	*Zhengming* (Hong Kong)
ZGFZB	*Zhongguo Fazhibao* (Beijing)

Introduction

Corruption means different things to different people. To some, it is individual moral degeneration; to others, it is a reflection of particular social structures; to still others, it is a cultural heritage. However, all these efforts at attribution are too general and malleable to specify the causes of corruption. Causes abound. The nature of corruption differs across societies and changes over time even within the same society. Thus an in-depth study of the contextual meanings, causes, and effects of corruption may serve us better in understanding corruption than any attempts at generalization.

This book addresses the problem of bureaucratic corruption that plagues China now as it has since ancient time. China becomes the focus of this study not because it is particularly prone to corruption. All societies, whether socialist or capitalist, developed or underdeveloped, religious or secular, are subject to corruption. However, China is unique in its ways of understanding, identifying, and combatting bureaucratic corruption. China is a socialist country with a long history of bureaucratic culture. The Chinese Communist Party (CCP) has put some constraints on the bureaucracy since assuming power because of the party's utopian idea of an egalitarian society. Yet, on the other hand, the party continued to rely on the bureaucracy to manage the centrally planned and hierarchically ordered economy. Administrative power and associated privileges virtually turned the bureaucracy into a powerful social class. The existence and development of corruption in China appear to be well connected with this bureaucratic Leviathan.

It is also interesting to note that no country in the world has engaged in so many nationwide anti-corruption campaigns as China. Immediately after the communist takeover in 1949, the CCP launched the Three-Anti's Campaign (1951) to eliminate the so-called three evils: corruption, waste, and bureaucratism. The campaign was immediately followed by the Five Anti's movement (1952) against bribery, theft of state property, theft of state secrets, cheating on contracts, and tax evasion. During the Socialist Education Movement (1963–1965), the whole country was once again immersed in a nationwide whistle-blowing exercise. The most drastic purge of the state apparatus took place during the Cultural Revolution, which was, to some extent, motivated by Mao Zedong's extreme worry about an inept and corrupt bureaucracy. In the late 1980s a new anti-corruption campaign (1988–1991) was in progress to redress the corruption problem which seemed more serious during the reform than before. Despite all these efforts, however, corruption as a social problem has never stopped plaguing Chinese society.

The wonder is how and, more importantly, why.

THREE TYPES OF POLICIES

To explore answers, this book relates the problem of corruption to China's political processes and the CCP's corresponding policies in the post-1949 period. It places the issue within a broad political context to see how corruption has been fashioned by "politics." More specifically, this study examines three types of policies.

General Policy

The first set of policies examined in the book is the CCP's three general policies in the post-1949 period: transformation, consolidation, and modernization.[1] The general policies set the direction for each phase of the party's social reconstruction and direct various political and economic programs. In the early 1950s the party set "transformation" as its general policy, aiming at quick economic recovery, full political control over society, and complete restoration of social order. After it had achieved remarkable successes in the first years of the People's Republic, the CCP relocated its focus of work after 1953 from transformation (i.e., destruction of the "old society") to consolidation (i.e., economic and administrative construction of a new society). A third intentional shift in general policy took place right after the Cultural Revolution, as the party committed itself to the four modernizations in 1978, a program designed not only to boost the economy but also to restore the party's own legitimacy.[2]

Organizational Policy

Organizational policies epitomize the general policies with regard to state institutions and cadre corps. During the transformation period, the CCP's organizational policies demonstrated a transitional tendency. Without enough personnel of its own, the CCP frequently employed the method of mass mobilization to accomplish its tasks. It also relied on government personnel and factory managers retained from the Kuomintang (KMT) regime to sustain normal production of the "new society." Accordingly, the building of a strong, professional, and loyal administrative apparatus became the focus of the party's organizational policies in the subsequent consolidation period. Efforts were directed at professionalizing, centralizing, and rationalizing the state apparatus. Lastly, during the modernization period, the CCP's organizational policies highlighted the party's determination to accommodate its cadre ranks to the four-modernization program. The party's organizational policies in this period included institutional differentiation, managerial decentralization, and a series of efforts to reform the cadre system.

Anti-corruption Policy

In each of the three phases mentioned above, the party had distinctly different policies toward corruption in terms of problem identification, campaign targets, and reform measures. But they all embodied the party's general policies and particularly its organizational policies. The Three and Five Anti's Campaign had a clear-cut focus on capitalists as the campaign targets, based on the party's perception of capitalist influence as a threat to the new-born regime. The Socialist Education Movement was principally based on Mao's illusion of a growing bourgeoisie within the party due to the bureaucratization of the cadre corps. During the Rectification Campaign, the party became less tolerant of corruption because it not only jeopardized the modernization program but also shook the party's political legitimacy.

QUESTIONS AND HYPOTHESES

Policy studies may center on origins of policy, policy-making processes, or policy outcomes. This study is particularly interested in policy outcomes: What are the outcomes of the aforementioned policies adopted by the CCP and, particularly, their impact on bureaucratic behavior? Do all the policy outcomes result from the actor's intention? If not, why do intended policies generate unintended consequences? Under what circumstances do unintended consequences tend to occur?

Given the CCP's ultimate political goal (i.e., to build a socialist China), these policies are its "rational" choices under certain circumstances. The three general policies (transformation, consolidation, and modernization) are necessary subsequent steps for a party that successfully seized power in a backward country. Ever since the birth of the People's Republic, the CCP has faced two simultaneous problems: it must transform society to secure and consolidate socialist control while at the same time promoting economic development to modernize the country (Lowenthal, 1970). These two tasks further determine the basic content of the party's organizational policies: the party must constantly reconcile the need for a professional bureaucracy as a tool to manage society with the need to keep the bureaucracy politically loyal to itself. Because of this dilemma, the party's penchant for political campaigns against bureaucratic corruption becomes understandable, though the content of the campaign varies.

However, behind these "rational" policies lie some problems which have troubled the CCP ever since it assumed power. They have not only affected the effectiveness of the party's daily policy performance, but also generated unintended policy consequences which counteract the party's original attempts. Among the most noteworthy are three contradictions and their connections with three institutional features of the CCP's rulership.

First, *the party's ideological affiliation conflicts with its practical needs.* As we mentioned before, the CCP has confronted the dilemma of political consolidation versus economic modernization ever since 1949. Though the two goals have often been at odds with each other (see Lowenthal, 1970; Sakwa, 1991), they are identical in one thing: that is, both require a strong state apparatus as the instrument of social control or management. This need has resulted in an institutional feature of CCP rule which contradicts its Marxist-Leninist roots: in the process of demystifying the professional monopoly of a bourgeois bureaucracy, bureaucratic socialism emerged with an ever larger and more hierarchical state apparatus. Nevertheless, given the monopoly nature of the party leadership, this bureaucratic apparatus has largely developed in line with the party organization. This then leads to a second contradiction of CCP rulership. That is, *the party's role as a political organization conflicts with its role as an administrative institution.*

A vanguard party, the CCP is supposedly built upon a set of Leninist principles—tightly organized, well disciplined, and dedicated to the revolution above all (Nagle, 1989). It emerged during the ordeal of wars and was chiefly composed of professional revolutionaries. Such a political group was nevertheless confronted with the responsibility for economic management after achieving power. To fulfill the task, the CCP has carried out purposive programs to transform itself from a purely revolutionary organization into an administrative institution. No matter these programs were successful or not, the party's dual role as both a political organization and a leading administrative organ resulted in a second institutional feature of the party's rule: tremendous economic and administrative powers are given to party cadres who are already laden with political privileges.

A third contradiction is that *the party's political goals conflict with its ability to implement them*. The CCP is highly capable of policy formulation, but it lacks a commensurable ability to implement policy. This is, first of all, because China's huge bureaucratic structure makes it extremely difficult for the party leadership to monitor every stage of policy implementation. Moreover, within the centralized and hierarchically organized bureaucracy, feedback is slow and information can be easily distorted. Thus, as Lampton (1987:8) correctly points out, as a result of the party's simplistic performance indicators and its multiple performance objectives, subordinate units and localities are able to emphasize a few objectives while ignoring others. Policy implementation becomes "the most effective avenue by which individuals, localities, and organizations express their interests and shape policy to fit the peculiarities of their situation." This is evident in a third institutional feature of the party's rule: the party and state bureaucracy becomes an elite group "in itself and for itself."[3]

Not surprisingly, the large-scale bureaucracy which combines political, economic, and administrative powers while enjoying autonomy in policy implementation, has become the major source of corruption in China. However, behind this phenomenon, which appears to be a truism to many, lies an even more important fact. That is, as this study argues, the bureaucracy and the corruption-conducive conditions associated with it are largely creations of the party itself intentionally and, to a larger extent, inadvertently. This study thus posits a paradoxical hypothesis: *the attempts of the CCP to transform society at the same time produce or reproduce certain political and economic relations conducive to corruption.*

PLAN OF THE STUDY

This book is divided into three parts. The first (Chapters 1–3) deals with theory. It surveys the major classical and contemporary theories on corruption and highlights the differences between this study's approach and the conventional ones. Chapter 1 reviews the various definitions of corruption. Chapter 2 deals with competing approaches in the analysis of bureaucratic corruption. These include the views of contemporary Western social scientists, classical Marxists, and Chinese ideologues. Chapter 3 comments on the methodological limitations of these theories, and the commentary further develops into a general introduction of this book's unique analytical model, the policy outcomes perspective.

The second part (Chapters 4–6) presents the history of corruption in China. Chapter 4 is a general description of how and why corruption appears to be a chronic problem for China, as seen in the cultural heritage and the CCP's wrestling with it before 1949. The following chapters present empirical findings on the two most important anti-corruption campaigns in China's post-

1949 history: the Three and Five Anti's Campaign in the 1950s (Chapter 5), and the Socialist Education Movement of the 1960s (Chapter 6). The third part of the book (Chapters 7–9) examines the corruption problem in China today. It pays particular attention to the relationship between the reform and corruption, a topic of interest to many scholars. Chapter 7 describes the CCP's general policy in the reform period and its organizational corollaries. How these policies generated unintended consequences, which in turn affected the patterns of corruption, is explored in Chapter 8. Chapter 9 provides a detailed analysis of the overt and hidden agenda and the process of the latest anti-corruption campaign, the Rectification Movement in the late 1980s. Finally, the conclusion (Chapter 10) summarizes the major findings of the study and delineates their broader implications for the study of corruption.

NOTE ON METHODS AND SOURCES

For data, this study concentrates on corruption cases reported by the *People's Daily* (RMRB) during anti-corruption campaigns. Though this does not exclude other sources, this study believes that the *People's Daily* is the most important source for understanding CCP policies. The *People's Daily* is the CCP's official newspaper, with which other newspapers have to conform. Sampling methods scarcely make sense in China, where the mass media show identical reporting patterns.

People may question the reliability of the data by asking how much serious coverage could be given to corruption in a communist country such as China. However, one should note that corruption in China has always been associated with "bourgeois liberalism." It is never treated as a social malady related to the socialist system. In other words, corruption is not taken as indigenous to socialist China but as imported from the capitalist system. The Chinese press, accordingly, is not hesitant to expose corruption cases. There seems no reason for the press to hide corruption cases since corruption is the fault of capitalism. Comments and analyses on the cases may be biased, but the cases themselves are still illustrative.

Moreover, this study uses the cases only to illustrate how the CCP has perceived, conceptualized, and identified corruption. It makes no attempt to use the cases as measurements of the exact degree of China's corruption (i.e., how serious corruption is). This reduces the risk of data spuriousness, since it is unnecessary for the party to conceal its perceptions and conceptualizations of corruption.

NOTES

1. The three tasks were originally identified by Kenneth Jowitt (1974) in his analysis of how the political culture of a Marxist-Leninist regime shaped its organizational character.

2. My study does not include the Cultural Revolution of 1966–1976, an abnormal period of post-1949 Chinese history. Although there were several attempts at opposing corruption during the Cultural Revolution (e.g., the Campaign of Cleaning Class Ranks and the One Anti and Three-Opposing Movement), data for these campaigns are hardly reliable given the chaotic situation during the period.

3. To a great extent, this explains why in today's China corruption tends to occur more in policy implementation processes than in legislative and electoral processes. In China, where there are no independent legislature and judiciary, the executive power is unchecked or, we can say, the real power resides in the party-state bureaucracy.

Part I

THEORY

1

Rethinking the Definition of Corruption

The term "corruption" has been widely used in the mass media, government reports, and daily conversations. But defining corruption has proven difficult for social scientists. Numerous efforts have been made, but little consensus exists on what is corruption. Even less agreement has been reached on the inquiries into whether all societies are the same in exhibiting corruption, why some societies or sectors are more prone to corruption than others, and why certain behavior qualifies as corruption in one place or period but not in another.

CONCEPTS OF CORRUPTION IN HISTORY

This is not because corruption is a new problem. Instead, the origin of corruption as a theoretical notion can be traced back to the founding fathers of Western political thought such as Thucydides, Plato, and Aristotle. The classical notion regarded corruption as a general disease of the body politic, a definition somewhat different from that of today. Plato viewed all government systems where sectional interests prevailed as corruption. In *The Republic*, he designed an ideal polity free of corruption (Hamilton, 1957). Aristotle, following Plato's notion, described three types of bad polity as corruption: "there are three kinds of constitution, or an equal number of deviations, or, as it were, corruptions of these three kinds." (Barker, 1946:373). According to Aristotle, the "corrupted" constitutions served the interest of the rulers instead of being guided by the law. They were corrupt in the sense that they exploited the ruled.

The concept of "corruption" as a bad polity was carried on by and central to the political thought of Machiavelli, Montesquieu, and Rousseau (Friedrich, 1972). But the agent of corrupt behavior shifted from constitution or body politic to individuals. Corruption was an important notion in Machiavelli's discussion of the cycles of government in *The Discourses*, where he distinguished three good forms of government and their "corrupt" counterparts. The language he used to describe each form, however, applied to individuals within each form.[1] In the same vein as Machiavelli, Montesquieu attributed the decline of the Roman republic to its corrupted public ethic, resulting from the imperial enterprise of the Romans. Rousseau was also deeply concerned with the corruption of his time. For him, though, it was not the corruption of man which destroyed political systems but that of the political system which corrupted and destroyed man. Apparently, Rousseau would agree with Lord Acton's statement that all power tended to corrupt, because he believed that political corruption was an inevitable consequence of the struggle for power (see Friedrich, 1972:128).

Clearly, corruption, as traditionally conceived, is closely related to politics. Nevertheless, it is more concerned with the "failure of government" than with the transaction between power and wealth, which, as we will see, appears to be more important to the scholars of modern times.

DEFINITIONS IN CONTEMPORARY CORRUPTION LITERATURE

The fundamental difference between the classical notion of corruption and the modern one is that the former focuses on institutions whereas the latter is behaviorally oriented. With the rise of modern bureaucracy, the conceptualization of corruption has shifted since then from a broader one, that is, "institutional decay," to a more delineated one which defines corruption in terms of public officials' obtaining money for personal gain.

In defining corruption, recent political scientists have been fairly consistent with the Weberian ideal type of bureaucracy.[2] They have focused their attention on transactions between private and public sectors which illegitimately convert collective goods into private payoffs (Heidenheimer et al., 1989). Under this seemingly obvious consensus, however, no particular definition of corruption enjoys substantial agreement among social scientists. Sometimes a variety of terms, such as kleptocracy, graft, embezzlement, profiteering, misappropriation, fraud, and scandal, are used to describe bureaucratic malpractice of the same type. Often, corruption scholars come to different definitions having obviously different foci.[3] However, the dissension is much more a matter of different emphases than of substantial disputes. Some scholars focus on the *actor* involved in corrupt practices; some pay particular attention to the *motivation* behind a corrupt act; others emphasize the *norm* used to judge corruption; and still others define corruption primarily according to its *consequence*.

Actor

Many authors find the role of public office the most essential to the definition of corruption. Jacob van Klaveren discusses the Inca society and concludes that, by definition, corruption does not exist in the Inca and other systems based on pure patrimonial domination. "Corruption is built on the underlying principle that the people are subjected to the control of officials. Thus there exists a regulating principle, which gives to the officials . . . a public existence." (Klaveren, 1989:75). The definition of corruption thus developed has a clear focus on the "formal" role of a public official. It can be as broad as "a general term covering misuse of authority." (Bayley, 1989:936), which includes all forms of power abuse attached to a public office (Mydral, 1968). The definition of corruption can also be narrowed to refer only to violations of certain "formally" defined obligations of public office. Corrupt behavior, for example, is defined by Ekpo (1979:3) as "role behavior in political institutions which violates formally defined role obligations in favor of personal roles that are extra-organizational." The role of public office is certainly important for a better understanding of the nature of corruption. However, an overemphasis on the role of public office would foreclose discussion of corruption in pre-bureaucratic systems where there were no formal official roles. It may also lead to a confusion of corruption and maladministration such as arbitrariness, inefficiency, and incompetence. Both of them result from a failure of the role of public office while having different connotations.

Motivation

Some definitions mainly concern the motivation behind public misbehavior. From this viewpoint, the intention of making personal gains conveys the very connotation of corruption. Robert Brooks (1974:41-54) argues, for example, that corruption can be defined as "the *intentional* misperformance or neglect of a recognized duty, or the unwarranted exercise of power, with the *motives* of gaining some advantage more or less directly personal" (emphasis added). Gerald Caiden tries to distinguish the notion of corruption from that of illegality as he comments (1988:8), "If they do not personally gain then their misconduct may be illegal and wrong but not necessarily corrupt, as no *improper considerations* have induced the violation of duty" (emphasis added). By the same token, the "market-centered" definition, as classified by Heidenheimer (1970:3), stresses the importance of the motivation of "profit maximization," considering corruption only another means of actively seeking economic resources (Rose-Ackerman, 1975, 1978; Beenstock, 1979; and MacRae, 1982). The merit of this conceptualization lies in its distinction of purposive dereliction of duty for personal gain from other careless maladministrative behavior and its sensitivity to the rationality that underlies corruption. However, not all corrupt acts have a clear-cut intention of personal profiteering at the very beginning. Some corrupt officials become greedy only in the process of exchange. More importantly, it is usually quite difficult to detect one's motivation until certain results become clear.

Norm

Students of corruption also devote a great deal of effort to seeking objective criteria or norms by which to judge corruption. While legalists believe in legal norms, moralists appeal to values. But the legalist definition is said to be more "operational" than the moralist one, for "laws are relatively precise and consistent," or "generally clear-cut" (Lowenstein, 1985). A well-accepted definition is offered by J. S. Nye (1967:419) who defines corruption as "behavior which deviates from the *normal duties* of a public role because of private-regarding (personal, close family, private cliques) pecuniary or status gains; or violates *rules* against the exercise of certain types of private-regarding influence" (emphasis added). This definition places an obvious emphasis on the formal duties of public officials and public rules regulating public officials. Other scholars rely on public opinion as a criterion to assess official conduct. For them, "corruption" means what people think it means, and exists where they think it exists. To be corrupt or not depends on the weight of public opinion (Rundquist et al., 1979). For instance, Wraith and Simpkins (1963:45) suggest in their analysis of corruption in developing countries that "an act is presumably only corrupt if society condemns it as such and if the doer is afflicted in a sense of guilt when he does it." Another example is Heidenheimer's distinction of "black," "grey," and "white" corruption. According to Heidenheimer (1970:26-27), an act is "black" corruption when both public officials and the public consider it corruption and wish it to be punished. An act is "grey" corruption when either public officials or the people want it to be punished. And, finally, if an act is judged by both public officials and the public as corrupt but neither side wants it to be punished, the act can be called "white" corruption. The norm-focused conceptions have some problems, however. Moral or public norms are not only subject to change, but also prove to be diverse. An act may be considered "corrupt" in one society, but "normal" in another society or in the same society at different times (White, 1988). Even in a given society and at a given time, the question remains whose norm should be used, because public opinion in a complex society is far from homogeneous (Carino, 1986). As for legality-based norms, as critics (Berg and Hahn, 1976; Moodie, 1980; Etzioni, 1984; Williams, 1987) point out, powerful groups are always able to influence legislation and likely to do so to exempt themselves from charges of corruption. Besides, the legalist definitions neglect the situation where certain behavior is generally considered corruption but no legal precedent has been established for it. Thus, Peters and Welch (1978) comment that not all acts that break rules are corruption and corrupt acts are not all necessarily illegal.

Consequence

Given that public norms tend to be heterogeneous while legal norms may be manipulated by the politically powerful, some writers feel it tempting to define corruption in terms of its consequences instead of some pre-set standards. It is likely that an act may be prescribed by law as corrupt but be beneficial to the common good, such as "fixing" the papers of an illegal alien who contributed his labor and skills to a rapidly expanding economy (Peters and Welch, 1978). Such an act should not be regarded as corruption. Hence, corruption should not be defined in terms of how it subverts public interests or common good for private ends. Carl Friedrich (1966:74), for example, holds that "the pattern of corruption can be said to exist wherever a power holder . . . is . . . induced to take actions which favor whoever provides the rewards and thereby does damage to the public and its interests." On another occasion, he (1972:127) points out, "whether this was the motivation or not, it is the fact that private gain was secured at public expense that matters."

However, it is not always clear whether corruption is detrimental to society in all cases. A corrupt official who accepts a bribe is not directly inimical to the public until he takes further action. In addition, the presumption of the existence of a well-defined "public interest" or "common good" is elusive and open to broad interpretations. In many cases, consequently, the common good or public interest is regarded as synonymous with the creation or maintenance of a specific set of political arrangements and corruption is hence identified as behavior likely to undermine such arrangements (Williams, 1987:18). There is no consensus among social scientists as to what constitutes the public interest; even if they do agree on a definition, criteria to determine whether certain actions undermine it remain amorphous.

CORRUPTION CONCEPTUALIZATION IN CHINA

Corruption has not been systematically studied in China. There is no well-accepted definition of corruption in China's intellectual circles. Nor has the CCP clearly defined corruption in any official documents. Indeed, though everyone is aware of the existence of corruption in China, no one really knows its exact scope or nature. To some extent, the difficulty of defining "corruption" accounts for this problem.

Western conceptualizations of corruption become ineffective when applied to China. The actor- and norm-focused definitions are inappropriate for several reasons. First, duties for office holders are usually not clearly defined in China. In most cases, cadres' responsibilities are decided only by their immediate superiors. Thus, though the Constitution of the People's Republic of China provides people with the rights of criticism, compliance, appeal, charge, and damage claim against malpractice of bureaucrats,[4] there are no criteria by which to judge what is wrong. Second, Chinese laws against corruption are underdeveloped: they are neither specific nor comprehensive. Worse yet, laws are subject to change according to political circumstances. Political considerations play an important role in the making and implementation of laws. In many cases, "power" outweighs "law" and public officials can even openly defy laws.

The consequence-focused definitions do not avail much in China, either. This is because to identify public interests appears to be more subtle in China than in other places. The CCP has long been considered the representative of public interests. Accordingly, party officials naturally assume the responsibility of expressing public interests, as they present themselves as the intermediaries between the government and the mass.

Finally, the motivation-focused definition lacks explanatory power in China because corruption in China is not always related to personal gain. For example, officials can be considered corrupt when they expand benefits of local units at the expense of the central government or when their acts deviate from some fundamental political principles of the party.

Table 1.1 provides a listing of eighteen types of activities considered "corruption" in China. It was compiled by the author based on newspaper editorials and reports of recent years. This list shows the broadness of the CCP's concept of corruption, which ranges from the value system to the life style of a person. Corruption includes not only economic wrongdoings but also political irregularities. Corruption is often used to describe "serious bureaucratism" or the dissolute life led by public officials. It can also be employed to accuse politically disloyal or unreliable officials.

A WORKING DEFINITION

The foregoing review of major definitions of corruption proves the difficulty of defining corruption. M. Halayya (1985:1) is right when he comments that "everyone knows what corruption is; but it is difficult to define it in exact terms." However, the problem is not that some serious controversies stand in the way of compromise among corruption analysts, but that different analysts have directed attention to different lines of inquiry. As

Table 1.1
A Recent Classification of Corruption Activities

1. Taking bribery or embezzling state funds and properties
2. Seeking benefits for dependents, relatives, and friends in recruiting, school admission, job assignment, cadre status, exit permit, and admission to the party
3. Neglecting one's duty and, thereby, causing great damage to the economy
4. Providing trusted followers with key official positions
5. Working inefficiently, shirking responsibility, and shifting blame onto others
6. Acting arbitrarily, retaliating, and framing cases against others
7. Making false reports, prone to boasting and exaggeration
8. Using public funds for banquets and gift-giving
9. Running businesses and profiteering
10. Taking advantage of one's position to occupy or build houses for oneself
11. Living lavishly
12. Mishandling sexual relationships
13. Forming cliques to pursue selfish interests
14. Gambling and visiting prostitutes
15. Spending extravagantly on marriage and funeral arrangements
16. Engaging in superstitious activities
17. Smuggling
18. Selling state intelligence

Sources: *Dangde Shenghuo*, September 1988:6; *Dangjian*, October 23, 1988; *BKWZ*, August 29, 1989; *Zhongguo Xingzheng Guanli*, April 1990:14–16; *RMRB*, February 21, 1991.

a result, the choice of definition simply reflects their different foci and purposes. Different perspectives and priorities ensure analytical diversity and reduce the possibility of consensus.

Despite the dispiriting complaint that "the search for the true definition of corruption is endless, exhausting and ultimately futile" (Moodie, 1980:209) and the proper warning that "corruption, like obscenity or beauty, could exist only in the eyes of the beholder" (Williams, 1987:11), it is still necessary and worthwhile to pursue a serviceable definition. Such a working definition, as I call it, suggests that the definition of corruption should reflect the question the analyst poses. It is not supposed to be a global definition, broad enough to include all informalities, yet precise enough to analyze each individual case. A "working definition" only reflects the direction in which the analyst wishes to go. Two general features stand out for the working definition of this study: one is its clear locus and the other its special context.

A clear locus of the concept. Clear locus means that we need a definition of corruption that, while allowing for describing corruption in many areas, nonetheless locates itself precisely as the corruption of somebody. That is, we cannot assume that one definition will apply universally, sufficing for various actors. This study is confined to bureaucratic corruption. The term "bureaucratic corruption" is purposely chosen on the assumption that there is a distinction between bureaucratic corruption and corruption in general. The former is corruption involving governmental officials (bureaucrats), while the latter, a broad term, includes corruption in all sectors. Thus, this study is only concerned with "bureaucratic corruption" committed by cadres, or *ganbu* in Chinese. It doesn't deal with such cases as ordinary workers stealing public assets from their work units and selling them on the black market.

However, this doesn't mean that we neglect the larger societal dimension of corruption. The scope of corruption practices extends far beyond governmental cadres. It involves groups and persons who deal with the government but themselves are not a part of its structure. Nevertheless, to restrict this book to bureaucratic corruption reflects the author's observation: bureaucracy constitutes the most corruptible and corrupted part of Chinese society.

A special context of the concept. Special context means that, to conceptualize corruption, one must take into consideration the impact that the changing context may have on the term. In the past decades, scholars have made great endeavors to search for a universal definition of corruption based on the assumption of the existence of an all-inclusive conception of corruption. In a great measure, this assumption neglects the fact that corruption is not a static notion, but a dynamic one which evolves over time and differs from society to society. Depending on the individual, ideology, paradigm, culture, or other context, the term "corruption" can mean different things to different people. Corruption, in particular, has to be analyzed within a political environment specific to a country. This is because politics not only affects the understanding and explanation of corruption, but also produces and identifies certain social behavior as corrupt. Hence, it is not enough just to investigate corruption practices per se. One should also investigate, as J. F. Medard (1986:117) suggests, the attitude and performance of the political system toward corruption: the exposure of corruption by the press, by the party in power, by different factions, and by the populist opposition, as well as the reaction of government to corruption, whether symbolic, administrative, or judiciary.

With all these considerations in mind, this book regards corruption as a kind of bureaucratic behavior which deviates from the norm stipulated by a given political context. This working definition is of particular help toward a better understanding of China's corruption problem.

NOTES

1. According to Machiavelli, the cycle begins with kingship decaying into corrupt tyranny, proceeds with aristocracy overthrowing the tyranny but soon itself decaying into corrupt oligarchy, and ends with a shift to popular rule, which in turn becomes mob rule (Shumer, 1979).

2. For Weber's view on bureaucracy, see H. H. Gerth and C. Wright Mills (1958:196–244).

3. Heidenheimer et al. (1989:8–10) identify three types of definitions: public-office-centered, market-centered, and public-interest-centered. There are also other typologies.

4. Article 41 of the Constitution of the People's Republic of China (1982) states: "Citizens of the People's Republic of China have the right to criticize and make suggestions to any state organ or functionary. Citizens have the right to make to relevant state organs complaints and charges against, or exposures of, violation of the law or dereliction of duty by any state organ or functionary, but fabrication or distortion of facts with the intention of libel or frame-up is prohibited."

2

Contending Approaches to Corruption

Where, then, does corruption come from? Or how is it to be explained? While the definition of corruption proves controversial and troublesome, there has been no general answer to the origins of corruption either.

Five contending approaches to corruption exist. They are: the moralist, modernization, economic, organizational, and Marxist approaches. This is certainly not an exhaustive list of the possible views of corruption. In addition, none of these approaches forms a unity; that is to say, each represents a heterogeneous body of ideas that shares some common points with the other approaches. However, an examination of these five approaches presents a general picture of today's corruption literature.

CORRUPTION AS MORAL DEGENERATION

Up to the mid-1960s, the question of corruption in the contemporary world had been taken up almost solely by moralists (Leys, 1965). The moralist approach to corruption centers on the evil motives of morally degenerate individuals. Corruption is viewed primarily as an individual moral problem, akin to engaging in "sinful" activities such as drug trafficking, stealing, prostitution. Paul Appleby was among the first to raise the ethical and moral issues of public service. He believes that the individual is morally ambiguous: "an individual who would defer to another individual in all things would invite on the part of the second immoral actions inconsiderate of the first" (1952:1–2). Because of the moral ambiguity, governance in some societies usually involves the establishment of special privileges for a few. Graft and corruption tend to become a price of governance. Appleby's logic falls into the same line of argument pursued by Reinhold Niebuhr, that "man's capacity for justice makes democracy possible, but man's inclination to injustice makes democracy necessary" (1944: xi).

While Appleby deals more with general moral principles than any particular moral behavior, two important works emerged in the late 1950s and 1960s to provide detailed analyses of moral deviation. One is *The Moral Basis of a Backward Society* by Edward Banfield (1958), and the other, *Corruption in Developing Countries* by Ronald Wraith and Edgar Simpkins (1963).

Based on a case study of the familist system in Montegrano, a small village in southern Italy, Banfield finds that "amoral familism" constitutes a social syndrome which makes the local people to "maximize the material, short-run advantage of the nuclear family; assume that all others will do likewise" (1958:83) and leads to the extreme poverty and backwardness of the village. Wraith and Simpkins have a more straightforward moralist position. According to their self-styled "moralizing approach," the flourishing corruption in some newly independent African countries can be attributed to the *appetitus divitarum intinitus*, the insatiable avarice of human beings. "Its simple cause is avarice; the wrong that is done is done in the full knowledge that it is wrong, for the concept of theft does not vary as between Christian and Muslim, African and European, or primitive man and Minister of the Crown" (1963:45).

Dissatisfied with the traditional concepts of the moralist school, Dobel (1978) develops an alternative account of the decay of trust, loyalty, and concern among citizens of a state. He regards corruption as the moral incapacity of citizens to make reasonably disinterested commitments to actions, symbols, and institutions which substantively benefit the common welfare. He believes that this moral incapacity comes from the interaction of human nature with systematic inequality of wealth, power, and status. Such disparities, spawned by the human capacity for selfishness and pride, generate systematic corruption. However, the privatization of moral concerns and the accompanying breakdown of civic loyalty and virtue are the cardinal attributes of a corrupt state.

In short, the moralist approach appeals to moral standards or values in its effort to describe corruption of public officials. Taking corruption as an individual lapse from universal principles of public ethics, the moralist approach tends to be more concerned with describing and condemning corruption than explaining it. It therefore fails to provide valuable insight into different causes and various patterns of corruption. Worse yet, when confronted with different and conflicting codes of behavior, moralists tend to assert the superiority or the universality of their own moral values (Williams, 1987).

CORRUPTION AS A BY-PRODUCT OF MODERNIZATION

The modernization approach has other labels, such as "revisionist" or "structural-functionalist." Each of them signifies an emphasis or a set of issues that an author wants to specify. Thus, to name this approach "revisionist" is to emphasize its effect on changing the then-current way of thinking of corruption as an unmitigated evil (Carino, 1986:163). We choose the term "modernization" because it states the essential assumptions of the approach.[1]

Where moralists see deficiencies in individual consciences, the modernization approach calls attention to the relationship between corruption and social development. Scholars of the modernization approach first transfer corruption from the realm of morality to that of legality, and then identify it as "functionally" determined by a society's modernization process. They suggest that when a society experiences social changes, regulations of public office will change and laws regarding official behavior will multiply. Accordingly, some groups are disadvantaged by new laws and have to seek alternative channels for benefits. These norm changes and the legal multiplication of laws are, after all, consequences of modernization (Huntington, 1968). As long as those societies, characterized as gift-giving, resource-scarce, and economically underdeveloped, seek modernization, they have to accept corruption as a by-product of political and economic development; corruption nevertheless withers away as their political systems grow mature. Corruption for these scholars is on balance beneficial, because it "greases" an otherwise inefficient bureaucracy (Waterbury, 1973), promotes the economy by allocating resources away from consumption and into investment (Leff, 1964; Nye, 1967; Bayley, 1989), helps political development by increasing political participation (Scott, 1969; Bayley, 1989), and offers an alternative to violence (Shils, 1962; Nye, 1967). Table 2.1 summaries the functions suggested by these scholars.

Analyzing corruption from a developing functional perspective has improved theoretical inquiry into corruption. It is true that corruption may make some contributions to the process of development on the given level, but the modernization approach suffers from some fallacies.

One fallacy lies in its assumption of corruption as a dependent variable of development processes. Contrary to the "withering away" tenet, corruption has proven to be a universal phenomenon in the world. Political scandals such as Watergate disclosed in the United States and those in other Western states indicate that corruption may well be endemic to all levels of economic development (see, for example, Amich, 1976; Berg and Hahn, 1976; Gibbons and Rowat, 1976; Benson et al., 1978; Blankenburg et al., 1989). Communist systems are not immune from corruption either, despite their denial of the existence of corruption in a genuine socialist state. According to Staats (1972),

Table 2.1
Functions of Corruption

Economic Functions:	
Capital formation	Entrepreneurialism
Resource allocation	Market force
Political Functions:	
National integration	Mass participation
Alternative to violence	Development of parties
Administrative Functions:	
Qualified personnel	Administrative elasticity
Governmental humanity	Efficient bureaucracies

Source: Compiled by the author based on the modernization literature.

corruption was an important systemic feature rather than a transient phenomenon in the former Soviet Union, where government officials hoarded materials, concealed resources, participated in the black market, and broke laws as much for organizational ends as for personal gains. China also admits (Xie, 1988) that corruption accounts for a high percentage of all cases of economic crime.

The overly optimistic view of functional corruption constitutes the second fallacy of the modernization thesis. As many critics point out, this view relies on "too much anecdotal evidence, hypothetical cases, and speculative linkages between corruption and social outcomes" (Johnston, 1986:459). Even assuming that corruption has beneficial functions, critics point out, it is necessary to distinguish between short-term and long-term consequences, to distinguish between benefits to society and those that go to a small elite, and to distinguish between objective and subjective effects.[2] Corruption generally has negative effects on the organization in terms of personnel satisfaction, administrative costs, rationality, and effectiveness (Carino, 1986). Though it may give people entry into politics, corruption always tends to favor the "haves" rather than the "have nots," and the possibility of fundamental changes is likely to be less than what might otherwise have occurred (Johnston, 1989). Table 2.2 presents a summary of the dysfunctions of corruption based on these scholarly analyses.

Table 2.2
Dysfunctions of Corruption

Economic Dysfunctions:	
Unproductive and wasteful pursuits	
Diversion of scarce resources	
Disincentive to legitimate business	
Political Dysfunctions:	
Demoralization	Ignorance of regulations and laws
Alienation	Exacerbation of social divisions
Administrative Dysfunctions:	
Unstable work situation	Distortion of policy implementation
Nepotism and spoils	

Source: Compiled by the author based on Ben-Dor, 1974; Carino, 1986; Hope, 1985; Johnston, 1989; and Alam, 1990.

CORRUPTION AS A RATIONAL CHOICE

The economic approach views corruption within a model of rational individual choice, based on the assumption that corruption is part of a rational calculus and an integral and often deeply rooted method by which rational individuals seek to promote their own interests in a competitive "market." It occurs because of two factors: a monopolistic condition on the side of the bureaucracy, and a black market to benefit profiteering activities of the bureaucracy. A modern bureaucracy is like a mandatory model of market economies: it is expected to fix price schedules based on costs and benefits of both sellers and buyers. In reality, however, supply and demand always go out of balance. When demand outpaces supply, a black market in government services may surface. "Whether it involves something as expensive as fur coats and free vacations for high administrators, or as modest as a fixed ticket at a local precinct, we know this bureaucratic marketeering as administrative corruption" (Tilman, 1968:440). James Scott (1969) further distinguishes between "parochial" corruption and "market" corruption: the former refers to the favors given by public officials based on ties of kinship, affection, caste, and so on, while the latter is based on the criterion of who "pays" the most, no matter who they are. Anne Krueger (1974) believes that when government officials perform services—such as allotting permissions or licenses—they are in fact conferring rents. To illustrate how the "rent-seeking" works, Sivalingam (1983) presents a case of bureaucratic monopoly in Malaysia, where the bureaucrats were granted the power to allocate shares to Malay individuals. The Malay bureaucrats could not only receive a percentage of the unearned rent in exchange for allotting the shares, but also use this power to benefit themselves or their relatives and friends.

In short, the economic approach believes that individuals engage in illicit economic activities based on carefully weighed cost-benefit considerations. This theory, however, has been criticized for its theoretical simplicities, especially its analogy between the market and the bureaucracy (MacRea, 1982:678). According to Rose-Ackerman (1978:3), the linkage between corruption and government intervention in the economy is more apparent than real. She points out that many of the market failures which make government intervention necessary are the real conditions of corruption. Because of the institutional distinction of bureaucracy from market situation, a simplistic application of the market model is not sufficient to disclose the genesis of bureaucratic corruption.

CORRUPTION AS AN ORGANIZATIONAL DEFICIENCY

Originating from Weber's theory of bureaucracy, the organizational approach regards corruption as an organizational pathology which results from impediments created by the bureaucratic structure. It takes as its essential theme the inability of bureaucratic organizations to accomplish public purposes because "there are certain inherent characteristics in every administrative system which are detrimental to honest behavior" (Ali, 1985:164).

Anthony Downs believes that bureaucratic officials have in general a complex set of goals. Some are "pure" manifestations of self-interest, while others are almost altruistic. Still others stand in the middle as "mixed" motives. Thus every official acts at least partly in his or her own self-interest, and some officials are motivated solely by their self-interest (1967:83–85). Downs also finds that the personal goals lie deeper in an official's goal structure. It is more likely for the official to sacrifice other, shallow layers than these deeper layers. This view accords with March and Simon's observation that in an organization most members are motivated indirectly by organizational objectives and directly by the incentive structure (March and Simon, 1958). It is clear, for Downs, that the bureaucracy is not so pure from the very "inside." So it is not surprising to find that "officials are motivated to create informational networks of friends, favor recipients, contracts, and communication links based upon primarily personal, rather than official relationships with others." Neither is it unusual that "organizations that cannot charge money for their services must develop non-monetary costs to impose on their clients as means of rationing their outputs." Downs calls this the Law of Non-Money Pricing (1967:188). Some scholars explicitly illustrate the linkage between bureaucratic corruption and characteristics of bureaucratic organizations. Banfield (1975) compares the main structural features of the "typical" business (a competitive organization) with those of a government organization and concludes that corruption as a feature of the latter can be readily seen. Robert Williams (1987:63) expresses the same concern: opportunities for bribery and nepotism increase as the scope and size of government expand, because of the impossibility of framing rules and regulations to meet every circumstance or contingency.

Susan Rose-Ackerman (1978:170–184) has a more refined analysis of the relationship between bureaucratic structures and corrupt bureaucratic behavior. By examining how alternative bureaucratic structures[3] affect the incidence and level of corruption, she stresses the necessity for reformers to "move on to propose more particularized structures—closer monitoring, higher pay, nonvested pension, rights, and so forth—that will increase the expected costs of peculation at the critical soft spots."

The organizational approach is mainly derived from the conception of the Weberian ideal-type bureaucracy. Such conception, however, may not apply appropriately to underdeveloped countries, as Robin Theobald correctly points out (1990:2–4). In addition, the organizational approach also fails to explain why under the same conditions (e.g., in the same bureaucratic organizations) some officials are corrupt, while others keep their integrity.

CORRUPTION AS A CAPITALIST DISEASE

In contrast to the organizational approach, the Marxist approach totally rejects the notion of a bureaucracy as proposed by Weberian scholars. Revolutionary Marxists by and large did not anticipate the survival of bureaucracies into post-revolutionary society, because capitalist bureaucracies represented exploitation, alienation, and parasitism. For Marx, the bureaucratic authority and the privatizing of the state are identical processes; the bureaucracy does not represent a general or universal interest but rather the interest of a dominant class. The bureaucracy, first of all, is exploitative, for it controls public resources in the manner of a private owner and uses them for its own purpose. Hierarchy, the central organizing principle of the bureaucracy, is not protection against power abuse, but a powerful source of it (Kamenka and Krygier, 1979). The bureaucracy is also alienational, felt by citizens to be distant, beyond control. Its relationship with the outside world is not cooperative but manipulative (Jacoby, 1973). Finally, the bureaucracy is corrupt and parasitic. "For the individual bureaucrat the state's purposes become his private purpose of hunting for higher position and making a career for himself" (Seshadri, 1982:185). Thus the social origins of senior bureaucrats are usually those of the ruling class, and many personal ties of influence, status, and experience exist to link members of the ruling class with members of the state apparatus, especially the bureaucracy (Miliband, 1969; Krislov, 1974). The bureaucracy is parasitic because it lives on the capital which comes into the world, as Marx describes, dripping from head to foot, from every pore, with blood and dirt.

The foregoing analysis of the characteristics of the modern bureaucracy logically led Marx and Engels to the conclusion that bureaucracy would not be needed after the proletarian revolution and there would be, therefore, no bureaucratic corruption under a communist system.

Lenin in general accepted Marx's interpretation of bureaucracy: it is a privileged group holding "jobs" remunerated on a high bourgeois scale (Lenin, 1963, CW, 24:39). For Lenin, the most important tenet of Marxism about state and revolution is that the proletariat should "break up the bureaucratic and military machinery" (Lenin, 1963, CW, 25:415). Thus privilege, "official grandeur," special allowances and high levels of remuneration would be abolished. The state of new society under socialism would be simplified into routine operations like registering, filing, and checking, and hence administrators would have no particular interests of their own. It is obvious that the socialist mode of state functionaries "will make possible the gradual abolition of all bureaucracy" (ibid.:425).

Almost immediately after assuming power, however, Lenin began to worry about the bureaucratization of the Soviet party and state, which led to such problems as abuse of power, corruption, inefficiency, and insensitivity. Nevertheless, he attributed these problems to three external causes. One was the dependence of the new regime on the personnel of the old; "our state apparatus is to a considerable extent a survival of the past and has undergone hardly any serious change" (CW, 33:481). A second cause perceived by Lenin was the new state's backwardness—the atomized and dispersed character of small production with its poverty, lack of culture, the absence of roads, illiteracy, and the absence of exchange between agriculture and industry. The final cause was the necessity of bureaucratism as a weapon for the bourgeoisie to sabotage the revolutionary movements, and "the capitalists of the advanced countries . . . are bribing [the workers] in a thousand different ways, direct and indirect, overt and covert" (CW, 22:194). Thus, for Lenin, if socialist administrators were steeped in "bureaucratic attitudes," the evil of previous regimes or the external influence of capitalism was to blame.

All this said, it is not an exaggeration to conclude that in Marxist-Leninist theory there is nothing to suggest that corruption is likely to flourish under communism where there is no ground for public officials to profiteer for themselves.

However, the evolutionary practice of communist states has proven to be at odds with the Marxist-Leninist explanation of corruption as mentioned above. Instead of disappearing, bribery, embezzlement, extortion, backdoor relationships, and favoritism continue to exist after the communist takeover. The privilege of using, enjoying, and disposing of collectivized property through the organizational medium of state administrative institutions, has proven quite common in socialist states (see, for example, Staats, 1972; Kramer, 1977; Lampert, 1985; Harris, 1986; and Klugman, 1986).

CHINESE INTERPRETATION OF CORRUPTION

Marx and Lenin's ideas have greatly influenced orthodox Marxists in China who deny any possible connection between bureaucratic pathologies and the communist system. For many years, especially when Mao was in power, the extent of bureaucratic corruption was concealed because a rigorous, austere morality was believed to have taken hold of society. Even today when corruption has to be openly admitted, apologists still contend that it should be attributed to either the moral degeneration of certain individual officials or extra-system influences, such as the imperialist policy of "peaceful evolution" (*heping yanbian*).

According to Chinese orthodoxy, corruption, first of all, should be seen as a problem of personal morality. "Corruption" means moral decadence or degeneration. Therefore the determinant factor for whether a person takes advantage of his power for private gains or not lies in his own morality (Chen, 1989). Corruption is also attributed to the influence of rotten feudalistic ideas left over from the old society. "All expressions of the phenomenon of corruption have, in varying degrees, something to do with the corrosive influence of feudalist vestiges" (Liu, 1990:3). According to this line of explanation, patron-clientelism has been well built into Chinese culture, because of China's long history of feudalism and its immediate past of semi-feudalism and semi-colony (He, 1989). Feudalism has not yet withdrawn from the people's thinking even though the feudal system was overthrown (Liu, 1990). The orthodox apologists believe that corruption is rooted in pre-revolutionary imperial times but the "long-finger nailed mandarins" always creep back into the modern public services (Liu and Wang, 1988).

More importantly for the orthodox apologists, however, corruption occurs under the influence of capitalist ideology and its way of life. Chen Yun, former chairman of the Central Discipline Inspection Commission, CCP, points out that "in the process of the opening up to the outside world, it is inevitable to bring in capitalist decadent ideas and corrupt life styles. They directly endanger our socialist cause" (GMRB, September 2, 1985). Other Chinese leaders have expressed the same concern about "germs" from outside.[4] For them, socialism is healthy while only capitalism sick. "The spreading of corruption . . . is unrelated to the socialist system; it is a result of the spread of bourgeois liberation" (Liu, 1990:3). A clear example of this can be found in an internal document of the CCP's Propaganda Ministry in 1986. The document prohibited the mass media from using the word "privilege" in describing corruption within the party. The reason was given as follows: the concept of privilege was closely connected with exploitative classes, for it reflected the special rights entitled to these classes; in a socialist country like China all people were equal and there were no "special rights" for certain people. Moreover, the document pointed out, "anti-corruption" was a sensitive political slogan and some people in the past took advantage of it to oppose the party; all comrades therefore must be alerted to such abuse (XCGZTX, August 1986:17). According to the Chinese ideologues, the communist party is the most honest organization to serve people's interests (QS, September 16, 1989:13–15). The socialist system under the leadership of the CCP is superior to all other types of social systems, for it has one distinctive characteristic—the public ownership. The system is able to restrain corruption because: (1) self-profiting is not the motivation of socialist enterprises; (2) the aim of socialist production (i.e., people's needs) helps restrain money-fetishism; and (3) national planning plays an important role in controlling illicit productive activities (Wu, 1989).

Finally, Chinese theoreticians admit that some loopholes in management may occur in the process of transition from the old system to the new. Unlawful elements tend to take advantage of these opportunities to commit criminal offenses (Xie, 1988:72). But, again, this is to a large extent due to the introduction of market mechanisms into China. An article in the *People's Daily* has the following analysis:

> In the economic activities in the form of commodity economy, operations continue to flow along the track of the old structure, especially that of power, thus shaping into a situation in which the commodity economy in the embryonic stage intertwines with the old structure characterized by excessive centralization. This has created a major hotbed for corruption within the party. (Luo, 1989:5)

Indeed, the Chinese interpretation of corruption is basically a sinicized version of the orthodox Marxist understanding of corruption. Corruption is related to certain particular social systems such as feudalism and capitalism. Under socialism, corrupt practices, if any, are "flies" that have gotten in because of the system's openness to the outside world.

NOTES

1. For example, Peter Lee (1981:167–198) suggests that one can begin to approach the problem of corruption loosely from two basic theoretical perspectives. One is to treat it as part of the attributes of traditional social structures, and other to examine it as a problem created in the process of political modernization.

2. In his analysis of intersections between corruption and inequality, Michael Johnston distinguishes the effect of corruption upon "objective inequality," the actual distribution of wealth and power within a society, and "subjective inequality," perceptions of, and reactions to, corruption and inequality by members of society. See Johnston (1989:13–37).

3. The four structures examined by Rose-Ackerman are the fragmental, the sequential, the hierarchical, and the disorganizational models.

4. See, for example, Hu Qili's talk on the CCP's 13th National Congress about the rectification of party style (Hu, 1986); Zhao Ziyang's speech at the workshop of Party Construction (RMRB, March 17, 1989); Li Peng's address to the National Procuratorial Work Conference, (*Jiancha yu Lianzheng* 1 [1990]:2–3).

3

A Methodological Alternative: The Policy Outcomes Perspective

Despite important differences, the established approaches fall into two polar positions in terms of ontology and methodology: the moralist and economic approaches rest on an individual ontology and methodological individualism, individualizing corruption as it comes from individual moral deviation or individual rational choice, whereas the modernization, organizational, and Marxist theses take a social ontology, searching for causal predicates beyond the individual level. This study sees from this polarization a need for methodological restructuring of corruption studies. It accordingly proposes a policy outcomes perspective to mediate the dichotomy. This perspective, then, sets the methodological underpinnings for the empirical portion of this book.

INDIVIDUALISM

Ontological/methodological individualism conceives of individuals as rational and reflective subjects. It explains social behavior strictly in individualist terms because "all acts involve actors who are, ultimately, specific individuals behaving in particular situations" (Pye, 1988:13). It is thus assumed away by ontological/methodological individualism that societies are *sui generis* entities with properties of their own. This line of inquiry can be traced back to classical social theories, such as Hobbes' "atomistic" methodology, and Popper's praise of psychologism.[1]

According to ontological/methodological individualism, "social processes and events should be explained by being deduced from (a) principles governing the behavior of participating individuals, and (b) descriptions of their situation" (Watkins, 1973:149). In the corruption literature, the moralist approach shows a clear tendency toward (a), while the economic approach is more prone to (b). Moralists are concerned with the impact on individuals of their compliance or noncompliance with moral norms. For them, the motive or state of mind of an individual is critical because morality, after all, is enforced from within. Thus the attributes of the individual (i.e., attitude, belief, disposition, appetency) become the sole explanatory variables. Social phenomena are treated as the mere reflections of individual psychological tendencies, qualitatively undifferentiated from individual phenomena (Haines, 1988).

The economic approach to corruption does not have as strong a commitment to reductionism as has the moralist approach. It takes into account macro-level situations such as those of the economic market. However, while trying to avoid micro-level reductionism, the economic approach indulges in the "rational-choice" model in which individuals are believed to act according to a cost-benefit calculus. Here, individuals and their actions are conceived in terms of a means-end scheme: individuals are goal-oriented (e.g., profit-maximizing) while their actions serve only as means to specify goals. Fletcher summarizes the position as follows:

> Men oriented their actions to each other in terms of *meaning*. They actively sought to achieve certain ends of which they were (often) consciously aware. They employed certain *means* (and discarded others) in striving to attain these ends. They exercised choice; they deliberated; they calculated; they took decisions; and they then acted in relation to other men to accomplish their purposes. They exercised *will* in disciplining their thought and emotions, in channeling their energies and resources, in the conscious pursuit of clearly foreseen objectives. (Fletcher, 1971, vol. 2: 383–384)

According to this line of enquiry, explanations of social phenomena are to be reduced to a study of the rationality of individuals.

Ontological/methodological individualism—in both its moralist and rational-choice versions—is behaviorist in character and reductionist in logic. As Hempel (1966:108) observes, "Behaviorism . . . in all its different forms has a basically reductionist orientation." The vital problem with this line of theorizing is "the programma of explaining all social phenomena solely with the aid of psychological theory" (Agassi, 1960:246). Steven Lukes (1968:122) has successfully falsified the logic of reductionism, as he points out: (1) If the logic assumes that in the social world only individuals are observable, it is evidently false: some social phenomena are also observable (for instance, procedure of a court); (2) if the logic is on that individual phenomena are easy to understand while social ones are not, it is also unpersuasive: comparing procedures of a court with motives of criminals; (3) if the logic stresses that facts about social phenomena are contingent upon facts about individuals, one can argue that the reverse is also true, as we can speak of soldiers because we speak of armies; and (4) if it resorts to the argument that only facts about individuals are explanatory, this simply is a statement rather than a reasoning.

STRUCTURALISM

Structuralism sits on the other end of the ontological/methodological polarization. It is embodied, to different degrees, in the modernization, organizational, and Marxist approaches to corruption.

Contrary to ontological/methodological individualism, structuralism concerns concepts of societies, institutions, and social groups of various kinds where these entities are viewed as *sui generis* wholes, irreducible to their parts. To illustrate the idea, it is worthwhile to quote Durkheim at some length:

> The liquidity of water, its sustaining and properties, are not in the two gases of which it is composed, but in the complex substance which they form by coming together. Let us apply this principle to sociology. If, as is granted to us, this synthesis *sui generis*, which constitutes every society, gives rise to new phenomena, different from those which occur in consciousnessin solation, one is forced to admit that these specific facts reside in the society itself that produces them and not in its parts—namely its members. In this sense therefore they lie outside the consciousness of individuals as such, in the same way as the distinctive features of life lie outside the chemical substances that make up a living organism. (Durkheim [1895]1982: 39–40)

Structuralism proposes to substitute social structures for individuals as the object of social science. Here, structures are not merely phenomenal patterns generated from more basic processes underlying them. At least, they have the same ontological status as individuals, embodying certain superindividual properties and regularities (Staats, 1975). Properties are composed of functional needs, requirements, imperatives, or prerequisites, while regularities comprise ways in which those needs are satisfied by the elements of the social wholes (Sztompka, 1979). They are considered as distinct and irreducible constraints or even determinants of individual behavior.

The modernization, organizational, and Marxist perspectives in corruption studies largely concur with this line of explanation though they conceptualize and interpret "structures" differently. Given the ontological priority of society (the whole) over individual (the part), the biological concepts of organism and development are crucial to the modernization thesis. This thesis involves analyses of how "a given structure rather than another contributes to the satisfaction of a given functional requisite at a given time." Thus "hypotheses of self-regulation and of developmental accommodation are necessary if this approach is to be useful" (Holt, 1965:84). Therefore it is not surprising to find that the modernization approach treats corruption as a by-product of social development at certain stages, which fulfills an important social function by providing alternative channels of interest articulation for those otherwise excluded. Moreover, for the modernization thesis, structural properties such as economic backwardness and a gift-giving culture are generative in the sense that they produce corrupt citizens.

The Marxist perspective of corruption shares the same line of "situational determinism": the existence of corruption and the identity of corrupt actors are associated with, and therefore can only be explained by, certain social structures. Just as the capitalists are effects of the structure of the capitalist mode of production, or slaves are effects of the structure of feudal relationships, corruption is the effect of economical conditions of capitalism where anything can be a commodity—power, influence, office, love, labor, knowledge, and conscience—and where money counts for everything.

While the modernization thesis and the Marxist perspective of corruption are more concerned with external, or social, structures, the organizational approach is more interested in internal, or organizational, structures. Corruption is perceived as situationally determined by characteristics of bureaucratic organizations, as reflected in Downs' Law of Non-Money Pricing (1967), Crozier's theory of "Vicious Circles" (1968), Banfield's account of corruption as a feature of governmental organization (1975), and Rose-Ackerman's four-model illustration of the relationship between bureaucratic structures and corruption (1978).

In spite of their explicit differences, these three approaches would conform with Parsons' assertion that "the most essential condition of successful dynamic analysis is continual and systematic reference of every problem to the state of the system as a whole" (Parsons, 1954:216).

Compared with ontological/methodological individualism, structuralism appears closer to a social theory of corruption. It removes speculations on human motives by introducing objectively determinable factors in social systems. But it suffers from the same weakness as individualism does: it makes only one entity determinant, while reducing others to its effects (Wendt, 1987:345). In other words, by taking social/organization structures as the primary causes, and thereby the only object of social inquiry, structuralism throws all other social components beyond the pale of analysis or distorts them to fit the a priori notion that all social phenomena are structurally determined. This approach renders human beings only passive subjects, while objectifying social/organizational structures.

What makes structuralism more vulnerable is its inability to answer some crucial questions. First of all, it does not explain why a system develops one set of structures over another and why they endure. In other words, where do the structural conditions conducive to corruption come from? Another, more crucial problem is its failure to elaborate and specify why, under the same social/organizational structures, some people become corrupt while others remain upright. Or why do some societies appear more corrupt than others at the same developmental stage? The separation and isolating of system structures from human activities cannot justify theoretical and explanatory claims of this line of reasoning. There are missing links between structural conditions and their social consequences. As Giddens (1984:227) rightly points out, these scholars seem interested in finding universal laws which can reflect the effects of social constraints. They presume that it is possible to formulate theorems of structural causation to explain the determination of social action in general.

A POLICY OUTCOMES PERSPECTIVE

The policy outcomes perspective of this work is a synthetic attempt to bridge the macro versus micro dichotomy in theorizing about corruption. More specifically, it tries to find answers to the question of where the social structures or conditions conducive to corruption come from.

This perspective rests on certain implicit assumptions, primarily the conceptualization of policy outcomes and the emphasis on the role of politics in shaping policy outcomes.

Public policy is usually defined as goal-oriented actions of authorities backed by widespread approval and/or threat of sanction. Public policy as such is often contained in governmental decisions. Policy further produces two types of outcomes: outputs and impacts (Dunn, 1981:280). Policy outputs are what a government in fact does to realize its policy goals. They may include concrete policies, programs, services, proposed sanctions. Policy impacts, on the other hand, are the effects of policy outputs on people's behavior and attitudes.

Policy is only partially a rational process, however. Policy outcomes (both outputs and impacts) do not necessarily reflect policy makers' intentions; the complicities of society often produce outcomes neither expected nor intended. Unintended policy outputs exist because different interpretations of a policy intention often lead to different ways of policy enforcement. Some of them may diverge from or even contradict the original intention. Unintended policy impact is even more likely to occur. This is because human knowledgeability is always bounded.[2] An anticipation of consequences can only be based on the existing state of knowledge, which may not apply to the future. As Anthony Giddens contends, unintended consequences usually arise when human beings are "bounded on the one side by the unconscious and on the other by unacknowledged conditions." (Giddens, 1984:282). However, the lack of knowledge is not the sole cause of unintended consequences. Unintended consequences may also be caused by what Robert Merton called "imperious immediacy of interest," when the actor's paramount concern with immediate outcomes makes him or her overlook future or other consequences of the same act (Merton, 1936:901). Finally, unintended consequences may arise from the interaction of coexisting policies; that is, some policies contradict other policies and therefore lead to unexpected outcomes. In other words, policy itself is the cause.

An analysis of unintended consequences also distinguishes unforeseen consequences from unintended ones. Unforeseen consequences refer to instances where the actor fails to foresee upcoming results, while in the case of unintended consequences it is possible that people may know that a certain outcome will ensue but may not intend for it to occur in the first place. This way, the unintended consequence is not related to the predictability. The actor may be simply indifferent to that consequence though he or she has sensed it. Or the actor may be prepared to accept that consequence for the sake of other, higher goals (Cohen, 1989:135). Thus unintended consequences should not be identified with the failure of foresight. Nor should they be identified with the failure of action, because undesired results do not mean undesirability. Unintended positive consequences also exist.

A second and related assumption of the policy outcomes perspective is that politics plays a key role in determining policy outcomes.[3] Policy outcomes express the value and material allocations of a society while these allocations are the chief products of the society's political institutions. The author endorses the complaint that political institutions are too often treated not as explanans but as explanandum, a complex dependent variable derived from other sources (Cerny, 1990: x). According to the perspective of this book, political agents, that is, institutions and actors, are able to make choices in policy-making processes and, therefore, influence policy outcomes. They nevertheless do not have much control over policy outcomes. This is because the action of the agent may be limited, not only by the existing distribution of resources and stakes but also by the agent's own perceptions of the environment at large.

These two assumptions seem to contradict each other: policy processes yield unintended outcomes while they are heavily influenced by intended activities of policy-making actors. Such a statement, however, reflects a critical synthesis of the either-or theorizing implied in individualism versus structuralism debate in the social science.[4] Political institutions are creative agents that are able to transform or reproduce the structures of their societies, but they are at the same time structured by social relationships or structures they operate within or attempt to bring changes to. Social structures, on the other hand, are generative in terms of both constraining and enabling political agents (Mouzelis, 1989). This reflects what Anthony Giddens (1984:375) terms the "duality of structure." Accordingly, neither political actors nor social structures constitute a dependent variable of the other. Rather, they are mutually dependent yet ontologically distinct entities, interacting dialectically in determining the actual outcomes of human beings' purposive action.[5]

Here therefore lie the ontological roots of the policy outcomes perspective. Because both the agent and the structure are independent but dialectically intertwined variables, politics can be conceptualized as a dynamic process of structuration in which society is shaped and reshaped via the interaction of political agents and social conditions in the context of unintended policy outcomes. The "context of unintended policy outcomes" is important because it points to the recurring incongruity between actions and structures which provide the real dynamic for their continuing interactions.

IMPLICATIONS OF THE POLICY OUTCOMES PERSPECTIVE FOR CORRUPTION STUDIES

The policy outcomes perspective described above provides important guidelines for the empirical research of corruption. The perspective offers a dialectical synthesis to transcend the dichotomy between ontological/methodological individualism and structuralism in corruption literature.

The policy outcomes perspective concurs with the moralist and economic approaches that see corruption as usually individualized or based on individual calculation, because of its form of activity and clandestine nature. But it does not agree with the moralist explanation that "the root of corruption lies exclusively in the *dialectical divitarum intinitus*, the insatiable avarice that is one of the human weaknesses" (Klaveren, 1989). Nor does it enshrine the economic explanation that corruption results from a rational calculus of "profit maximization." The policy outcomes perspective pays particular attention to the social context of corruption and regards it as a social phenomenon generated and shaped by political environments. It emphasizes the impact of the evolution and fluctuation of a society's political and economic relations and the cultural formations that underlie society on the genesis, formation, and intensity of corruption.

The policy outcomes perspective endorses the focus of the modernization, organizational, and Marxist approaches on the organizational and social structures that produce and identify certain behavior as corruption, and shares with them the assumption that certain structures provide opportunities for corruption and make it possible. Nevertheless, the policy outcomes perspective differs from these structuralist approaches in an important aspect. It does not consider organizational and social structures as given or inherent, though it emphasizes the structural constraints on policy choice. This is because the very existence of these structures themselves can neither account for their own continuity nor explain why one set of structures prevails over another.

A fundamental distinction between this study's approach and the structuralist ones is that the policy outcomes perspective goes one step further than the structuralist to inquire where the structures conducive to corruption come from in the first place and in what ways they influence people's behavior.

Here are actually two issues. One is the nature of social structures. One should not blame history, culture, and the like, for the existence of certain corruption-conducive structures. Rather, they should be seen as the outcomes of human agents' goal-oriented policies. The second issue is the nature of these policy outcomes, intentional or otherwise. They are the *results* of contradictory interactions between political agents and social structures. Thus, speaking of corruption-conducive conditions as policy outcomes does not mean that they are purposely created by political agents. Rather, they may well be unintended by-products of intended policies.

Let us specify how the policy outcomes perspective differs from others. There are three types of inquiry about corruption with different explanans. The first type of inquiry (Inquiry I) mainly focuses on individuals. It answers the question of *how* corruption actually happens through individuals. The individual-oriented approaches (namely, the moralist and economic approaches) center on this type of inquiry.

Inquiry I

(a) Because human actors tend to take advantage of corruption-conducive conditions;
(b) these conditions exist;
(c) therefore corruption happens.

In contrast, the second type of inquiry mainly concerns the domain of social structures. It narrates *how* certain social conditions lead to corruption. This type of inquiry is conducted by structure-oriented approaches (namely, the modernization, organizational, and Marxist approaches).

Inquiry II

(a) Because certain social conditions are conducive to corruption;
(b) these conditions exist;
(c) therefore corruption happens.

Yet the policy outcomes inquiry (Inquiry III) is not content with either of these explanations. It further sets out a series of "why" questions. Instead of accepting them as given, it questions where those corruption-conducive conditions come from in the first place, and why these conditions affect certain individuals but not others. By doing so, the policy outcomes perspective attempts a more convincing historical exploration of the causes of corruption. An illustration of the policy outcomes inquiry is as follows:

Inquiry III

(a) Why certain social conditions exist and why these conditions generate corruption;
(b) these conditions exist;
(c) therefore corruption persists.

The policy outcomes perspective suggests for this book a context-oriented study of China's corruption. Three programmatic features of this perspective are worth mentioning: (1) policy making as a structuration process of agent-structure interactions; (2) contradictions implied in the process; and (3) resultant yet unintended consequences. These programmatic features help set an analytical trajectory for the empirical parts of this book. To begin with, this study regards the post-1949 Chinese history as composed of the three policy-making and implementation stages of transformation, consolidation, and modernization. It then investigates how the process has been associated with contradictions because of the incongruity of the policy-making agent and social conditions and analyzes how corruption has been produced as a consequence of these contradictions. And finally, it examines how the CCP was forced to launch political campaigns against corruption as it appeared, threatening the party's leadership, and analyzes the effects of these campaigns. This study thus presents a four-part analysis of bureaucratic corruption in post-1949 China: the CCP's policy efforts, the organizational corollaries, resultant bureaucratic corruption, and anti-corruption campaigns. Such a dynamic analytical framework goes beyond formal structures and individual morality to identify the origins and conditions of corruption in China.

NOTES

1. Hobbes claimed that "it is necessary that we know the things that are to be compounded, before we can know the whole compound," for "everything is best understood by its constitutive causes" (see Lukes, 1968:119, note 1). Popper wrote, "we must not overlook the great merits which psychologism has acquired by advocating a methodological individualism and by opposing a methodological collectivism; for it lends support to the important doctrine that all social institutions should always be understood as resulting from the decisions, actions, attitudes, etc., of human individuals" (1966:98).

2. The term "human knowledgeability" has been used by Anthony Giddens and others to refer to what actors know (or believe) about the circumstances of their actions and those of others (see Giddens, 1984:375). This word may be better than "rationality." Rationality usually connotes reasoning and calculation, which may not be present in all cases.

3. This sounds like a truism, but reasoning for it is not easy.

4. The agent-structure problem, that is, the conceptualization of the ontological and explanatory relationship between social actors and social structures, constitutes the core question of some classical social sciences (e.g., Spencer and Weber). Recent social science literature has reflected a resurgence of interest in reinterpreting the relationship of individualism and collectivism (or agent and structure, parts and whole, micro and macro, actor and system) for the purpose of explaining contemporary social behavior. For details, see O'Neil (1973), Knorr-Cetina and Cicourel (1981), Smith (1983), Wendt (1987), and Haines (1988).

5. The author is indebted to Anthony Giddens' structuration theory on this point.

Part II

HISTORY

4

Corruption in China: A Legacy?

A famous Chinese economist once pointed out that "the entire Chinese history was a history of embezzlement" (Wang, 1987:117). It is true that as early as during the Western Zhou Dynasty (1027–771 B.C.), there were already some written records of corruption. Since then, through dynasty after dynasty, corruption appeared routinely not only as a fact of life but also as a way of life for bureaucrats.[1] Accordingly, there evolved in the public mind a stereotype of officialdom in which no one was immune from corruption ("*wu guan bu tan*"). It was believed that "a three-year term of office could earn an extra income of 100,000 taels[2] of silver even for a 'clean' magistrate" ("*sannian qinzhifu, shiwan baihuayin*"). As a Chinese proverb states, just as "whoever is near an official gets honor and whoever is near a kitchen gets food" ("*jinguan degui, jinchu deshi*"), a person close to public office could always benefit from his authority.

THE DUAL NATURE OF THE CHINESE BUREAUCRACY

China is one of the oldest bureaucratic countries in the world. Chinese society for thousands of years was dominated by an elite of scholarly officials and local notables. The traditional Chinese bureaucracy retained certain features common to other bureaucracies: absolute authority, hierarchical structures, rigid operations (Laaksonen, 1988). Its millenarian endurance only added refinements to these features "generally in favor of increased centralization, more minute regulations, strict surveillance, and tight control" (Hsiao, 1960:3). However, the Chinese bureaucracy in its millenarian history developed and demonstrated certain political patterns different from or even contrary to those of Western bureaucracies.

Power integration was one important feature of the Chinese bureaucracy. Unlike their Western counterparts, Chinese bureaucrats were not subject to checks and balances from other government branches. Rather, the organization of the traditional Chinese government was quite simple and easy to schematize: at the top ruled the emperor surrounded by bureaucrats who were entitled administrative, legislative, and judicial powers. Power thus was highly integrated in the hands of bureaucrats. They performed multiple functions, acting as "parent officials" (*fumuguan*) over their "children citizens" (*zimin*). This would not be surprising given the deep-rooted Confucian emphasis on vertical human relations. In China, the original place of Confucianism, the sense of law was weak. Checks on and division of power became hardly necessary, as government was believed to rest on the "rule of virtue."

It would be misleading, however, to view the imperial Chinese bureaucracy as an integral whole. Significant differences existed between those whose bureaucratic status was secured and those who held office on a precarious tenure, and between the influential and the less influential. In the West, government bureaucrats are usually granted certain protection in terms of their salaries, retirement, and other rights. In imperial China, on the contrary, most government officials lived with trepidation, fearing an imminent dismissal. Being dismissed from office meant not only losing all the official privileges one had enjoyed, but also jail, servitude, exile, property confiscation, even death and implication of relatives and friends. A dismissal could occur virtually at any time, unless an official pandered to the liking of the people above him. Thus insecurity became a second feature of traditional Chinese bureaucratic life.

The dual nature of the bureaucracy thus became clear. On the one hand, bureaucrats stood high in the social order, well above the artisans, merchants, peasants while just below the emperor. The identity as a privileged notability enabled them to penetrate society in ways they preferred. Yet, on the other hand, they had to strive to maintain their positions, power, and privileges and prevent themselves from falling into disfavor. These two simultaneous yet different images of the bureaucracy could be easily identified when seen as opposite sides of the same coin: the more powerful, the more fearful of losing power.

Since losing power meant losing everything and it could happen at any time, a reaction among imperial bureaucrats was to create as much fortune for oneself as possible when in power. While the fear of losing power made fortune seeking necessary for bureaucrats, their powerful status in society made fortune seeking possible. Thus came a third distinction between the Chinese bureaucracy and the Western ones: political office was more used to achieve wealth than wealth was used to achieve political office. It was an important observation of Samuel Huntington (1968:66) that in a society where opportunities for the accumulation of wealth through private activity are limited by traditional norms, politics could easily become a road to wealth rather than the other way around. In imperial China, "power" was more important than "wealth." Power could generate wealth, while the reverse did not necessarily hold true. The Chinese phrases "*sheng guan fa chai*" (get promoted and then become rich) and "*zheng guan duo li*" (scrambling for power and then seeking privileges) reflected the close relationship between power and fortune.

AVENUES TO WEALTH

The form of scrambling for wealth varied in imperial China. A common way of fortune accumulation was accepting bribes. In traditional China, "parent officials" were expected to provide government services and personal security for their "children citizens." In return, they received material rewards as well as deference and respect from the citizens. An official at the ministry level dared to take bribes as much as worth ten times his annual income (Liu and Wang, 1988). Such patrimonial relationships, to say the least, lacked the separation of "private" from "official" spheres (Weber, 1971:1028). While officials took solicitation or bribes for granted, clients believed it normal to bribe officials.

Bureaucrats did not just passively wait for gifts and bribes to come; they often engaged in extortion. As recorded in the *Veritable Records of the Qing Emperors, 1796–1911* (*Taqing Huangdi Shilu*),[3] extortion of money from the public was the most frequent form of corruption during that period (Lau and Lee, 1981). But official extortion had a much longer history. For example, in the Southern Song period (1127–1279) a *chengxiang* (an official equivalent to Prime Minister) could publicly request money or gifts from his subordinates who made petitions; if no money was attached, petitions would not be processed (Liu and Wang, 1988).

Misappropriating public funds was another common avenue to wealth. In ancient China, while the state imposed heavy taxes and goods levies on the public, officials often took advantage of tax collection for personal gain. This double-edged exploitation threw the general public into dire poverty, while allowing government officials to amass huge fortunes. For example, He Shen, a senior official in charge of the Boards of Revenue and the Civil Office in the Qian-long period (1736–1795), plundered state properties for twenty-five years. His confiscated fortune was estimated at 223 million taels, an amount five times more than the total state revenues of that year (Jin and Liu, 1983). Government officials squandered public funds for banquets and sightseeing. They also enjoyed luxurious residences with private servants, guards, and sedan carriers with public funds.

Corruption thus became an indispensable component of officialdom in imperial China. It could enrich a person in ways much faster than other avenues. Amassed wealth through corruption was often used for further political investment, such as buying a higher office or bribing to cover wrongdoing; or, as many officials did, for economic investment such as purchasing land or for practicing usury.

Accompanying corruption was the development of the network of *guanxi*, literally meaning social connection. Scholars have long argued that one of the most significant features of Chinese culture was its emphasis on the appropriate arrangement of interpersonal relationships (see Abbott, 1970). But an often neglected fact was that such arrangement was usually based on political considerations. The network of *guanxi* did not arise in a vacuum, nor was it a mode of interpersonal relations without political context. It usually grew out of the necessary of bureaucratic self-protection. A *guanxi* network, more accurately, was a social mechanism through which an individual could extract desirable resources for himself. The relationships based on the *guanxi* network thus were instrumental and reciprocal: an exchange of services for rewards or personal protection.

After bureaucrats started their official careers, they quickly had to establish a network of *guanxi* to protect themselves. This was usually done by bringing more relatives, friends, and townspeople of theirs into the officialdom. The Chinese proverb "*yiren dedao, jiquan shengtian*" (when a person gets power, even his pets ascend to heaven) vividly describes this. Another way to secure a *guanxi* network was to fawn on one's superiors. Two most frequently used tactics for this were presenting gifts and holding feasts. By these tactics, lower-level officials could obtain political resources controlled by their superiors, which would in turn bring them some benefits or help them evade certain punishment. This was why the phenomenon proverbially expressed as "*guanguan xianghu*" (officials protect officials) prevailed in traditional China.

RESTRICTIONS ON CORRUPTION

Corruption in traditional China did not develop without restrictions, however. Paramount rulers of dynasties often put certain controls on bureaucratic behavior, for fear that rampant corruption led to social unrest.[4] The most noticeable measure was that of civil service examinations, a system considered "unique in traditional political systems for its universalistic standard and open accessibility" (Liu, 1986:10). Under the system, state officials were recruited through a series of competitive examinations. The contents of these examinations mainly consisted of the Confucian classics in their orthodox interpretations. It was believed that the regular use of examinations to recruit officials would curb the privileged and permit the rise of the "talented."

Other measures included the system of accountability and the rule of avoidance. The system of accountability subjected officials at lower levels to the close surveillance of their superiors, but it was not effective in checking nepotism. The rule of avoidance accordingly developed to forestall it and other illegal affinities. The system emerged in the Spring and Autumn Period (770–476 B.C.) and was extensively used in the Han, Tang, and Qing Dynasties. It involved (1) avoiding assigning officials to their native places; (2) avoiding recruiting relatives in the same government department; and (3) prohibiting collusion between central and local officials (Li and Yang, 1989). The system of avoidance also included prohibiting nepotism in civil services examinations. During the reign of Emperor Yongzheng, for example, separate examinations were held for the offsprings and relatives of examining officials.

Punishments for corruption were usually quite harsh. *Zangzui* (literally meaning the crime of illicit gaining) was used to describe economic wrongdoing of government officials, and was explicitly prohibited by the laws of Tang, Song, Yuan, Ming, and Qing Dynasties. The punishment for *zangzui* was usually more severe than those for other crimes, and in many cases *zangzui* was not subject to parole. For example, in the Qing period (1644–1911), the embezzlement of less than 1 tael would invoke a penalty of 80 bamboo strokes, while the sum for strangulation (that is, the death penalty) was 40 taels (Cheng, 1983).

These measures, though tough, were not so effective as expected. The examination system actually did not provide equal opportunities for all. Wealth, influence, and family background as powerful factors continued to favor privileged social strata. Instead of preventing corruption, the system ironically facilitated corruption activities. "For the examiners, this was their opportunity to profit. For the examinees, the risk of being caught and punished for cheating and bribery was outweighed by the greater chance of success in the examinations" (Chang, 1963:26). In addition, examinations tended to have a strong psychological impact on a candidate since he had to devote painful preparation efforts to them. By the time he passed the examinations and became a government official, he was very likely to expect some material returns (Lethbridge, 1985). The system of accountability did not help curb corruption too much, either. On the contrary, it contributed to the development of organized corruption networks in which superiors demanded payments from their subordinates who sought protection. The rule of avoidance might help curb nepotism, but it could not stop other forms of corruption.

Corruption flourished in traditional China to such an extent that it frequently triggered popular rebellions. The Taiping Rebellion (1850–1864) denounced the Qing Dynasty's rule as protecting corrupt officials and permitting them to exploit the public (Shao, 1983). During the 1911 Revolution, bourgeois revolutionary leaders condemned the last empire in China because it failed to straighten out administration, openly encouraged bribery, and "exploited the people in a way more fierce than tigers and wolves" (Li, 1989:5).

The 1911 Revolution successfully overthrew the imperial system, but it did not put an end to China's corruption. Bureaucratic corruption continued to flourish after the Revolution throughout the Republic (1911–1916), Warlord (1916–1927), and Nationalist (1927–1949) periods. According to some scholars, "if anything, the republican period was more misery and lawless than before" (Hsu, 1975:588). The KMT government extorted small businesses for "donations" and confiscated them when they refused. Through the government's Opium Suppression Bureau, the racketeers divided up the profits from the sale of the drugs and from the "registration fees" paid by known addicts (Spence, 1990:362). Local KMT officials acted as tyrants in tax collection and service requisition. Corruption also plagued the nationalists during their war with the communists. KMT officials and soldiers conducted corrupt seizures of assets as they took over Japanese-occupied areas. Some even publicly auctioned relief goods for personal gains. Corruption activities of the KMT government increased the burden of taxation and requisition on the citizens and, hence, alienated the government from the general public. John Fairbank (1985:264) commented that the nationalist government "represented the worst form of 'bureaucratic capitalism,' in which officials feathered their nests at the expense of the public." It is not surprising that corruption became one of the important causes of the nationalist defeat in 1949.

CCP REVOLUTIONARY HERITAGE AGAINST CORRUPTION

At the time when the ravages of the Japanese war brought incredible economic disorder for the nationalists in the cities, the communists successfully gained access to vast areas of the countryside. While corruption alienated the KMT government from citizens, the communists obtained political and material support from tens of millions of peasants. It was on the shame of the KMT government—militarily defenseless in face of the Japanese invasion, politically corrupt, and economically incompetent—that the communists established their public images: heroic sacrifice, diligence, courage, unselfishness, and self-discipline. The negative lessons of the KMT paved the way for the development of a strategy of "mass line" by the CCP. From the CCP's determination of winning over the masses emerged a constellation of rectification techniques aiming at consolidating party ranks.

As early as in the late 1920s and early 1930s when the nationalist government of the KMT was encumbered with corruption, the CCP started to create a new popular image for itself, which, to say the least, would help it survive the war. A good example was the Campaign against Embezzlement and Waste in the Soviet areas (*suqu*). The Central Worker-Peasant Democratic Government directed its campaign efforts at waste, negligence, bureaucratism, and embezzlement among cadres. The official newspaper, *Hongse Zhongguo* (*Red China*), reported that waste had become a common problem at all levels of government. The General Service Bureau of the central government was cited as an example of this, for it spent 10,000 yuan more than needed to purchase clothing. The central authority also found that some of its cadres falsified accounts, forged documents, or destroyed incriminating evidence, in order to embezzle public funds. A small county of Jiangxi province exposed twenty cases of embezzlement in a period of less than one year, involving the county's party secretary, chief executive, military minister, minister of treasury, and some other high-level officials.

Against this backdrop, the central government launched the campaign to check "unhealthy phenomena." The Worker-Peasant Inspection Committee issued a series of directives regarding the scope, targets, and reform methods of the campaign. It also established a special bureau to accept complaints against corrupt cadres and government agencies. The Ministry of Treasury, Labor Ministry, Land Ministry, General Service Bureau, the General Print Shop, the Mint of the government, were all accused of corruption. Several cadres were sentenced to death while some were jailed. It was also during the campaign that the CCP for the first time established auditing agencies at different levels of the government.

The largest rectification campaign before 1949, however, took place in the Yanan era, that is, the CCP's Zheng-Feng (rectification) movement of 1942–1944. The movement was the first open rectification in CCP history. It not only proved very important for the succeeding revolutionary victory of the CCP, but also had a significant impact on the CCP's post-1949 rectification policies.

The Yanan Zheng-Feng, first of all, was an effort to "revolutionize" the party's spirit and working style. In the 1930s, disappointed with the KMT government, thousands of students, intellectuals, and city residents migrated to the base areas to join the communist movement and the CCP.[5] However, as the party perceived, many of them did not belong to the working class. It was estimated that of 800,000 CCP members, nearly 90 percent of the members were of "petty bourgeois" origins (Hu, 1962:422). Some of them, though anti-Japanese-oriented, were less sure of committing themselves to the communist course. The coming of these fellow-travelers expanded the revolutionary forces, but also brought along the influence of bourgeois thought. As Mao (SW, 1965,3:294) saw it, "in the expansion of the party organizations, a good many careerists and enemy saboteurs succeeded in sneaking in despite the fact that the central committee stresses the slogan 'expand the party boldly, but do not let a single undesirable in.'" Thus, in 1939 the CCP's Political Bureau made the "Decision on the Consolidation of the Party" to alert the whole party to the necessity of ideologically "remolding" the party. Mao listed eleven bad manifestations of "liberalization" and traced them to the fundamental error of "petty bourgeois selfishness," which "places individual interests first and the interests of the revolution second" (SW, 1965,2:32). To solve the problem, the party resorted to thought education. The Yanan Zheng-Feng thus started with a study of twenty-two official documents. One major document was Mao's work on *Reform Our Study*. The work made specific analyses of the origins and characteristics of the "petty bourgeois ideology and style of work" and stressed the importance of building consensus on and commitment to the party's ultimate goals within the party. Studies of political documents were coupled with intense self-criticism and criticism. Cadres, especially those accused of various errors, were subjected to "thought struggle" under psychological stress. However, "the goal . . . was to reconstruct and reincorporate them within the movement rather than to eliminate them as enemies through exile, concentration camps" (Selden, 1971:194).

The Yanan Zheng-Feng was also a crisis-solving attempt. It was, after all, born of the political and economic hardship triggered by the Japanese invasion and KMT blockade. In the base areas, inflation and tax increases brought tensions between the CCP's government and peasants. Pressed with material shortages and low allowances, some cadres engaged in corrupt activities to seek personal gains. In the Huaibei base area, for example, a town head embezzled 300 hectoliters of public grain; a head of a submilitary district misappropriated hundreds of thousands of yuan in only three or four months. Other forms of corruption also developed, including forging bills and receipts, extorting money, evading taxes, harboring smugglers. Some cadres even absconded with public funds from the base areas (Yao and Luo, 1989).

These problems called for disciplinary sanctions in addition to persuasive methods. In 1941 the party issued the "Organizational Rules of the Administrative Prefectural Commissioner's Offices in Shan-Guan-Ning Border Region" to tighten its discipline. Other base areas also passed their own anti-corruption laws. Take the "Provisional Regulations of Corruption Punishment of Huaibei-Suwan Border Region" (March 1943) as an example. It stipulated that "a person who embezzles 500 yuan or more is subject to five years in prison up to death penalty"; that "for the embezzlement under 100 yuan, the punishment is one year or less in prison"; and that "any cadre who knows about corruption activities but does not report them would be found guilty of malfeasance." Besides the criminal sanctions, disciplinary punishments (*jilu chufen*) were also available. They ranged from formal warning, demotion in grade or in office, dismissal from office, to permanent expulsion from the cadre ranks.

A more severe but informal coercive measure was the "struggle meeting" (*douzhenghui*). It was usually conducted publicly with a number of representatives of the "most serious evils" being targets. These "struggle meetings" brought public humiliation and physical intimidation to the targets, and could also produce psychological pressure on the audience. However, in most cases, targets were carefully chosen and limited in number.

However, Zheng-Feng was more than a thought education movement or a crisis-solving effort in the face of economic hardship. From the very beginning it was well connected with the consolidation of the party leadership, or more accurately, the leadership of one faction headed by Mao. The Long March (1934–1935) brought Mao to the supreme leadership of the party. But it was during the Yanan period that Mao firmly established thought control over his followers. The Yanan era was the most productive period of Mao's lifetime, in which he wrote many of his important works.[6] What was later termed "Mao Zedong Thought" actually took shape during this period. Derived from Marxism and Leninism but more concerned with the Chinese practices, these writings brought Mao the image of an independent Marxist theoretician. It was during the Yanan time that "for the first time his writings and the example of his leadership were widely projected as the embodiment of party policy and spirit" (Selden, 1971:198). Mao's writings dominated the "study documents" assigned to cadres to read and study. Others included Liu Shaoqi's *Training of the Communist Party Member* and *On the Intra-Party Struggle*, and Chen Yun's *How to be a Communist Party Member*. There were pressing reasons for CCP leadership, especially Mao, to consolidate party organization. First, though Mao had established his leading position in the party, for many years many "Russian returned students" still held key positions of the leadership (Harrison, 1972:324). Their ideas appeared at odds with the indigenous orientation of Mao Zedong Thought. Besides, there was mounting concern over security, traitors, or KMT spies. A prominent example was the case of Wang Shiwei. Wang became a victim of the rectification as he was accused of being a KMT spy as well as "Trotskyist." He was severely criticized, arrested, and later executed.[7]

On the whole, the Zheng-Feng movement was a success for the CCP. Though it did not wipe out all the policy differences in the leadership, the party significantly disciplined its members. Zheng-Feng strengthened the CCP from the inside and inspired the party to still greater efforts to take over the whole of China. Five years later, the founding of the PRC signaled the final victory of the CCP over the KMT.

The Yanan legacy has proven important to the development of CCP rectification methods. First of all, the party has learned from its Yanan experience how to use rectification as a way of solving a crisis. A rectification movement such as the Yanan Zheng-Feng can consolidate cadre ranks in the face of mounting pressure from external sources, for two reasons. First, it helps reunite the party on some new ideological bases; and second, it cleans party ranks by educating wavering members and expelling corrupted elements. Moveover, the Yanan Zheng-Feng sets a good example of effective combination of different rectification techniques—coercive and persuasive, formal and informal, public and behind-closed-doors, and group-oriented and self-conscious. The requirement for skillfully using different methods reflects the complex nature of the CCP's rectification campaigns as illustrated by the Yanan Zheng-Feng.

Another equally important heritage from the early rectification is the "mass campaign" method. Out of the experience of difficult survival in the base areas developed the CCP's conviction that "however active the leading group may be, its activity will amount to fruitless effect by a handful of people unless it is combined with the activity of the masses" (Mao, SW, 1965,3:118). The Yanan period demonstrated the party's first systematic effort to apply the "mass line"[8] to concrete situations and to use mass campaigns to implement its policies.[9] Since then, drawing in the broad masses for the supervision of cadres has become one of the most important techniques of rectification.

IS CORRUPTION A CULTURAL LEGACY?

The findings of this chapter pose an important question: Is corruption an inherited problem or component of Chinese culture? Or is it part of history, having emerged under certain political conditions?

My analysis supports the latter interpretation. Corruption was persistent in imperial China, tormented the KMT's government, and also appeared in the communist base areas before 1949. But we hardly found any consistent patterns and methods of corruption. Even the concept of corruption (what constituted corruption) changed from one period to another. Imperial bureaucrats engaged in corruption under the pressure of political and physical survival. The KMT's corruption occurred more at the top level of government than the lower ones and was, to a large extent, due to the formation of the "bureaucratic capital," namely, the combination of big capitalists with the public office. Finally, as we depicted, the CCP's corruption problem emerged in some particular political and economic environments in which the party had been struggling for survival. Even the party's interpretation and countermeasures were heavily circumscribed by the political situation of that time.

Another fact that invalidates the "legacy doctrine" is that, as we have seen, throughout Chinese history there were anti-corruption movements as well, either government-sponsored campaigns or popular rebellions, denouncing official corruption. If corruption is a legacy of Chinese culture, then why is not another part—anti-corruption? What decides that some part of Chinese culture becomes a legacy while other parts do not?

Finally, the term "legacy" is too general to be convincing, for it fails to specify the *mechanisms* through which corruption was handed down from generation to generation.

Cultural heritage certainly bears upon corruption, but it is not a *cause* of corruption. The chief causes of corruption can only be found in its immediate context and, more specifically, as we will see in the following chapters, the politics of a given time.

NOTES

1. This means that bureaucrats lived more on graft than on their regular salaries.

2. From 1600 to 1814, a tael was equal to one and half or two dollars in current terms. In the late Qing, the value of the tael gradually dropped to half and then one-third of its original value.

3. *Taqing Huangdi Shilu* (2,247 volumes) recorded significant events within the Qing Dynasty, including all the cases of punishment of official offenses.

4. Many scholars have suggested that positive relationships existed between corruption and political instability in traditional China. See, for example, Lau and Lee (1981).

5. As reported, the population of the base areas grew to more than 100 million by the end of 1940.

6. Mao wrote, for example, *On Practice, On Contradiction, Combat Liberalism, On Protracted War, The Chinese Revolution and the Chinese Communist Party, On New Democracy, Reform Our Study, Rectify the Party's Style of Work, Talks at the Yanan Forum on Literature and Art*, and *Some Questions Concerning Methods of Leadership*.

7. For the case of Wang Shiwei, see Goldman (1967) and Dai Qing (1988).

8. Mao explained the "mass line" as "from the masses to the masses"; namely, "take the idea of the masses and concentrate them, then go to the masses, persevere in the ideas and carry them through, so as to form correct ideas of leadership—such is the basic method of leadership" (SW, 1965,3:120).

9. Besides the Zheng-Feng movement, there were the *Jingbing-Jianzheng* campaign (reducing army and government personnel), the *Xiafang* campaign (sending "intellectual" cadres to the countryside), the *Jainzhu* campaign (reducing rent for peasants), the *Hezhouhua* movement (reorganizing the village economy), the *Dashengchan* movement (increasing production), and the *Dazhong-Jiaoyu* campaign (spreading literacy). These campaigns were designed to "enable the party to forge closer ties with the masses" (Mao, SW, 1961,4:186). See Selden (1971:210–211) for a full account of these campaigns.

5

Transformation and the Three and Five Anti's Campaign

The proclamation of the People's Republic of China on October 1, 1949, marked the beginning of another long march for the Chinese Communist Party. As Mao (SW, 1965,4:374) himself saw it, "to win country-wide victory is only the first step in a long march of ten thousand *li.*" Indeed, immense work awaited the CCP. However, the party leadership was confident in its ability to bring the country political stability and economic prosperity. As early as in 1945 in a talk with a well-known educationist, Mao had made this very clear.[1] When asked about the CCP's view of the cycle from victory to corruption, and then to disintegration, throughout Chinese history, Mao replied confidently, "we have found the way out of the cycle. The new way is 'democracy.'. . . Only under public supervision, can the government not slack off; only by making everyone responsible, can we avoid failure" (Yao and Luo, 1989:58). Mao's conclusion was overly optimistic. After the founding of the PRC, corruption continued to haunt Chinese society. China was dragged into a large-scale anti-corruption campaign only two years after the CCP took power. What went wrong? What happened to a party which had successfully established a "clean" image in the public before taking power? An outline of the CCP's general policy and organizational policies during the early years is offered in this chapter. These policies provide good answers on the causes and nature of the first large-scale anti-corruption campaign in the PRC history—the Three and Five Anti's Campaign, 1951–1952.

GENERAL POLICY: TRANSFORMATION

Upon taking power, the new leadership in China faced "a huge country where traditional forms of political authority had long ago disintegrated, where modern forms of government had existed only incompletely and superficially even in the best of times, where during most of modern times and in most places the Chinese people had been 'governed' by marauding warlord armies, by foreign invaders and occupiers, and by corrupt and inefficient KMT bureaucrats and militarists" (Meisner, 1977:59). The CCP set "transformation" as the general policy during the first years of its leadership, which involved some tough tasks. Among the most important was the need, facing the war-torn economy, for the party to achieve "a fundamental turn for the better in the financial and economic situation" in order to demonstrate its ability to lead the country.

The economic situation in 1949 appeared to be worse than ever. Devastated by the civil war for years, the output of the country's industrial and agricultural production dropped significantly. According to official statistics, the production of investment goods and consumer goods declined by 70 percent and 30 percent respectively as compared with their previous peak levels. Trade was sluggish whereas speculation flourished. Transportation was almost at a standstill. By the end of 1949, although about two-thirds of the railways were open, the army requisitioned a large part of them; almost all commercial ships had gone to Taiwan, while civilian motor transportation was virtually nonexistent (Guillermaz, 1976). Given such bad transportation, it was very difficult to distribute the limited supply of goods to areas in urgent need. Thus, when the People's Liberation Army (PLA) took over Shanghai in May 1949, the quantity of coal there could last only five to seven days, and rice was only enough for half a month (Jin Dexin, 1989).

Unemployment increased because of massive displacement during the collapse of KMT government. In Shanghai, in less than one year between June 1949 and May 1950, about 240 big capitalists fled, and more than 1,800 enterprises and 7,100 businesses petitioned for shut-out. As a result, the figure of unemployment in Shanghai alone soared to 190,000 (XHYB, April 1952:36). The most serious problem, however, was that of chronic hyperinflation. Inflation had upset the Chinese people for twelve years since 1937, as the country experienced a continuous expansion of the money supply and a rise in the demand for goods and services which far outpaced increases in production (Eckstein, 1977). According to official statistics, if one took the index of money issuance in December 1948 as 1, then only one year later, in December 1949, the index reached 287. The rise in price was even sharper. If one took the wholesale price in December 1948 as 100, the index went up to 153, 267, 1059, and 5376 in January, April, June, and November 1949 respectively. To make matters worse, the country was suffering the worst natural disaster since 1931. Some 120 million *mou* of land and 40 million people were affected by floods (Jin, 1989:5).[2] In short, in 1949 China's economy "by practically all available measures was near the bottom of the world development scale" (Eckstein, 1975:174).

Moreover, the party was also pressed with the urgency of social reform. Entering the cities, the communists found themselves in an environment totally different from that of their base areas. They saw in cities great disparities, disorganized masses, and reckless crimes. Society was rife with opium addiction, gambling, and prostitution. In Shanghai alone, more than 800 brothels existed at the time of liberation. In a single month in June 1949, the police reported 173 major robberies (White, 1988). Having suffered from social disorder for many years, people in the urban areas were longing for peace and stability. The situation in the rural areas was not much better. The CCP's early land reform had won over vast masses in some base areas. Because of military operations, however, the party could not quickly extend land reform to those newly liberated areas. Consequently, when the party came to power, the old agrarian order was still intact in almost four-fifths of the country (Rodzinski, 1988).

Thus, in addition to the economic recovery, the establishment of a stable social order also fell under the party's general task of transformation. To attain full control over society, the party was to suppress all public and hidden "reactionary elements." The "public enemy" referred to the 400,000 KMT remnants who were still conducting "bandit guerrilla warfare" against the communists (Mao, SW, 1977,5:29), while "hidden reactionary elements" practically involved all those who showed a hostile attitude to the new regime. Equally important for the party was to develop a national consciousness in place of traditional localistic and regional loyalties, and to bring ideological conversion to a weary, indifferent, and illiterate population.

Gullermaz (1976:xv–xvi) nicely summarizes the CCP's task of transformation in the early years. As he points out, in order to establish a "new society," the CCP faced the problem of transforming (1) organization, socioeconomic structures, social relations, and production relations; (2) moral values, mental and intellectual habits; and (3) customs, and the content and forms of cultural expression, starting with the writing system, and moving on to art and social studies.

To fulfill these tasks, the party made great efforts to establish new rules and redistribute resources. It launched campaigns to suppress those suspected of having close ties with the KMT or former American agencies. From December 1950 to the end of 1952, the party executed 710,000 "reactionaries," imprisoned 1270,000, and put 230,000 under public surveillance (Ma and Huang, 1989:737). In cities, it confiscated all industries and services owned by KMT government, including factories, mines, stores, banks, warehouses, ports, railways, post offices, utilities, and farms. In rural areas the party carried out land reform to redistribute land and destroy clan authorities. The party also reformed the nation's educational system, issued a new marriage law, extended control over publication and art, and set restrictions on religious activities. All these efforts reflected the party's determination to transform the old society at a good pace.

Obviously, the party needed a highly competent administrative apparatus to realize its ambitious goals and to carry out these transformation policies. The apparatus should first of all be politically reliable so that the party could have all its policies faithfully implemented. But the apparatus should also be administratively skillful so as to enable the party to effectively utilize limited resources of that time. Finally, the apparatus was to be highly disciplined lest it became itself a source of waste, corruption, and exploitation. Unfortunately, however, such a state apparatus was far from ready for the CCP during the early years.

EARLY ADMINISTRATIVE STRUCTURE AND PERSONNEL

The establishment of PRC state apparatus began with the First Plenum of the Chinese People's Political Consultative Conference in September 1949. Held just before the formal proclamation of the PRC, the conference blueprinted the new state's administrative organization. It promulgated the Organic Law of the People's Republic of China and established the Central People's Government. The Central Government Council, composed of fifty-six members and headed by Mao, was the supreme authoritarian organ. Below the Central Government Council came the State Administration Council (the state executive organ) and three other important institutions—the People's Revolutionary Military Council as the supreme military command of the state, the Supreme People's Court as the highest judicial body, and the Supreme People's Procuratorate as the highest supervisory organ of the country.

The State Administration Council consisted of four committees, which in turn, controlled twenty-nine ministries and six departments (Figure 5.1).

Vertically, the new state had a four-tier system. At the first tier, the country was divided into six large administrative regions. According to the Organic Rules of the People's Government Council in the Large Administrative Regions (December 16, 1949), the regional administration committees were the supreme authorities of local governments but directed in all important aspects by the central government in Beijing. After the regions came the other three tiers—province or district, city or *xian* (county), and *xiang* (town) (Figure 5.2). By September 1950, people's governments were established in 28 provinces, 9 districts (equivalent to province), 67 cities, 2,087 *xian*, and more than 280,000 *xiang* (Zhu and Zhu, 1989:34).

Given the immense tasks facing the CCP and given its structural designs to fulfill these tasks, the party apparently ought to have had enough administrative elites to staff the administrative organizations. During the early years, the party's administrative personnel was composed of four groups: (1) party members; (2) the PLA; (3) newly graduated students; and (4) retained

Figure 5.1
The PRC's Early Administrative Structure

- People's Political Consultative Conference
  - People's Central Government Council
    - State Administrative Council
    - People's Revolutionary Military Council
      - Committees and ministries
    - The Supreme People's Court
    - The Supreme People's Procuratorate

Figure 5.2
Vertical Administrative Structure in the Early PRC

Central Government
|
Large Administrative Region
|
Province or District
|
Xian (county) or City
|
Xiang (town)

administrative elites.

Party Members

After the party took the reins of government, its members naturally became the most important and reliable administrative forces to manage society. Of them, the Yanan generation constituted the core, because the people of this generation had been tested in harsh political and military struggles. However, this generation only accounted for about one-fifth of the total membership. A majority of party members joined the party during or after the Liberation War (Table 5.1). It was by no means surprising that the party organization expanded more quickly than ever as the communists approached nationwide victory. As Table 5.2 shows, in the year 1949 alone, the party recruited over 1.4 million new members.

The reliance on party members as a source of administrative personnel had some problems, though. First, many of the new members did not have the same high moral affinities for communist ideology as those early guerrilla leaders. Moreover, party members in general lacked technical skills or intellectual capabilities for economic management. The overall education level of CCP members was very low. Fewer than half reportedly only had the level of junior high school education or below, and a good many were illiterate (Harding, 1981:35). As a result, the party's leadership only considered 720,000 or percent of its party members as cadres (An, 1952:55). In terms of geographical distribution, in the early years a majority of party members (52 percent) remained in rural areas, while only 12 percent worked in government units (Table 5.3). Although the party provided some in-service training for its cadres, the training alone still could not solve the urgent need for qualified personnel.[3] Hence the party had to supplement its administrative force with the PLA.

The People's Liberation Army

In addition to its usual functions of defending governments, the military in China played an important role in managing society in the early years of the PRC. The PLA's mixed military and managerial function could be traced back to the Yanan era when economic, educational, and military activities were highly integrated and when army units actively engaged in production to make both ends meet. Even before the founding of the PRC, Mao had pointed out that the army could be a major source of cadres for the new communist government:

Table 5.1
Generational Distribution of CCP Membership in 1949

Period	Number	% of Total Membership
1st Revolutionary Civil War (1921–April 1927)	600	0.012
2nd Revolutionary Civil War (April 1927–July 1937)	30,000	0.6
Anti-Japanese War (July 1937–Aug.1945)	1,100,000	22
Liberation War (Aug.1945–Oct.1949)	3,800,000	76

Source: Compiled according to the data in Chen and Zhang, 1989:61.

Table 5.2
Numerical Growth of the Chinese Communist Party, 1921–1950

Year	Number
July 1921	57
July 1922	195
June 1923	420
January 1926	994
April 1927	57,900+
July 1927	10,000+
July 1928	40,000+
January 1930	65,000+
1934 (before the Long March)	300,000+
1937 (after the Long March)	40,000+
July 1940	80,000+
July 1942	73,000+
July 1944	90,000+

Table 5.2 (continued)

Year	Number
April 1945	1,210,000+
1946	1,350,000+
January 1947	2,220,000+
December 1947	2,700,000+
July 1948	3,000,000+
December 1949	4,500,000+
June 1950	5,000,000+

Source: Ma and Huang, 1989:685–686.

Table 5.3
Sector Distribution of Party Members, 1951

Sector	Number	% of total membership
Rural areas	3,000,000	52
Armies	1,600,000	27.5
Government units	700,000	12
Industries	200,000	3.4
Other	300,000	5.1
Total	5,800,000	100%

Source: Compiled by the author according to the Party's Working Report delivered by Liu Shaoqi at the First National Conference of Organizational Work, March 1951.

There is a possibility that before very long the entire People's Liberation Army will be turned into a working force, and we must take this possibility into account. The 53,000 cadres now ready to leave with the army for the south are very inadequate for the vast new areas we shall soon hold, and we must prepare to turn all the field armies, 2,000,000 strong, into a working force. In that event, there will be enough cadres and the work can develop over large areas. We must look upon the field armies with their 2,100,000 men as a gigantic school for cadres. (SW, 1965,4:363)

Thus, in the early years of the PRC the army discharged hundreds of thousands officers and soldiers to civilian posts equivalent to their previous military ranks.[4] In the process, the army was requested to choose some politically reliable, well-educated, and physically fit cadres to strengthen local governments. However, a great number of those demobilized officers and soldiers actually belonged to the following categories: local armies, insurrectionary troops, military women, and those officers who were no longer suitable for military work because of bad health, low education, and old age (Chao, 1985). The discharged officers fell short of the expectations of local governments in both quality and quality.

Newly Graduated Students

In the early years of the PRC, a number of newly recruited cadres came from higher educational institutions. According to An Ziwen, then Minister of Personnel, there were altogether about 66,000 graduates from 1949 to 1952; 99.4 percent of them were assigned as cadres to government organizations, enterprises, and other work units (An, 1952:56). Given the urgent needs of economic reconstruction, many of them were sent to economic sectors. For instance, among 27,000 graduates in the summer of 1952, 56 percent were assigned to factories and mines (ibid.).

These school graduates had relatively high level of technical competence, but the size of this group was really small, especially compared with China's population size (Table 5.4).

As it became clear that the CCP did not have enough institutions to train its own technical intelligentsia, the party had to turn to old managerial elites for administrative help.

Retained Administrative Elites

The older administrative elite consisted of two groups of people. One was lower- or middle-level former officials of KMT government, and the other intellectuals and technicians graduated from old educational institutions. Before the establishment of the PRC, Mao (SW, 1965,4:364,373) had promised the

Table 5.4
Enrollment and Graduation in China's Higher Education, 1949–1952 (in thousands)

Year	Enrollment	Enrollment as % of Total Population	Graduates
1949–50	11.7	0.023	18
1950–51	13.7	0.024	19
1951–52	15.3	0.027	32
1952–53	19.1	0.033	48

Source: An, 1952; Richman, 1969:164.

nonparty administrative elites and intellectuals an important role in later economic reconstruction. In September 1949 the party formally appealed to all previous officials to stay on and serve the new regime (RMRB, September 18, 1949). When the party took over Shanghai, it inherited over 49,000 officials, a number equal to 70–80 percent of the former KMT officials there (White, 1988:54). While the exact national figure of the retained personnel for the whole country was not available, some source suggested that about 3 million civil servants who had worked for the KMT remained in place in 1949 (Chesneaux, 1979:10).

The policy to use old managerial elites was, first of all, due to the shortage of the CCP's own administrative talent upon taking power. At the time, the estimated official vacancies were about 2 million, while the CCP had only 720,000 civilian cadres at its disposal. In addition, a majority of CCP cadres were concentrated in those earlier liberated areas. The party had to transfer cadres from the sectors and areas in relatively less urgent need to those where cadres were badly needed. The party accordingly made several major cadre reallocations. In October 1948, 63,000 cadres were transferred to the regions of east and central China; in 1949, 38,000 cadres were sent to the northwest, southwest, and south; and in 1952 the party again dispatched 700 cadres to southern China to carry out land reform. Given the extreme shortage of cadres in industrial sectors, the party altogether transferred about 163,000 personnel there from other sectors during the period of 1952–1954 (Gao, 1987:99).

There was another important reason for the party to retain old managerial personnel. In the initial period of transformation, the party only nationalized a small proportion of enterprises, mainly those larger ones which had been under control of the notorious Four Families.[5] In 1949 the private sector still accounted for 63.3 percent of the total industrial output, while 85 percent of trade was in private hands (Rodzinski, 1988:22). The private sector even expanded in the next several years. In 1951, for example, the number of private enterprises, employees, and output increased respectively by 11, 11.4, and 39 percent, as compared with the year 1950. The growth in the private trade sector was also impressive: 11.9 percent in the number of private businesses, 11.8 percent in their employees, 35.9 percent in the volume of wholesale, and 36.6 percent in the turnover from private retail trade (Zheng and Zhu, 1980:523–524). Because these private enterprises and businesses were small and scattered, it was extremely difficult for the party to take over all of them by its own cadres. What the party could do was to encourage old managerial personnel in these places to remain and work for the new regime.

CORRUPTION IN THE EARLY YEARS

The foregoing discussion reveals a profound dilemma of the CCP's early administration policies—the contradiction between the party's ambitious goals of transformation and its insufficient administrative capabilities. The party quickly realized the dilemma as it was confronted with some serious problems from both inside and outside the government organization.

Problems from the Inside

As illustrated, the party's cadre corps was actually composed of three layers (Figure 5.3).[6] At the top were the old cadres who joined the CCP during those early days when the party's victory was still uncertain. They were small in number, though no actual figure is available. New cadres constituted the next layer. This group included newly recruited party members and young graduates of higher educational institutions and other professional schools; they were not necessarily party members, though. The third and largest layer was retained KMT personnel, and intellectuals and technical specialists.

These groups in one way or another fell short of the party's ideological criteria and especially the party's high expectations for them to fulfill the tough tasks of transformation. Rather, they created some problems for the party from the inside of the government organization.

Figure 5.3
The Composition of CCP Administrative Elite During the Early Years

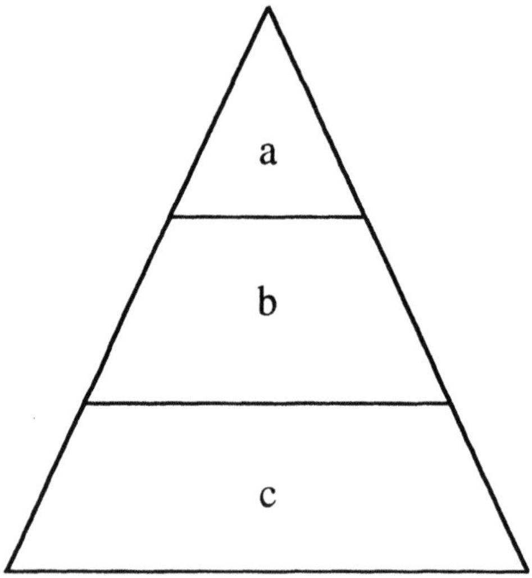

a = Old party members
b = Newly recruited members
c = Retained administrative elites

Old cadres

Old cadres had politically respectable backgrounds, for many of them had risked their lives for the communist cause and were therefore naturally regarded by the party as the core group of the new administrative elite. However, the party leadership perceived an increasing mood of conceit and pride among these cadres, which contravened the party's cause. Regarding themselves as heroes, some old cadres became arrogant, indolent, fearful of hard working and living conditions, and unwilling to cooperate with others; they looked down on new cadres, especially those who worked in newly liberated areas, whom they called "retained party members" or "liberated workers" (XHYB, November 1950:27). As a party newspaper said, "some of our party members only have limited education and little knowledge of science, but they are reluctant to learn from nonparty colleagues. They are intoxicated with their revolutionary experience, with their seniority in the party, and with such titles as 'old revolutionary' or 'old cadre'" (SYRB, September 18, 1950). Meanwhile, some of these cadres began to seek material shares from the fruit of victory, believing that their seniority should have brought them more privileges. Some even openly complained that "the fruits of victory which we paid for in blood and flesh are now being enjoyed by those who contributed nothing and deserve less" (XX, January 1, 1951:9). The party gave high publicity to two cases of old cadre degeneration: the cases of Liu Qingshan and Zhang Zishan. Liu and Zhang both joined the revolution in the early 1930s and had fought for the party's cause during the Anti-Japanese War and the Liberation War. After 1949 they served as party secretaries at the district level in Tianjin. Taking advantage of their positions, Liu and Zhang allegedly embezzled public funds and properties of more than 1,550,000 *yuan*, kept close personal contact with capitalists, and lived lavishly. They were both sentenced to death during the early stage of the Three Anti's Campaign (Cheng, 1986). The Party Bureau of East China Region also fired several high-ranking officials of the region for taking bribes, misappropriating public funds, or protecting unlawful elements. Among them were a deputy minister, the head of the region's press bureau, and a vice-president of the region's People's Revolutionary University (RMRB, March 20, 1952). The Party's Shanghai Committee removed its secretary general, the secretary general of the Shanghai General Federation of Trade Union, the deputy secretary general of the Shanghai People's Government, and several other higher-level officials. These old cadres with many years' party standing were all accused of engaging in corrupt activities (JFRB, January 31, 1952; March 2, 1952).

Upset by these problems, the party felt an urgent need to "check the grave danger of many party members being corrupted by the bourgeoisie" (Mao, SW, 1977,5:64). As the party perceived it, "many comrades who had successfully manifested their courage in the fight against imperialism, feudalism, and bureaucratic capitalism have now succumbed to bourgeois tricks and temptations, and have changed, degraded, and even betrayed the revolution" (XX, Feb. 10, 1952:17).

New cadres

New cadres, the second layer of the administrative elite, were problematic, too. As mentioned previously, new cadres mainly came from two sources: (1) newly recruited party members, usually of peasant origin; and (2) newly graduated students from schools. As they were new, they had different problems from their seniors. The first group, the new party members, primarily emerged from mass campaigns and, therefore, were presumably politically reliable. Yet the party found that they had less political knowledge and experience than old cadres on the one hand, and lacked the culture and skills of school graduates on the other. As revealed by party newspapers, some new party members did not know the party's "working class" nature; others identified communism with common property, eating out of the same bowl, and wearing the same clothes (Teiwes, 1979:94–95). The party also found that many new cadres were entangled in the complex web of particularistic ties, as they often relied on their relatives and fellow townsmen to make decisions. As reported by the *Northeast Daily*, the director of a department of the Northeast People's Government employed sixteen relatives or friends as cadres without the approval of the party; among them, some were serious political suspects, others were liquidated landlords in exile, and still others had been dismissed because of poor work elsewhere (*Northeast Daily*, December 1, 1951). A problem like this was believed to result from the lack of education and political indoctrination, since a large proportion of new party members were of peasant origin. The party admitted that the past recruitment had paid too much attention to mass activists so that the quality of new members was not secured. It then decided that from 1951 on, recruitment should focus on urban workers, while in rural areas the main work was to educate new party members and rectify party organizations (Chen and Zhang, 1989:63–64).

In contrast to worker-peasant cadres, young graduates had professional skills. Fresh out of schools, however, they lacked "revolutionary experiences." The party believed that "although they had relatively high initiative and revolutionary enthusiasm, they were vulnerable to bourgeois thought and style" (ibid.:61). At the Third Plenum of the Central Committee held in June 1950, some party leaders publicly expressed their concern over the fact that too many young intellectuals were serving as cadres (Harding, 1981:37).

New cadres, judged by the party leadership, were no less vulnerable to corruption than their seniors. Because they were young and inexperienced, they were more likely to become victims of bourgeois influence. The case of Chen Juhong was publicized by the party to illustrate the vulnerability of young cadres. Chen was a new cadre who joined the revolution in the summer of 1949. When he was put in charge of purchasing materials by the Industrial Ministry of the Southwest Region, he spent tens of thousands of yuan of public funds on speculation, sightseeing, and women. He was later sentenced to death by the Beijing People's Court (XHYB, September 1950:1019). The Central Committee of the Communist Youth League also reported a number of cases of embezzlement by young cadres. According to the statistics from 17 provinces and cities, among more than 600 punished League members, 120 were charged with graft. In Beijing alone, 45 League members were expelled from the organization because of their involvement with embezzlement. (XHYB, January 1952:33).

Retained personnel

The party never relaxed its vigilance against retained personnel, presumably because of their class background and bourgeois ideology. While relying on them for professional skills, the party was eager to reinforce their loyalty. All retained personnel were required by the party to take special courses to remain in administrative posts. During the first three years, about 100,000 "old intellectuals" were sent to the People's Revolutionary Universities, institutions aiming at thought reform. The party believed that "these old intellectual cadres retained from the old society have cultivated hireling mentality, technocratic tendency, and political apathy. All of these weaknesses may not have been solved" (An, 1952:58). As the party perceived, while these people served public offices, they carried over with them corrupt ways of life from the KMT period and would continue to seek private gain. On January 6, 1952, *People's Daily* disclosed the case of Wang Chanwen, a retained former KMT official who stole 200,000 yuan in public funds and properties. It was believed that Wang's corruption had something to do with his past because he was from a landlord family and had once worked for the KMT as an English interpreter and technician. After 1949 when he was asked to take charge of electric product inspection in a government unit, he profiteered by stealing and reselling electric machines and goods. After his case was brought to light, people found in his home 20 valuable machines, a great many electric products, 3,150 grams of gold, 50 American dollars, and 20,000 yuan in cash. Other reports showed that, of 650 cases of embezzlement exposed in two major inspections in Beijing between 1949 and 1950, 514 were conducted by retained personnel (Li, 1984:54). In the East China Region, from June 1950 to November 1951, the judicial organ altogether handled 615 corruption criminals; of them, 365 were retained personnel (JFRB, December 30, 1951).

Problems from the Outside

Since its victory in 1949, the CCP had worried about the actual and potential threat from external sources such as the bourgeoisie. A class with huge fortune but suddenly without political influence, "the bourgeoisie doubts our ability to construct [the country]," as Mao pointed out before the nationwide victory,

> The policy of restricting private capitalism is bound to meet with resistance in varying degrees and forms from the bourgeoisie, especially from the big owners of private enterprises . . . . It has been proved that the enemy cannot conquer us by force of arms. However, the flattery of the bourgeoisie may conquer the weak-willed in our ranks. There may be some communists who were not conquered by enemies with guns and were worthy of the name of heroes for standing up to these enemies, but who cannot withstand sugar-coated bullets; they will be defeated by sugar-coated bullets. (SW, 1965,4:374)

Though on other occasions Mao included the "petty bourgeoisie" and the "national bourgeoisie" in the category of "people," regarding them as friends of the working class (Mao, SW, 1965,4:417), the difference between friendly bourgeoisie and enemy bourgeoisie was indeed a matter of political relativity, as there had never been any fixed criteria for the distinction (Brady, 1982).

The resistance of private businesses to the CCP's restrictions intensified when the party began to confiscate bureaucratic capital, exercise financial control, regulate domestic and foreign trade, and centralize the allocation of important resources and major industrial and agricultural goods shortly after liberation. Scared by the party's ambitious transformation goals and worried about profit, capitalists resorted to various means to resist the CCP's control. The party found that "the bourgeoisie in China, for the self-interests of the class itself and in disregard of the interests of the state, launched a fierce attack on the Chinese working class and the Chinese Communist Party during the past three years (1949–1952)" (XX, February 10, 1952:14).

A number of means were identified as used by the bourgeoisie against the party's transformation efforts:

Tax evasion

Tax evasion was believed the most common means used by capitalists to escape the party's control. The report of the East China Region revealed that cases of tax evasion kept increasing from 1949 to 1951. In 1949 the region handled a total of 49,175 cases of tax evasion; the number increased to 117,360 in the next year and reached 139,068 by November 1951. According to the investigation of the Shanghai Tax Bureau in 1951, about 99 percent of the city's taxable businesses evaded taxes in one way or another.

Stealing public assets

The party also found that besides passive resistance through tax evasion, many capitalists engaged actively in profit-seeking activities. Xue Kunshan was an example. Originally an ordinary fur merchant, Xue made off with about 400,000 yuan's worth of state assets after he became a government cadre and reinvested them in nineteen businesses as private properties. He was later sentenced to death (XHYB, March 1952:7).

Cheating in labor and materials

Capitalists also took advantage of loopholes in the state administration to profiteer, as disclosed by the party. For example, after they signed governmental contracts to produce military raincoats, twelve factories started a series of illegal activities; they used excessive gasoline, exaggerated costs, delayed delivery, and more seriously, produced many defective goods (XHYB, January 1952:45). As China's engagement in the Korean War in 1950 brought an urgent need for military supplies, the party saw cheating increasing among private industrialists and merchants. It publicized several major cases to alert the nation: the manager of Huafu Absorbent Cotton Factory used nonsterilized cotton for military orders; the bosses of two beef-processing factories sold bad beef to armies; and in Shenyang, nineteen factories reportedly mixed chaff and sand into rice when they were processing food for armies (XX, February 10, 1952:19).

Stealing state economic intelligence

Stealing state intelligence was identified by the party as an important means of capitalists to profiteer for themselves while doing damage to the state economy. In early 1952 Wushun city uncovered five cases of this nature. Among them, Wang Kechun, a merchant, stole the special skill of grease processing and then opened a processing factory himself. The skill helped him earn huge profits. In another case, the blueprints of a unique type of planing machine were stolen by a merchant for personal gain (ibid.).

Bribery

Of particular concern for the party, however, were bourgeois "sugar-coated bullets." As the party perceived, the bourgeoisie was taking advantage of the fact that old cadres were eager to enjoy the fruits of victory while young ones were inexperienced in management. Many private entrepreneurs overtly or secretly searched for their protectors or representatives within the party. They were doing this with two general tactics called "pulling out" (*la chu qu*) and "sending in" (*da jin lai*). "Pulling out" referred to buying cadres by means of banquets, gifts, sales commissions, and beautiful girls. For example, the manager of Dakang Pharmacy, Wang Kangnian, "pulled out" 65 cadres from 25 different government units by these means. It was reported that he was immensely proud of this, as he told others that "Dakang is a thought reform place for cadres. All cadres who came to Dakang for business will be reformed" (Liu, 1989:5). "Sending in" was a method of the bourgeoisie to send its own people into government organs as personnel. Some of these people got in because they pretended to be more revolutionary than others; some were introduced in by their relatives or friends who had already worked in government; still others sneaked into government ranks in the name of cooperation with state enterprises (Qi, 1952). As reported, in the Dairen General Goods Company, the chiefs of six departments were big merchants; of the 1,300 employees there, 1,200 were employed or appointed though the introduction of private merchants (RMRB, January 24, 1952). Among nine department heads of the China Medicine Corporation in the East China Region, four had a merchant background and two others were sent in by private businessmen (DBRB, March 1, 1952).

THE THREE AND FIVE ANTI'S CAMPAIGN

These problems, as perceived by the CCP, not only hindered the fulfillment of the party's transformation goals but also threatened the new regime's survival. The CCP believed that a capable and reliable state apparatus on the one hand, and the obedience and cooperation of private enterprises on the other, were the two prerequisites for a successful socialist transformation (NFRB, January 1, 1952). Without an administratively capable and politically reliable state apparatus, the transformation might lose its socialist traits. On the other hand, the full obedience and cooperation of private enterprises were indispensable, given the urgent task of economic recovery. However, for the party the two issues were closely connected. Bourgeois evils (such as those listed above) and values had corroded the party's organization to an intolerable extent. They shook or weakened the political conviction of some party members, those self-complacent old "revolutionaries" and those inexperienced young ones, and corrupted them. Hence the struggle against corruption was interpreted as a class struggle with the proletariat on the one hand and the bourgeoisie on the other (RMSC, 1952:48). It was a counterattack against bourgeois attacks on the new-born regime, and hence an important component of the party's overall program of transformation.

The party thus launched the earliest anti-corruption campaign in PRC history, the Three and Five Anti's Campaign between December 1951 and June 1952. The campaign started with the Three Antis—anti-corruption, anti-waste, and anti-bureaucratism among government officials. Not surprisingly, it quickly stormed the private enterprises by a Five Anti's movement against bribery, tax evasion, theft of state assets, cheating in labor and materials, and stealing of state economic intelligence.

The campaign was first carried out on a regional basis in the Northeast Region. On November 2, 1951, when commenting on the region's report of "Increasing Production and Austerity and Furthering the Struggle against Corruption, Waste, and Bureaucratism," the Party Central Committee declared that the experience of the Northeast Region had nationwide implications (Li, 1984:56). The *People's Daily*'s editorial on November 23 then systematically introduced that region's experiences of performing the Three Anti's. However, it was Mao himself who set the course, guiding principles, and policies for the campaign, as he made a series of important instructions during the months of November and December 1951. On November 30, 1951, Mao pointed out, "We need to have a good clean-up in the whole party, which will thoroughly uncover all cases of corruption, whether major, medium, or minor, and aim the main blows at the most corrupt while following the policy of educating and remolding the medium and minor embezzlers so that they will not relapse" (SW, 1977,5:64). On another occasion, he again suggested,

> The broad masses, including the democratic parties, and also people from all walks of life, should be mobilized, the present struggle should be given wide publicity, the leading cadres should take personal charge and pitch in, and people should be called on to make a clean breast of their own wrongdoing and to report on the guilt of others. In minor cases, the guilty should be criticized and educated; in major ones, the guilty should be dismissed from office, punished, or sentenced to prison terms (to be reformed through labor), and the worst among them should be shot. The problem can only be solved in these ways. (SW, 1977,5:65)

On December 1, 1951, the party issued the Resolution on Better Staff and Simpler Administration, Production Increase and Austerity, and Anti-Corruption, Anti-Waste, and Anti-Bureaucratism. The document marked the beginning of the campaign which could be further divided into four phases—mobilization, confession and accusation, expansion, and disposition. In many ways, the campaign resembled the CCP's previous rectifications.

First phase: mobilization (December 1–31, 1951)

In the first phase of the campaign, the party issued a series of directives to urge the public to participate. Other leading government organs such as the Chinese People's Political Consultative Conference and the State Council also followed suit by issuing similar directives. The *People's Daily* published several editorials to elaborate the party's guiding principles on why and how to mobilize all party members and the general public to take part in the campaign. People were then asked to gather together to study Mao's works and party documents, while cadres were expected to make self-criticism for waste, bureaucratism, and other rightist tendencies.

Second phase: confession and accusation (January 1–25, 1952)

As the campaign entered into its second phase, the party urged all those who had engaged in corruption to confess. In the meantime, the party encouraged the public to expose and denounce cadres involved with corruption, waste, and bureaucratism. People could do it publicly or secretly, orally or in writing, and anonymously or with their names. At any event, the party guaranteed, they would be protected against retaliation. According to some statistics (Wang, 1990:34), during the first month of confession and accusation in Beijing, 556 people from 24 different administrative units, and 250 from the army's logistic units, confessed their corruption related problems; in addition, 823 people from 18 administrative units, and 566 from military units informed against others and exposed a total of 359 cases.

Third phase: expansion (January 26–March, 1952)

As mentioned above, from the very beginning when the party found the problems of its administrative elite, it had considered them the consequence of bourgeois sugar-coated bullets on unsophisticated party members or nonparty cadres. "The 'sugar bullets' used by the bourgeois class today are especially dangerous for our party" (XX, February 10, 1952:16). With the campaign going on and more and more cases explored, the party's concern further increased. An editorial in *Tianjin Ribao* told businessmen that "the movement must be carried to you people. This is only because you are often the parties directly responsible for these criminal acts" (TJRB, January 15, 1952). On January 26, 1952, Liu Ren, the chairman of the Economy Inspection Committee of Beijing Municipality, claimed that 80 percent of the discovered corrupt elements had connections with private industrialists and merchants: some of them were agents of the bourgeois class, while others themselves were of bourgeoisie origin (XX, February 10, 1952:16). It was thus not surprising that the campaign soon swept over the private enterprises and business circles. On January 26, 1952, the party issued the Directive on Launching a Large-Scale, Resolute, and Thorough "Five Anti" Struggle in Urban Areas. It requested that all cities should start the struggle against the "Five Evils" in the first ten days of February (Mao, SW, 1977,5:66). The campaign was immediately intensified at this point, demonstrating more characteristics of a mass movement. Numerous "working teams" or "tiger-hunting teams" emerged, composed of workers and mass activists selected from ordinary staff members.[7] These teams went to individual private entrepreneurs to investigate the five "illicit activities" mentioned above, and then organized struggle meetings against those "dishonest" ones. Very few private entrepreneurs and merchants were exempt from the investigation. The investigation results of nine big cities suggested that 76 percent of private capitalists engaged in one or more type of corruption (Ma and Huang, 1989:739).[8]

The party also mobilized propaganda machines to expose before people how bourgeois elements were engaged in profiteering, stealing, cheating, bribing, and wasting. The public exposure of numerous corruption cases of big or small "tigers" intensified public hatred of the bourgeois class, while putting old KMT personnel under great psychological pressure.

Fourth phase: disposition (April–June, 1952)

In mid-March and April 1952, the party published a series of documents regarding how to handle those exposed cases, including Provisions on Handling Corruption and Waste and Overcoming Bureaucratic Mistakes (March 8, 1952), Provisions on the Establishment of the People's Courts in the Three Anti's Campaign (March 8, 1952), Provisions on Recovering Stolen Money and Properties (March 8, 1952), and Act of Corruption Punishment of the People's Republic of China (April 21, 1952). The Beijing People's Government also issued the Criteria and Measures of Classifying Private entrepreneurs and Merchants. These documents highlighted general principles and detailed guidelines for disposing of cases. For example, penalties for graft were divided into several categories, depending on the amount of money: (1) under 100 yuan: no penalty; (2) 100–1,000 yuan: disciplinary sanction;[9] (3) 1,000–5,000 yuan: 1–5 years' imprisonment; (4) 5,000–10,000 yuan: 5–10 years' imprisonment; and (5) above 10,000 yuan: from 10 years imprisonment up to the death penalty. However, in meting out the penalties, the fundamental criterion was that of "leniency to those who confessed their crimes and severity to those who refused to confess." As a result, among 1,203,590 cadres who were exposed as embezzlers, only some 43,330 or 3.6 percent were sentenced. The party's reluctance to severely punish its cadres reflected its bad need for managerial personnel during the early years. Table 5.5 showed the results of case handling during the campaign. As for private entrepreneurs and businessmen, through strict inspections they were grouped into five categories: law-abiding; basically law-abiding; unlawful; very unlawful; and totally unlawful (Table 5.6). There were no penalties for those private entrepreneurs and businessmen of the categories B, C, and D, but they were requested to return all illegally gained money or goods. For those in the category E, penalties involved confiscation, imprisonment, and also possibly the death penalty (Liu, 1989:8).

Table 5.5
Results of Disposing of Graft Cases

Total No.	Above $1,000 No. & %		Party Members No. & %		Results No[a]	Dis.[b]	Criminal[c]
1203590	105916	8.8%	196000+	16.3%	75.7%	20.7%	3.6%

Source: Ma and Huang, 1989:738.

[a] No=no penalty
[b] Dis.= disciplinary sanction
[c] Criminal= criminal charge

Table 5.6
Classification of Private Entrepreneurs and Businessmen (Beijing and Shanghai)

City & No.	A		B		C		D		E	
Beijing (58,000) 100%	5,000	10%	30,000	60%	12,500	25%	20,000	4%	500	1%
Shanghai (163,400) 100%	24,510	15%	81,700	50%	49,020	30%	(8,170	5%)[a]		

A=law-abiding
B=basically law-abiding
C=semi-unlawful
D=very unlawful
E=totally unlawful

Source: Jin, 1989:258.

[a] In Shanghai, the groups D and E altogether accounted for 5 percent.

On June 13, 1952, the State Administrative Council of the Central People's Government issued the Directive to Conclude the Five-Anti's Campaign. The directive further interpreted some policy issues in disposing of cases while declaring that the campaign had entered its concluding stage. The document laid down the guiding principles for concluding the campaign as "sternness in struggle, magnanimity in disposal of cases; sternness as deserved, magnanimity as deserved" (XHYB, June 1952:49). In the following months, more focus was put on establishment of new and efficient work systems. The Three and Five Anti's as a mass campaign thus ended in June 1952.

IMPLICATIONS OF THE CAMPAIGN FOR THE PARTY'S OVERALL POLICY

The foregoing review of the Three and Five Anti's discloses some unusual patterns of the first anti-corruption campaign in PRC history. First, the targets of the Three and Five Anti's Campaign reflected the party's overall transformation effort as well as its particular concern over the problem of corruption. Tables 5.7 and 5.8 classify the 127 cases reported by the *People's Daily* during the campaign according to the sector and the type of activity. We

Table 5.7
Sector Distribution of Corruption Cases

Sector	Frequency	Percentage
Production	95	74.8%
Trade	17	13.4
Government	9	7.1
Tax bureau	6	4.7
Total	127	100%

Source: Compiled by the author based on the 127 major cases reported by the *People's Daily* between December 1951 and April 1952.

Table 5.8
A Classification of Corruption Cases by Activities

Activity	Frequency	Percentage
Embezzlement	34	26.8%
Stealing state assets	34	26.8
Graft	32	25.2
Cheating in labor and materials	15	11.8
Speculation	4	3.1
Luxury	3	2.4
Others	5	3.9
Total	127	100%

Source: Compiled by the author based on the 127 major cases reported by the *People's Daily* between December 1951 and April 1952.

can see from the tables that, given the priority of economic recovery, the party centered its anti-corruption drive on the production and trade sectors. The cases reported were mainly from these two sectors (a total of 88.2 percent). Among these cases, moreover, the acts which brought direct damage to the state economy were usually given special publicity, such as embezzlement (26.8 percent), stealing state assets (26.8 percent), and graft (25.2 percent). They were given great publicity because these activities caused the state direct financial losses and thereby hurt the party's overall goal to achieve "a fundamental turn for the better in the financial and economic situation" in the early years. Other types, such as luxurious life style, speculation, smuggling, and feudal rites, might not bring direct and heavy economic damages to the state's treasury as long as actors spent their own money, though they also fell short of the party's ideological requirement.

Second, given the deep concern with the transformation program and the "pureness" of its cadre corps, the party's main objective to carry out the campaign was to cut off connections between party officials and private businessmen, which were perceived as the major cause of corruption. The party expressed its campaign objective clearly:

to purge all speculative bourgeois elements who had infiltrated into the leadership organs and revolutionary forces for the sabotage of national reconstruction; to purge all elements within the ranks of the leadership organs and revolutionary forces who had suffered so seriously from the encroachment of the bourgeois class, and had become corrupt elements beyond remedy; to thoroughly eliminate the evil bourgeois practices of corruption and waste within the ranks of the leadership organs; and to firmly oppose the evil influence of bureaucracy and other bourgeois ideological concepts. (XX, February 10, 1952:13)

Not surprisingly, as we saw before, retained personnel and capitalists became the most frequent targets. Table 5.9 is a background report of those accused during the Three and Five Anti's. It shows that both retained officials and capitalists accounted for about 76 percent of all those widely publicized corruption cases.

Finally, as a result of the first and second patterns, punishment given to a corrupt cadre tended to have a closer relationship with the monetary amount involved in the case than with the person's position level. The statistical results (Table 5.10) show that the relationship between the position level of an accused person and the punishment he or she received is quite weak (G=0.068), while the relationship between the money amount he or she grabbed and the punishment seems moderately strong (G=0.28). The lower

Table 5.9
A Background Report of Corruption Cases During the Three and Five Anti's Period

Category	Frequency	Percentage
Old cadre	15	12%
New cadre	15	12
Retained personnel	24	19
Capitalists	73	57
Total	127	100%

Source: Compiled by the author based on the 127 major cases reported by the *People's Daily* between December 1951 and April 1952.

Table 5.10
A Statistical Test of Association Between Punishment and Other Variables, the Early 1950s

Gamma	Position level	Money
Punishment	0.07	0.28

N=127

Note: The statistic is based on the 127 cases in the author's database. Gamma is a statistical measurement of the association between two variables. Gamma has a possible range of -1 to 1. A gamma of 0 would indicate that information supplied by the independent variable does not improve our ability to predict the dependent, and therefore there is no association between the variables. A gamma of 1 would mean that it is possible to predict Y without error from X. A gamma close to -1 means that the two variables are negatively associated.

(gamma) value for the relationship between the position level and the punishment confirms that the main target of the campaign was capitalists and retained administrative personnel instead of high- or middle-level government cadres. The higher G value between the money amount and the punishment, on the other hand, indicates the party's high concern over economic loss caused by corruption for the already debilitated national economy.

The statistics indicate that on the whole, the Three and Five Anti's Campaign mostly struck the bourgeois class, though it also disciplined the CCP's own administrative ranks.

It is clear from the above that the development of the first anti-corruption campaign in PRC history was closely linked to the party's ultimate goal of that period: transformation. But it also brought to the surface a profound contradiction in the CCP's organizational policies. During the early years, because of the pressure of economic recovery and reconstruction, the party had to organize cadre corps in a way significantly different from that of wartime by recruiting intellectuals without affiliation with the party and by retaining the personnel of the former KMT regime. This shift of organizational policy based on practical concerns, however, created problems for the party itself. The more the party relied on the administrative elites, the more it was worried about the loyalty of the latter. The diversity in the cadre composition presented the cadre corps in a less controllable manner and therefore further reinforced the party's concern. The CCP, after all, was a Leninist party with strict ideological affiliation and class restrictions. The mood of conceit and pride, indolence, arrogance, misappropriation of public funds, bureaucratism, waste, negligence, profiteering, all these practices were in sharp contrast with the images of diligence, courage, and self-discipline which the party had enjoyed and itself been proud of. The dilemma of the party's organization policy during the early years therefore was that, on the one hand, the party's general policy of transformation required a professional administrative elite, which, at that time, could only come from nonparty groups. Yet, on the other hand, the party had to maintain people's good faith in itself by keeping those Yanan images alive. This to a large extent explained the nature of the Three and Five Anti's Campaign. The campaign was a result of the party's early organizational policy which brought in, from the party's viewpoint, disloyal and untrustful elements. The campaign was also a part of the CCP's general transformation policy, which would, at least as anticipated by the party, make its cadre corps healthy and strong enough to lead the transformation of the country. However, as we shall see in the next chapter, the campaign created unexpected problems for the party as well.

NOTES

1. In July 1945, Mr. Huang Yanpei, a well-known educationist and the chairman of the China Democratic National Construction Association, visited Yanan and had a conversation with Mao.

2. One mou equals 1/6 acre.

3. During the early years, there were numerous programs designed to improve the qualification of cadres, such as "government personnel schools," "worker and peasant accelerated schools," and "continuation schools for worker and peasant cadres" (Chao, 1985:63).

4. According to some source, by the year of 1958 the number of cadres transformed from the army to civilian posts had reached 7 million (Zhang, 1989:162).

5. When the KMT held power in China, there were so-called four Big Families of the Jiang, the Song, the Kong, and the Chen. With strong political backing, the Big Four ran vast business empires amassing enormous fortunes at a time of political and economic chaos.

6. In China, cadre corps, different from party ranks, refer to those people who assume leading administrative positions. They may not necessarily be party members. Nor all party members are government cadres.

7. During the Three and Five Anti's, the term "tiger" was used to refer to those private businessmen who "ate" (stole) public funds or property.

8. The nine cities included Beijing, Tianjin, Shanghai, Hanko. Altogether 450,000 private enterprises were investigated; 340,000 were reportedly involved in corruption of some kind.

9. Disciplinary sanction included six categories: warning, recording demerit, demoting rank, demoting position, dismissing from post, and discharging from job.

6

Consolidation and the Socialist Education Movement

After three years in power, the CCP could indeed look back with pride on its significant achievements. With the actual and potential enemies suppressed and the cadre corps disciplined, domestic threats to the new regime started to recede. In the international arena, the end of the Korean War brought some relief to the party's burden. While social life returned to normal, the first three years also witnessed the successful rehabilitation of the nation's economy. Industrial production and handicrafts rose by 144.9 percent from 1949 to 1952 (an average annual increase of 34.8 percent). Agricultural production exceeded its previous peak level. Foreign trade expanded steadily, increasing from the index number 100 in 1949 to 155.5 in 1952. Inflation was under control and the currency was stabilized (Eckstein, 1977:191–211; Guillermaz, 1976:25–35).

The achievements of the three-year transformation allowed the CCP to further consolidate its power by securing its leadership, constructing new production relations, establishing a solid economic base, and reinforcing its political and administrative apparatus. Accordingly, the party shifted the focus of its general policy from transformation to consolidation, aiming at more systematic construction and steady political and economic development.

GENERAL POLICY: CONSOLIDATION

Beginning in 1953, some changes in the party's working emphases highlighted the shift of CCP general policy and its new effort at power consolidation.

From Revolutionary Destruction to Social Reconstruction

To achieve massive transformation in the first years, the CCP concentrated its efforts on destroying old institutions and authorities before 1953. A fundamental Marxist principle well recognized by the CCP leadership was that any lasting revolutionary success required a thorough destruction of the political institutions of the old regime (Meisner, 1977:73). This was exactly what the CCP did in the first years: the Land Reform of 1950 aimed at landlords; the Campaign of Suppressing Counterrevolutionaries in the same year targeted KMT spies and American agents; the Thought Reform of 1951 put intellectuals under strict ideological control, whereas the Democratic Reform in the next year shook up old labor unions; and, finally, the Three and Five Anti's disciplined the party's own cadre corps and struck urban business people. As Alan Liu (1986:41) points out, "at the end of each campaign an old institution and the social groups connected with it, such as landlords, urban businessmen, liberal intellectuals, and labor unions, were either destroyed or totally discredited."

On the ruins of the old social structures, the party embarked on social reconstruction in 1953. In rural areas, social relations were reorganized through collectivization. In December 1952 the Party Central Committee issued the Resolution on Mutual-Aid and Cooperation for Agricultural Production, which marked the beginning of large-scale collectivization in the countryside. Since then, the "mutual-aid teams" (*huzhuzu*), originally small in scale, limited in number, and scattered in scope, rapidly spread from area to area.

Agricultural collectivization was a three-stage incremental process: (1) from temporary and seasonal mutual-aid teams to long-term teams, in which several peasant households cultivated fields jointly in the form of mutual-aid teams and shared agricultural tools and machines; (2) from mutual-aid teams to lower-level agricultural production cooperatives (APCs), a cooperative system in which members received their shares in accordance with the landed property they brought in as well as their work rates; (3) from lower-level APCs to higher-level APCs where the members were paid according to their work rates, with all tools, machines, and fields belonging to collective ownership, and only houses and vegetable gardens left for individuals.

Table 6.1 shows the process of agricultural collectivization in China from 1952–1956. The first stage of development virtually took place in 1953. The transformation of temporary mutual-aid teams into long-term teams proceeded rather easily, since it did not involve any change in the ownership of property. Collectivization accelerated during 1953–1955 as lower-level APCs increased from 15,000 to 1,905,000. By the end of 1956 when the party completed its collectivization campaign, 96.3 percent of the Chinese rural population had been organized into either higher-level or lower-level APCs.

Parallel to collectivization in rural areas, nationalization of private ownership of the means of production refashioned social relations in cities. By the end of 1952, China's socioeconomic structure had still been a mixture of five economic components: state enterprises (19.1 percent), cooperative enterprises (1.5 percent), state-private joint enterprises (0.7 percent), national capitalist enterprises (6.9 percent), and privately owned and managed handcraft enterprises (71.8 percent) (Zhu and Zhu, 1989:100). Industrial nationalization to change the economic relations was also a step-by-step process. Private ownership of the industrial means of production was first transformed into state-private joint property and then into state property. Table 6.2 shows the gradually increased share of state-owned industry in the gross national income (GNI).

Table 6.1
Process of Agricultural Collectivization, 1950–1956

Year	Mutual-Aid Teams		Lower-Level APCs		Higher-Level APCs	
	No.	%[a]	No.	%	No.	%
December 1952	8,000,000		3,644		—	
1953	47,900,000	43	15,000	0.13	—	
June 1955	—		650,000	14.2	500	
December 1955	—		1,905,000	63.3	17,000	4
January 1956	—		219,726	49.6	136,000	30.7
February 1956	—		165,883	36.0	235,000	51.0
June 1956	—		312,000	63.2		
September 1956	—		380,000	72.7		
December 1956	—		216,000	8.5	540,000	87.8

Source: Compiled by author according to the data in Zhu and Zhu, 1989: 108–111; 146–152; 198–202.

[a] % = percentage of the total agricultural households.

Table 6.2
Changing Proportions of Five Economic Components in GNI,[a] 1952–1957

Year	State	Cooperative	State-Private	Capitalist	Individual
1952	19.1	1.5	0.7	6.9	71.8
1953	23.9	2.5	0.9	7.9	64.8
1954	26.8	4.8	2.1	5.3	61.0
1955	28.0	14.1	2.8	3.5	51.6
1956	32.2	53.7	7.3	—	7.1
1966	33.2	56.4	7.6	—	2.8

Source: Ma and Huang, 1989:163.

[a] The total value of GNI = 100.

The socialization of trade proceeded along the same lines. By 1956, in wholesale trade, state and joint state-private commerce accounted for 97.2 percent of the turnover and private commerce only 2.8 percent. In retail sales, the share of state commerce was 68.3 percent, state-private joint and cooperative commerce 27.5%, and private commerce only 4.2% (Xue, 1981:31). Thus, in only a few years, the CCP consolidated China's socioeconomic relations for socialism.

From Political Mobilization to Economic Development

As a senior CCP leader admitted in 1952, the Chinese communists had mainly lived by political movements in the past (see also Chow, 1960:92–93). Indeed, as we saw in the preceding pages, from 1949 to 1952, the nation was involved in sequential political movements. These movements relied on forceful measures against traditional power holders on the one hand and politically oriented large-scale mass education on the other. They aimed not only to suppress opponents, but also to submit all sectors of the population to the CCP's control. However, the party leadership was fully aware of the importance of economic development as its power base. It also saw the necessity of rapid and successful modernization for survival in a still-hostile international environment. Equally essential for consolidating its leadership, the party had to increase the number of nonparty citizens who would loyally accept the regime for its contribution to their welfare, to general progress, or to the strength of the motherland (Lowenthal, 1970:50). Accordingly, the party leadership claimed that after the basic goals of economic rehabilitation were achieved, and especially after the social conditions returned to normal, the nation's principal task should be economic development (Mao, SW, 1977,5:29).

To promote economic growth, the CCP looked to the Soviet Union as a model. In 1953 the party adopted a "general program of transition to socialism" with the first Five-Year Plan (FYP) as its instrument. Soviet experts and advisers participated in drawing up the plan. It was thus not surprising to find a strong resemblance between the basic premises of the plan and the Soviet ones.

The first FYP demonstrated two prominent characteristics (Guillermaz, 1976:78–79): (1) heavier emphasis was laid on industry than agriculture; and (2) heavy industry, particularly the means of production, was in favor. The party offered some explanations for the imbalances in the plan. It claimed that agriculture did not seem ready to absorb extensive investment, while light industry lacked modern equipment, which it relied on heavy industry to supply. At any rate, CCP assumed that the first plan, followed by a second and a third, would provide Chinese socialism with a solid economic base and lead China well onto the road to rapid economic modernization. At the same time, the party also promised to promote the people's living standard by increasing average wages by 33 percent in cities and doubling peasant purchasing power by the end of the plan.

From Mass Mobilization to Regularized Bureaucratic Practice

Indeed, one of the important lessons drawn by the party leadership from the first three years of transformation was that it must standardize the party and government apparatus. In the earlier years, the party's administration had typified what Harding (1981:65) called "ad hoc-racy": it was understaffed, small, informal, and provisional. As a result, the party had to resort frequently to mass mobilization to implement its programs or policies. This was why the Land Reform, the Suppression of Counterrevolutionaries, the Three and Five Anti's Campaign, and other political movements during 1949–1952 all followed the same pattern of mass mobilization: pressure to denounce others, including one's neighbors, friends, and even relatives; mass "struggle meetings"; public condemnations and executions of numerous culprits; quick expulsion from cadre ranks of persons whose performance fell short of the party's expectations; and immediate recruitment of political "activists" into the party.

In addition, the numerous cases of cadre corruption exposed by the Three and Five Anti's Campaign further enhanced the party's dissatisfaction with its administrative elite in several aspects. First, the mixed sources of cadres, especially the retention of old personnel, made the administrative elite less reliable than the party had anticipated. Moreover, the irregular and decentralized administrative structures created difficulties for the party to tighten control over its administrative elite. Finally, as the party perceived, the low administrative capabilities of cadres furnished loopholes for various types of corruption. The party was thus convinced that a formal, powerful bureaucracy was indispensable for its rule. To consolidate its power, the CCP had to rely, as the party's newspaper put it, on "systematic and methodical" bureaucracies rather than "direct action of military forces and the masses" to fulfill the tasks of the new era (RMRB, May 21, 1954). However, "if the Chinese communists were not burdened by old bureaucratic structures, they soon were to be weighed down by new ones of their own" (Meisner, 1977:73).

BUREAUCRATIZATION OF THE ADMINISTRATIVE ELITE

The shift of the party's general policy from transformation to consolidation led to changes in its organizational policies. From 1953 on, China's administrative elite entered the process of transformation from a revolutionary organization into a professional bureaucratic apparatus. This process was characterized by institutional proliferation, administrative regularization, cadre professionalization, and power centralization.

Institutional Proliferation

Centralized economic planning and the party's involvement in economic activities inevitably brought about bureaucratic proliferation and hence the emergence of a new elite of bureaucrats in China. In September 1954 the first session of the National People's Congress in Beijing adopted several important documents: the first state constitution of the PRC, the Organic Law of the State Council, and the Organic Law of Local Governments. Replacing the Common Program of 1949, these laws started a new round of institution-building under the State Council: (1) eight offices were created in place of the previous four committees immediately under the State Council to assist the premier to control the ministries; (2) the number of ministries increased to 35; and (3) 20 new departments were established within the State Council in charge of particular issues. With a secretariat, thus, the institutions under the State Council increased from 42 to 64. Although there were some small-scale institutional reorganizations in 1955 and 1956, they all followed the same pattern: replacing one ministry by several. Not surprisingly, by the end of 1956, the number of institutions under the State Council reached its peak level of 81 in the pre-reform period (Table 6.3).

Institutional proliferation occurred at local levels too. Provincial organizational set-ups matched the innovations at the national level. County governments also increased their institutions correspondingly (Song and Lei, 1988).

With the proliferation of government institutions, the number of party and state cadres increased dramatically. While in 1949 the party only had 720,000 (0.13 percent of the population) cadres at its disposal, the number of cadres rose to 5,270,000 (0.86 percent of the population) in 1955. The percentage of

Table 6.3
Numerical Change of Institutions under the State Council, 1949–1965

Year	Ministry	Department	Office	Total
1949	29	6	—	35
1950	30	6	—	36
1952	38	4	—	42
1954	35	21	8	64
1955	39	23	8	70
1956	48	25	8	81
1957	48	24	8	80
1958	40	19	9	68
1959	39	15	6	60
1960	40	16	5	61
1961	39	17	6	62
1962	39	19	6	64
1963	42	24	7	73
1964	45	25	7	77
1965	49	23	7	79

Source: Su, 1987:32; Ren, 1989:17.

government payroll in the national budget went far beyond the originally planned figure of 5 percent as it amounted to 10 percent in the mid- and late 1950s (Kau, 1971:106). In the city of Shanghai, for example, while total employment between 1949 and 1957 grew at an annual rate of 1.2 percent, health and government cadres increased by 16 percent per year (Johnson, 1982:924). According to Yinmaw Kau (1968:269), the number of cadres in China increased by 139 percent from 1952 to 1958, a rate much higher than that of the gross national product.

Administrative Regularization

To establish a formal and systematic bureaucracy required regularizing cadre ranks and routinizing administrative procedures. As early as 1952, the central government had taken a series of measures to formalize governmental management with regard to transmission and protection of government documents, maintenance of state archives, and establishment of administrative organization committees to plan for the size and structure of the state bureaucracy (Harding, 1981:71). The Second Conference on Organizational Work held in September 1953 passed the resolution to establish a new system of cadre management. The system classified cadres into eight categories: (1) military cadres; (2) cadres of cultural and educational work; (3) cadres of planning and industrial work; (4) cadres of finance and trade; (5) cadres of transportation work; (6) nonparty cadres; (7) political and judicial cadres; and (8) others, including those working in mass organizations. However, this nine-fold classification was only one of the ways, and perhaps the least popular way, to stratify Chinese cadres. In China, while "cadre" generally referred to all those who lived on state salaries, conducted mental work, and held formal authority, many distinctions existed within this group:

Distinction between political and administrative cadres (xingzheng ganbu) and technical cadres (jishu ganbu). Depending on the purpose of the work, the two groups had different authority: political and administrative cadres managed people, while technical cadres dealt with various technical matters.

Distinction between party cadres (dangyuan ganbu) and nonparty cadres (feidang ganbu). This distinction was based on the fact that in China not all party members served as cadres and not all cadres had party membership. But party membership was important in deciding a person's position. Party cadres usually served as the chief of an office where nonparty cadres worked as assistants.

Distinction between leading cadres (lingdao ganbu) and ordinary cadres (yiban ganbu). Based on ranks, leading cadres took more responsibilities than ordinary cadres. Leading cadres' work usually involved major decisions, while ordinary cadres handled daily routines.

Distinction between older cadres (lao ganbu) and new cadres (xin ganbu). The key criterion for the distinction was the length of a cadre's revolutionary experience, or the number of years of his or her party standing. As we shall see later, this distinction gradually became an important part of official nomenclature.

Distinctions between state cadres (guojia ganbu) and local cadres (difang ganbu). The former referred to cadres who were on government payroll, while the latter were paid by collective institutions.

All these distinctions, official or nonofficial, reflected the regularization and rationalization of the CCP's cadre corps. They indicated that the party and state apparatus in China was not only increasing in number and size, but was also becoming more and more stratified.

In addition to classification of cadres, another important step in regularizing the bureaucracy was to formalize the ranks and wage scales of cadres. Prior to the mid-1950s, the ranking and salary systems in China were quite confusing. In terms of salaries, three parallel systems existed (Chao, 1985:246–247): (1) supply system (*gongjizhi*)—inherited from the Yanan model yet modified, the supply system provided room, board, clothing, and a small allowance for veteran cadres; (2) wage system (*gongzizhi*)—retained personnel were paid in cash; their salaries were based on their average monthly wages in the last three months before 1949; and (3) semi-supply and semi-wage system (*bangongji bangongzi zhi*)—this type of system was mainly applied to newly recruited cadres.

A mixture of the three systems, each with its own ranking method, not only brought confusion but also generated irrational ratings and inequalities among cadres (Harding, 1981:72–73). As a result, in 1956 the party removed the supply system and adopted a unified system of ranks and wages, called the "rank-wage system" (*jibie gongzizhi*). The system subjected each party and government cadre to one of thirty grades. The upper twenty-six were administrative grades, while the lower four were nonclerical service grades. Salaries were first standardized according to grades and then adjusted by eleven major area categories to compensate for regional varieties in living costs (Chao, 1985:258).

Cadre Professionalization

With the increasing weight of economic development in the national priorities, the party became more and more concerned with the professional knowledge and administrative skills of its cadres. According to official sources, in 1954 only 8 percent of cadres were professionals; about 15 percent had a senior-middle-school education, while college and university graduates only accounted for 7 percent (RMRB, September 16, 1989). Beginning in 1953 when the party's general policy shifted from transformation to consolidation, it began to emphasize education and skills as one of the important criteria for recruiting party members and cadres. The party called for a full recognition of the importance of technical personnel in industrial construction. It encouraged party and government organizations to consult professionals in their administrative work (RMRB, March 21, 1954). For the sake of needed skills, the party suggested, technical persons could be accepted regardless of their class backgrounds, as long as they demonstrated "ideological consciousness." It would not be tolerated for party members to be "active in politics and backward in production" (Martin, 1981:20–22). In 1956 the party launched a major drive to recruit intellectuals and professionals. In Meaney's analysis, this was "due to a CCP desire to co-opt engineers and technicians so that dependence on Soviet experts could be reduced" (Meaney, 1988:44). As a result, as Table 6.4 shows, between 1956 and 1957 the percentage of intellectual party members[1] increased from 11.7 to 14.8 percent as against drops in the percentage of worker and peasant members. Intellectuals actually outnumbered workers in the party. Up to half of the nation's higher and lower "intellectuals" were party members in 1956–1957. This meant that though the percentage of intellectuals in the party still appeared low, the party had actually absorbed a large proportion of available professionals (Harrison, 1972:458).

Table 6.4
Social Backgrounds of CCP Members, 1956–1957

	1956		1957	
Background	No.	% of total	No.	% of total
Worker	1,502,814	14.0%	1,740,000	13.7%
Peasant	7,417,459	69.1%	8,500,000	66.8%
Intellectual	1,255,923	11.7%	1,880,000	14.8%
Others	558,188	5.2%	600,000	4.7%
Total	10,734,384	100%	12,720,000	100%

Source: Lewis, 1966:108.

During this period, the party put more emphasis on in-service administrative and technical training and cultural education than before. On December 24, 1953, the party issued the Directive of Strengthening the Cultural and Educational Work for Cadres and decided to start cadre training in rotation (SCMP, 1954,740:16–20). Several measures were accordingly taken: (1) reorganizing the curriculum of the existing party schools to upgrade the requirements of cadres' administrative skills and educational levels; (2) establishing specialized cadre schools; and (3) trusting universities to organize special classes of science and technology for cadres. By 1956 there were 694 cadre schools at different levels, which had trained 1.275 million in-service cadres since 1953 (Chao, 1985:65).

Power Centralization

The bureaucracy not only grew in size, but also became increasingly centralized. This was, on the one hand, due to "the requirement of planned economic development," as explained by the CCP (SCMP, 1954,832:18–19). The construction of large-scale industrial projects under Soviet advice required center-directed resource redistributions. Yet, on the other hand, an unspoken reason was the party's growing apprehension of "dispersionism" (*fenshan zhuyi*), "departmentalism" (*benwei zhuyi*), and "independent kingdoms" (*duli wanggao*).[2] The numerous cases of cadre corruption exposed in the Three and Five Anti's enhanced this concern among the party's top leaders.[3]

Centralization was manifested in two trends: vertically, power shifted from localities toward the center; and, horizontally, from nonparty organizations toward the party.

Since late 1952, the party leadership had taken a series of measures to weaken the regional governments.[4] In June 1954 it finally abolished the six administrative regions. The decision brought little surprise as it came right after the party leadership accused two high-level party officials, Gao Gang and Rao Shushi, of trying to establish personal control over their regional governments and demanding compromise from the central party and state leadership.[5] During the period, the Party Central Committee issued a number of documents to emphasize the importance and necessity of administrative centralization. On March 10, 1953, for example, it made a decision to strengthen the reporting system, which required all government sectors to request instructions from and report their work to the central government on all important issues (Chen, 1988:35).[6] Other texts included the "Resolution on Party Unity" (February 1954) and the "Resolution on the Gao-Rao Anti-Party Alliance" (March 1955). Both documents urged provincial and local cadres to draw lessons from Gao Gang and Rao Shushi's mistakes and to obey the party's central direction (SCMP, 1954,751:1–8; SCMP, 1955,1026:3–9).

In addition, Article 26 of the 1954 Organization Law provided that "when setting up, amalgamating, or abolishing any administrative organs of the People's Councils of municipalities . . . the People's Councils concerned must report the matter to the People's Councils at the next higher level for approval." The power of appointing and dismissing bureau heads of municipal governments was also given to the People's Councils at the next higher level rather than left at the disposal of the municipal governments concerned. In terms of economic and financial control, after the elimination of the regional governments, all state-owned industries were put under the jurisdiction of central ministries.[7]

Horizontally, power became more and more concentrated in the hands of the party. In the name of opposing "dispersionism," the party increased its involvement with administrative daily routines. Mao (SW, 1977,5:109) made it clear that "all the principal and important issues must first be discussed and decided on by the party committee before its decisions are referred to the government for implementation." Only in so doing, the party leadership claimed, could it check the tendency that some cadres "always prefer to be left alone." The most important measure in this regard was to establish within party bureaus corresponding departments to supervise their counterparts in government. For example, in addition to government ministries, the party's Central Committee and provincial committees all established their own industry ministry, transportation ministry, treasury, ministry of trade, and ministry of education. City and country party bureaus were asked to follow this pattern and thereby to control their counterparts at lower levels of government (Pang and Han, 1988:24–25). The party also had all the say in judicial affairs. Under the "system of party approval" formally established in 1954, all arrests, verdicts, and executions should be examined and approved by the party committees at corresponding levels (ibid.). The concentration of power in the party was termed "the party's unified leadership" (*yiyuanhua lingdao*), one of the fundamental principles of China's political system after the mid-1950s.

CONTRADICTIONS AND TENSIONS

Having been regularized, rationalized, and systematized, a large-scale and formal bureaucracy finally took shape in China in the mid-1950s. For many, the emergence of a vast bureaucratic apparatus in China was by no means a surprise. For instance, Meisner (1977:261) identifies some important factors that contributed to the growth of an independent bureaucracy in China: a smaller and less politically mature proletariat; a large and deeply ingrained bureaucratic tradition; a nationalistic and revolutionary process and spirit; and a fragmented and impoverished economy. All these conditions, according to

Meisner, necessitated the participation of the state in the socioeconomic life and thereby led Chinese society onto the road of bureaucratization.

Yet bureaucratization generated by practical needs had profound contradictions with Maoist ideological commitments. Edward Friedman (1984:11–45) distinguishes three visions of Marxism in socialist countries. One is Stalinism, which rests on Marx's faith in rational centralized administration. The second is Titoism, which reflects Marx's commitment to the wisdom and power of freely associated producers. Maoism constitutes the third. It "builds on Marx's insistence that the exploitative divisions, oppressive conflicts, and painful inequalities of modern society result essentially from capitalism and its institutional forms (private property, division of labor, urban-rural split, bourgeois families, etc.) which must be abolished to create true egalitarian human solidarity" (1984:12). Growing out of the Yanan experience, Richard Kraus (1984:49) adds, the Maoist model demonstrated great inclination to mass mobilization and ad hoc political campaigns, based on its suspicion of, and an aversion to, formal and hierarchical bureaucratic channels.

Thus, as the Soviet influence pushed China gradually away from the Maoist strategy of mass mobilization, Mao himself became increasingly vexed. He saw growing inequalities in socioeconomic relations resulting from bureaucratization. Mao's speech "On the Ten Major Relationships" in 1956 reflected his concerns. Mao brought to the party's attention a number of tensions embodied in the relationships between heavy industry and light industry, between industry and agriculture, between industry in the coastal regions and industry in the interior, between the state, the units of production, and the producers, between the center and the local, between party and nonparty, and so on (SW, 1977,5:284–307). Mao's criticism was not without foundation. During the first FYP, imbalances developed between industry and agriculture, heavy and light industries, advanced regions and less advanced regions, and large production units and small or middle-sized units.

Mao's concern was even deeper. Underlying the text was his criticism of the entire administrative apparatus which, in his opinion, had become too bureaucratic—rigid, ill-informed, inert, overcentralized, and uncooperative. In addition, "one-man management"[8] emerged with the Soviet model. For Mao, the socioeconomic management appeared to stratify the privileged from the less privileged and to rigidify the division under bureaucratic rule.

Tensions also grew within cadre ranks. Regional leaders resisted the imposition of central administrative and financial controls upon them; technical cadres feared the growing monitoring of their work by political (party) cadres; some cadres disliked being transferred from administrative positions (office work) to managerial posts in factories (front line) or from assignments in big cities to small cities or rural areas (Harding, 1981:85). The establishment of formal ranks and the corresponding salary system also created problems. Some were disappointed with their new ranks, while others were discontented with salary differentials between high-ranking and low-ranking cadres.[9] In addition to salary differentials, the system entitled each level to precisely defined privileges, including access to information, housing, transportation, medical service, and even office furniture. Butterfield's description was not groundless, though a bit exaggerated, "Only cadres above grade thirteen are allowed a leather swivel chair, like those used by Western executives. Officials in the grades thirteen to sixteen range get a soft and upholstered chair with springs and a velvet-covered seat. Grade seventeen cadres are entitled to a wooden chair with a cushion; those below that, only a plain wooden seat" (Butterfield, 1983:67).

In 1956, several events had Mao finally make up his mind to bridle the tendency of bureaucratization. One was the Twentieth Congress of the Communist Party of the Soviet Union (CPSU). The Congress and the ensuing Hungarian revolt forced Mao to devote almost exclusive attention to the question of the party's relation with the masses as a problem in its own right (MacFarquhar, 1974:48), as he saw the leadership's loss of contact with the masses as the major cause of the errors of Stalin's years and the events in Hungary. Moreover, from September 1956 to March 1957, worker strikes and student demonstrations took place in several cities in China. Even worse, in some rural areas, peasants started to quit or dismantle APCs. Though small in scale, the turbulence was unprecedented in PRC history. Mao regarded this as the consequence of increasing bureaucratism at lower levels as well as the influence of international situations (Zhu and Zhu, 1989:89). For Mao, reactivating the mass-line principle became a must.

Many scholars in favor of the factional model of CCP politics have speculated on Mao's political intentions as to why he appeared so eager to restrain the institutionalization and systematization of bureaucratic power (Harrison, 1972; Teiwes, 1979; Fairbank, 1986; Nathan, 1990). They put Mao's countermeasures against the bureaucracy in a context of "two-line struggle" with Mao's mass-mobilization-oriented faction on the one hand and the bureaucratic-technocratic faction headed by Liu Shaoqi and Deng Xiaoping on the other. Notwithstanding different interpretations of Mao's intention, one thing was quite clear: Mao himself took two important initiatives which interrupted, but did not stop, the bureaucratization process in China in the late 1950s. One was the Hundred Flowers movement (1956–1957); the other, the Great Leap Forward (1958–1960).

The first movement, the Hundred Flowers, invited people to criticize the administrative performance of the party and state organizations in the name of helping the party reform its working style. Given the party's history of rectifications, there was perhaps nothing new in doing so. However, as Harding (1981:152) points out, in spite of many organizational rectifications before and after the CCP's triumph, this time Mao traced problems not just to the fact that the party was approaching victory or was in power, but more specifically to the bureaucratic establishment (SW, 1977,5: 378–379, 436–437). It was not just a coincidence that in 1957, Mao listed the "bureaucratic practices of certain functionaries in their relations with the masses" as one of the major contradictions in Chinese society (SW, 1977, 5:386).

The Great Leap Forward was another de facto attack on the bureaucracy. Economically, the GLF marked a significant departure from the Soviet model that China had adopted since 1953. The movement also had anti-bureaucratic implications as it demonstrated clear egalitarian and populist tendencies. For Mao, the essence of the Leap was unleashing rather than organizing the energies of the masses, as he told cadres in 1958,

> First of all, one should learn from the people and follow them. The people have so much energy, [they are imbued with the spirit of] more, faster, better, and more economically, [they are the source of] many inventions and creations . . . . This is why we follow the people first, and afterwards the people follow us. (MacFarquhar, 1983:54)

During the GLF, the most popular slogan was "From the Masses, to the Masses." Cadres were often criticized for lagging behind the masses. People believed in the imminence of communism in China. Even Mao himself was quite optimistic, as he told his colleagues that if China had been at the gate of communism, "we need not try to be the very first to enter the communist society; even if we first get in, we'd better not announce it" (Li, 1989:9).

Nevertheless, neither the Hundred Flowers nor the Great Leap Forward produced positive consequences in solving China's bureaucratic problems. The Hundred Flowers soon merged with the anti-rightist movement and changed its original purpose. Ridiculously, many nonparty intellectuals (professors, students, artists, and so on) were accused of being "rightists" simply because they had responded to the party's call to express contending views. According to official statistics, during the years 1957–1958, altogether 552,877 people were labeled "rightists" (Ma and Huang, 1989:751).[10] Among them many were minor party members.[11] The GLF, while aiming at modernizing and communizing the nation with "greater, faster, better, and more economic results," ended up with serious economic and social dislocations across the country. While Chinese official estimates were not available, foreign sources put the death toll somewhere between 16.4 and 29.5 million. It was reported that the mortality rate doubled from 1.08 percent in 1957 to 2.54 percent in 1960. In one county of Guangdong alone, about 20,000 people starved to death (MacFarquhar, 1983:330).

UNINTENDED ORGANIZATIONAL CONSEQUENCES

Significantly for this study, the episodes of the Hundred Flowers and the GLF brought unintended consequences for the party organization. Much to the party's disappointment, what it saw in the years following the GLP was not so much a revitalization of the mass line as originally expected but a demoralization of its own cadre corps and later a restoration of bureaucratism.

First of all, the irregularity and spontaneity advanced by the GLF weakened the party's discipline of its cadres. Having experienced political uncertainty and economic recession, some cadres became frustrated or even scared; they would rather resign from official posts to take care of private pursuits than remain in office to wait for the next political movement. Others believed that requirements on cadres' performance restricted their involvement in private economic activities. Still others became greedy and sought every possibility for personal gain in case they would lose power in the next political campaign, which could occur at any time. Thus, while retreating from the GLF with a general relaxation of its centralized control, the party saw a tendency toward "moral degeneration" growing among its basic-level cadres, especially in the rural areas.

More specifically, the party perceived three "evil" tendencies among its cadres: capitalism, feudalism, and extravagance (Chen, 1969). Capitalist tendencies referred to those activities aimed at enriching oneself at the expense of the public; examples were excessive private pursuits, abandonment of farming for peddling, and lending money at high interest. These practices were termed "capitalist tendencies" because the party believed that they originated from the influence of capitalist ideology. Feudalist tendencies included those practices conducted under the influence of old culture or traditions; for example, some cadres were engaged in marriages-by-sale, gambling, and superstitious activities. Finally, the tendency of extravagance involved practices considered overconsumption and therefore harmful to economic investment and expansion, such as lavish drinking and eating or luxurious housing. In addition to the "three evils," the party also identified other types of power abuses, such as decadent behavior and bad work attitudes. A summary of the malpractices identified by the party is presented in Table 6.5.

A second problem which emerged unexpected by the party was the revitalization of bureaucratism. As the strategy of mass mobilization actually suffered setbacks during 1957–1958, the post–Great Leap period witnessed a rapid restoration of bureaucratic rule. The revitalization was nothing but a continuation of the bureaucratization process from before 1956. To begin with, there was a new round of institutional proliferation, particularly at the upper levels. The state apparatus, whose size was reduced during the Great Leap years, expanded again in the 1960s and reached 79 ministries and committees in 1965, a size almost as large as the pre–Great Leap peak level.

Table 6.5
Identified Basic-Level Cadre Malpractice During the Socialist Education Movement

Type of Tendency	Activity
Capitalism	Favoring individual enterprise
	Abandoning agriculture for peddling
	Emigrating to work elsewhere
	Opening uncultivated land
	Lending money at high interest rates
	Excessively owning private plots
	Hiring labor
	Practicing labor contracting
	Not handing over fertilizer to the collective
	Speculation
Feudalism	Gambling
	Marriages-by-sale
	Religious exercises
	Worshipping idols
	Superstitious practices
	Making or repairing tombs
	Bridegroom married into the home of the bride
	Bringing up girls in home of fiance
Extravagance	Feast to celebrate births, weddings, etc.
	Giving parties and sending presents
Other abuses	Unauthorized borrowing of public funds
	Graft
	Theft
	Misappropriation
	Decadent behavior
	Privately slaughtering hogs
	Excessively cutting trees
	Extortion
	Refusal to act as cadres
	Bad work attitude

Source: Compiled by the author based on Chen, 1969:48–49, 178–180, 192.

Accompanying the proliferation of institutions was an increase in the size of cadre corps. Shanghai was a case in point. As Table 6.6 shows, the staff of the party and government organs in Shanghai increased more quickly during the periods of 1954–1956 and 1959–1961 than other periods, indicating two high tides of institutional proliferation before the Cultural Revolution. In 1962 the party's Central Committee stipulated that the authorized number of cadres in a city government should be limited to 4.5 percent of its population. The Shanghai government requested increasing its quota to 4.8 percent but was refused by the Central Committee. As a result, the party committee in Shanghai had to sharply reduce the size of its government agencies.

Meanwhile, the center resumed much of the authority which had been transferred to lower levels. For example, the number of center-controlled enterprises increased from 1,075 to 10,530 during 1958–1965. In the same period, the proportion of the government budget at the disposal of the central government also expanded from 20 to 60 percent (Wang, 1988:2). In 1960 the party restored the regional party bureaus. However, in contrast to the regional governments of the early 1950s, this time the regional bureaus were directly attached to the party's Central Committee. Their job was to supervise local governments on behalf of the center. Again, centralization after the GLF had

Table 6.6
Cadre Numbers in Shanghai's Party and State Apparatus, 1949–1965

Year	Number	Year	Number
1949	26,740	1958	44,251
1950	49,199	1959	62,739
1951	—	1960	59,226
1952	48,479	1961	59,338
1953	49,813	1962	37,600
1954	53,675	1963	36,505
1955	54,640	1964	36,864
1956	51,425	1965	36,910
1957	48,385		

Source: *Changes of Shanghai's Party and State Apparatus, 1949–1986*, Shanghai People's Publishing House, 1988:236.

a clear focus on unified party leadership. Mao made it very clear that "among all the sectors—worker, peasant, merchant, student, army, administration, and the party, the party takes the lead in everything" (Pang and Han, 1988:17).

The revitalized bureaucracy was actually top-heavy, for the state apparatus at lower levels were often understaffed. It was reported (SCMP,1965,3509: 8–12) that among 6,000 supply-marketing offices at the county level and below in Heilongjiang province, more than 1,900 did not have enough staff. Some had two cadres, while others only had one staff member. It was difficult for bureaucratic organizations as such to provide efficient services. As a result, the party leadership saw its cadres more and more occupied by paperwork, meetings, and other formalistic office routines. The party also identified the tendency among its cadres of being fearful of hard work, short on creativity, and indifferent to the suffering of the masses. The party leadership was quite upset that cadres at higher levels were divorced from the masses and reluctant to make tours of inspection in local areas, especially in the countryside, while those at lower levels tended to hold back unpleasant reports or simply to provide distorted information to their supervisors (SCMP, 1965,3589:1–4).

However, what disturbed the party most, particularly Mao, was the tendency of "production in command" among cadres. Because of the disastrous results of the GLF and the sudden withdrawal of Soviet experts in the early 1960s, the party had to renew its mid-1950s call for help from specialists and intellectuals. This instrumental concern was reflected in Deng Xiaoping's statement in 1962 that "Black cats, white cats, what does it matter? So long as they can catch rats, they are good cats." Many experts were thus placed in leading party or nonparty positions. Party recruitment jumped from 13.5 to 17 million between the summer of 1959 and mid-1961, after a decrease during 1957–1958 (Table 6.7). Like the years immediately after 1949, the great influx of new members, particularly those with nonproletarian backgrounds, together with the revitalized bureaucratism, created problems for the control of the party.

THE SOCIALIST EDUCATION MOVEMENT

For the reasons just given, as the nation began to recover in the early 1960s from both manmade and natural disasters, maintaining the revolutionary spirit of the cadres became a primary concern of the party. Consequently, from late 1962 to spring 1966, the party launched a mass campaign against what it called "unhealthy tendencies" among cadres. Two factors determined the timing. First, by 1962, China had, by and large, recovered from the economic setbacks. The descending spiral in production and consumption had largely been arrested, as the 1962 harvest brought a significant improvement in the supply of food and agricultural raw materials (Eckstein, 1975:290).

Table 6.7
Numerical Growth of the Chinese Communist Party, 1950–1961

Year	Number
December 1950	5,800,000+
1952	6,000,000+
October 1953	6,389,000+
February 1954	6,500,000+
February 1955	7,000,000+
June 1956	10,730,000+
December 1956	12,000,000+
September 1957	12,720,000+
November 1958	12,450,000+
Summer 1959	13,500,000+
June 1961	17,000,000+

Source: Ma and Huang, 1989:685–686.

The great relief from economic degeneration allowed CCP leaders to turn their attention to the internal organizational problems.

A second factor was the worsening and increasingly publicized debate between China and the Soviet Union. For Chinese leaders, especially Mao, the conflict was not simply a reflection of the differences between Chinese and Soviet views and strategies of socialist construction, but a struggle between Marxism-Leninism and revisionism. Mao saw from the Soviet experience the danger of bureaucratization and thereby the urgency to restrain bureaucratic tendencies on the home front. For him, the failure of the GLF, after all, was attributable to the incompetence of bureaucrats rather than deficient policies. More importantly, in Mao's opinion, bureaucratization was the wellspring of revisionism which would inevitably lead to capitalist restoration (Baum, 1975:4). It was noteworthy that during the Socialist Education Movement those concepts which were used to criticize the Soviet Union (e.g., bureaucratization, revisionism, capitalist restoration) were for the first time applied to Chinese domestic politics.

The Socialist Education Movement started as a reexamination of official behavior in the context of cadre-mass relationship. Only several months later, however, the campaign escalated into a campaign against capitalism and revisionism. The word "anti-corruption" virtually dropped out of the party's phraseology of the campaign. An examination of the process of the Socialist Education Movement revealed a distorted anti-corruption movement.

Mild Beginning

From late 1962 to the spring of 1963, some counties in Hebei, Henan, Hunan, and Zejiang provinces carried out small-scale commune rectifications. Through investigations in 90 counties, the party committee of Hunan reported 1,300 cases of counterrevolutionary group activities, 2,600 cases of landlord retaliation, and 8,000 cases of secret societies. In addition, account check-ups uncovered hundreds of thousands of cases of economic speculation. Investigations in other provinces presented similar results (Zhu and Zhu, 1989:390–391). In February and May 1963, as a result, the party's Central Committee held two work conferences to discuss these problems. The leadership came to a conclusion that the problems among basic-level cadres were so serious that a systematic "socialist education movement" must be waged. The conferences also produced the first important CCP directive for the campaign—the "Draft Resolution of the Central Committee on Some Problems in Current Rural Work," known as the Early Ten Points.[12]

The Early Ten Points dwelled on the rationale of "socialist education" by listing nine manifestations of class struggle in rural areas, ranging from class revenge by landlords and rich peasants to cadre corruption, from secret society activities to sabotage of public properties, and from exploitation of hired hands to speculation and profiteering. Of the nine, at least five were related to corruption. The document pointed out the importance of cleaning up account books, public granaries, collective properties, and work-point assessment. From here came the popular name of the Socialist Education Movement—the "Four Clean-Ups." Given its prevalence, the document suggested, cadre corruption was the principal cause of peasant dissatisfaction and hence the major target of the Socialist Education Movement.

The document went on to lay out reform proposals. What it prescribed was rather mild, though, including (1) establishing poor and lower-middle peasant organizations to supervise the administrative work of communes, brigades, and production teams; (2) engaging all cadres at the county level and below in regular collective productive labor and, therefore, having them form close ties with the masses; (3) dwelling on "four histories"—the individual, family, village, and commune historical records—to arouse class consciousness and hatred for capitalist tendencies; and (4) urging cadres who had conducted corruption to "wash hands and bodies" by intensive study of party doctrines and vigorous criticism and self-criticism. However, the principal objective was education rather than punishment. In terms of implementing the party's resolution on the Socialist Education Movement, the Early Ten Points stipulated three steps: first, training cadres; second, training activists among the poor and lower-middle peasants; and third, carrying out all-out efforts. As if reluctant to immediately immerse the whole country in a large-scale political campaign, the document added that in taking each of these steps, "spot testing" was necessary. In short, the Early Ten Points which signified the formal beginning of the Socialist Education Movement prescribed for the movement an anti-corruption orientation, an optimistic estimate, a mild therapy, and a limited scope.

First, an anti-corruption orientation was clear in the document, as it defined the movement mainly as an anti-corruption campaign, aiming at strengthening rural party organizations that had decayed in the years following the GLF. All the proposed measures were oriented toward rectifying cadre performance and forging closer relations between rural cadres and peasants.

Second, although the movement was carried under the broad rubric of "class struggle," the document had an optimistic evaluation of the cadre ranks. The party had two conclusions as reflected in the document: first, those "unhealthy tendencies" listed in Table 6.5 were "contradictions among the people" in nature; that means, those offenders should still be treated as comrades instead of enemies; and, second, more than 95 percent of cadres were free from corruption and the party, hence, should rely on them to oppose bureaucratism and corruption.

Third, the document suggested a mild therapy for cubing corruption. The major measures it proposed fit in a formula: propaganda plus education. The reform policy was summarized by the party as "education by persuasion; washing hands and bodies; going to the front with a light load; unity against the enemy" (Baum and Teiwes, 1968:66).

Finally, the document stipulated that the movement should not expand to all levels of the government and all areas of the country. It should be confined to a limited scope—rural areas only. It was also made clear that even if in the concerned areas the movement was to focus on studying documents and training activists rather than accusing each other.

Quick Unfolding

In September 1963, the party's Central Committee held another work conference in Beijing. After evaluating the ongoing movement and discussing the problems raised during "spot-testing," the party issued a new directive—"Some Concrete Policy Formulations of the Central Committee of the Chinese Communist Party in the Rural Socialist Education Movement." The directive was again in the form of ten points, and was therefore referred to as the Later Ten Points.

The Later Ten Points was similar to its predecessor in its diagnosis of the rural situation and campaign targets. Cadre problems were believed to be mainly those common mistakes such as "excessive eating, excessive possessions, and petty theft" (Baum and Teiwes, 1968:85). These problems, or other even more serious ones, were still considered nonantagonistic contradictions among the people. Hence reform methods should be relatively mild and aimed at "treating the illness to save the man" (*zhibing jiuren*).

Although the Later Ten Points kept the basic guiding principles of the Early Ten Points and made them more specific, it proposed a significant change with regard to the campaign strategy. While the Early Ten Points called for spontaneously formed peasant organizations to conduct rectification of basic-level cadres, the Later Ten Points emphasized the necessity of dispatching "work teams" from higher levels to guide the movement. It remained controversial as to what the party's real consideration was behind the change. Some scholars believe that it had something to do with the difficulties of establishing effective peasant associations. For example, Harry Harding (1981:203–204) points out, this was because, on the one hand, many peasants dared not speak out against cadre corruption, for fear of retaliations and, on the other hand, many local cadres tried very hard to change the supervisory function of peasant associations and put the latter under their own control. Other scholars interpreted the change along the line of "intra-party struggles." According to Meisner (1977:291), the real purpose of sending "work teams" was to keep the movement under the party's hierarchical control, as the Later Ten Points was mainly drafted by the then Party Secretary-General Deng Xiaoping. Different from Mao, leaders like Liu Shaoqi and Deng Xiaoping were more concerned with maintaining production and the party's organizational viability. They believed that it was the responsibility of higher party and state organs to rectify errors of basic-level cadres who, in turn, would lead and educate the masses.

The Socialist Education Movement quickly unfolded after the Later Ten Points was issued, especially after the party made the decision to make the two Ten Points known to every household in November 1963. As the New Year editorial for 1964 stated that "we must carry forward the Socialist Education Movement in even greater depth and breadth" (RMRB, January 1, 1964), the movement came to its full swing. In contrast to the mass mobilization strategy during the Three and Five Anti's, however, cadres and masses throughout the country participated in the movement "in an organized and planned manner" (ibid.). At this stage, the movement still tried to keep its anti-corruption momentum.

Dramatic Escalation

During the first half of 1964, the movement seemed to develop smoothly. However, when more local reports on the seriousness of class struggle, especially the report from the Taoyuan production brigade,[13] came to the attention of the party's Central Committee, the mood of the leadership became gloomy. While in the past the party's top leadership had estimated that only 5 percent of its local cadres were corrupt or lax, now it believed that about one-third of the basic-level posts were not in the hands of the CCP.[14] Thus the party issued a third important directive for the Socialist Education Movement in September 1964. This document was actually a revised version of the Later Ten Points, based on "new experiences" of the campaign. It was therefore known as the Revised Ten Points. As before, the document was first circulated within the party as a policy guide to the movement. All party members were required to attend study meetings to master its essence. The document was then relayed to the masses through unit meetings but not newspapers.

The Revised Ten Points escalated the movement in several important aspects. First, it raised the problems of rural basic-level cadres to a higher plane of principle. While previous documents considered petty economic corruption as the major problem among cadres, the new document warned that

> many basic-level rural cadres have . . . not only committed the four uncleans economically, but have also failed to draw the line between friend and enemy, lost standpoints . . . thus committing the four uncleans politically and organizationally . . . . Some have even degenerated into agents and protectors of class enemies. (Baum and Teiwes, 1968:112)

Second, the new document called for a reclassification of class backgrounds of the rural population. This revealed the party's deep concern that because "a certain number of landlords, rich peasants, counterrevolutionaries, and bad elements have sneaked into cadre ranks, class ranks in the rural areas have become muddled." The document requested that

> since there is widespread confusion about class background in villages, it is necessary to clearly define class ranks as a part of the work of the Socialist Education Movement. The background of each rural household should be examined and classified after full discussions by the masses, and a class file should be established. (ibid.: 1968:110)

Finally, given the dilemma that both basic-level cadres and masses were not reliable, the new directive specified the unique leading role of work teams. The party thus changed its previous stress on relying on basic-level organizations and cadres, and virtually deprived basic-level cadres of leading power in the movement.

The Socialist Education Movement intensified after the third document. The movement entered the stage of what Richard Baum (1975:130) has called "the most intensive purge of rural party members and cadres in the history of the Chinese People's Republic." Thousands of work teams were organized and sent to the countryside to investigate local cadres' malpractices. In contrast to the previous "back-to-back" policy,[15] "unclean" cadres were now asked to confess in front of the masses and accept the latter's open and usually sharp questioning. Many cadres were then removed from their posts or demoted in rank.

In October 1964 the party Central Committee explicitly called for a power takeover "wherever the leadership was manipulated or seized by corrupt elements" (Zhu and Zhu, 1989:395). In November, the party further ordered that all government organs under the county level hand over their power to work teams.

New Orientation

The changes in the Revised Ten Points inevitably brought confusion on the nature and purpose of the Socialist Education Movement. Some people still stuck to the original understanding that the movement intended to resolve the problem of basic-level corruption, defined as "contradictions among the people." Others now believed that the movement involved struggle against enemies as well as "contradictions among the people." According to the party's highest leadership, however, both perceptions were wrong. The struggle in question was nothing but the struggle between socialism and capitalism. This view was expressed clearly by a new party document in January 1965—"Some Problems Currently Arising in the Course of the Rural Socialist Education Movement," known as the Twenty-Three Points.[16]

The new document was a reorientation, or a "reunification of presentation" as the party called it, of rectification policies. In Harry Harding's analysis (1981:211–213), the reorientation was mainly based on Mao's three types of dissatisfaction with Liu Shaoqi's way of handling the Socialist Education Movement: first, Mao believed that the movement had so narrowly focused on the problem of cadre corruption as to set aside the general revisionist tendency among cadres and the masses; moreover, Mao was also concerned with excessively targeting basic-level cadres; and, finally, and perhaps most troublesome for Mao, was the way in which work teams had controlled the Socialist Education Movement from above. Secret investigations and arbitrary disposal of cases employed by some work teams were in sharp contrast with Mao's favorite strategy of mass mobilization. Thus, besides the confirmation of antagonistic contradictions as the main focus of the campaign, the document made several noticeable changes.

First, as opposed to the previous focus on basic-level cadres, the document now declared that "the key point of this movement is to rectify those people in positions of authority within the party who take the capitalist road . . . there are some people in the communes, districts, *xians*, special districts, and *even in the work of provincial and central committee departments, who oppose socialism*" (Baum and Teiwes, 1968:120) (emphasis added).

Second, there was a renewed call for relying on peasant associations to carry on the movement. "In those places where basic-level organizations have atrophied or became paralyzed . . . we may implement all power to the poor and lower-middle peasants' associations." Those problems raised during the movement "shall be judged and decided by the masses" and "not be decided from above" (ibid.:124–125).

Third, and most importantly, the Four Clean-Ups, formerly interpreted as cleaning economic accounting, public granaries, collective property, and work-point assessment, were now redefined as cleaning politics, economics, organizations, and ideology—a more politically oriented definition. The previous goal of opposing corruption finally disappeared from the party's campaign agenda. The movement was recolored with Maoist ideology.

The new document was undoubtedly in Mao's favor. The rhetoric of class struggle was much louder than before. Although the shift appeared to be merely a matter of language at the moment,[17] the document nevertheless served as a theoretical preparation for the later radical Maoist "democracy"—the Cultural Revolution. In Meisner's words (1977:292), "it was, in effect, a declaration of political war against the party bureaucracy and its top leaders."

DISTORTION OF THE MOVEMENT

Table 6.8 presents the major developments of the Socialist Education Movement. As the table shows, the movement diverged step by step from its original focus—corruption among the basic-level cadres. As the movement became more and more class-struggle oriented, especially after Mao's ever-increasing perception of "the bourgeoisie within the party," the Socialist Education Movement was no longer an anti-corruption campaign as it was originally intended. Partially because of this, few corruption cases were publicly exposed. But even from the very beginning, the party had no intention of making the movement a wide-ranging and well-publicized one. Having recovered from the turmoil of the GLF and economic recession, the party was cautious about any political and economic instability. However, this did not necessarily lead to the party's leniency toward problematic cadres. It was estimated[18] that during the Socialist Education Movement, about 1.25 to 2.5 million cadres were either expelled from the party or were criminally charged.

Table 6.8
Major Developments of the Socialist Education Movement

Date and Document	Target	Focus	Reform Force
10/1962–8/1963 Early 10 Points	Corruption	Basic-level	Peasant association
9/1963–8/1964 Later 10 Points	Corruption	Basic-level	Work team
9/1964–12/1964 Revised 10 Points	Political decay	Basic-level	Work team
1/1965–1966 23 Points	Capitalist roaders	All levels	Peasant association

Source: Compiled by author.

The figure accounted for 10 percent of the cadres at the level of commune or below. It was higher than the officially estimated 4.5 percent cadre corruption rate during the Three and Five Anti's.[19] In certain keypoint areas, the percentage of cadres who were removed from positions even reached 50-80 percent. If in the past, (e.g., in the Three and Five Anti's), the party had been lenient toward its cadres because it faced a shortage of managerial personnel, now it could no longer put up with any divergence from its rule because the party believed that its control had been consolidated.

The second anti-corruption campaign, however, had more in common with the first. As in the Three and Five Anti's, the corruption that the Socialist Education Movement originally targeted resulted from the CCP's own policies. In the mid-1950s as the party's general policy shifted from transformation to consolidation, it saw the necessity to formalize a large-scale state apparatus to manage the new society and to promote the economic development as required by the general policy. The corresponding organizational policies reflected the party's intention, as the bureaucracy became more and more formalized and absorbed more professional staff. Yet, on the other hand, the increasing powerfulness of the bureaucracy inevitably challenged the party's self-claimed commitment to the "mass line." Mao was especially troubled by his sense of a growing bourgeoisie within the party, and more so after the destalinization by the Communist Party of the Soviet Union and the failure of the GLP. The party leadership faced a bureaucratic Leviathan created by itself and was forced to wrestle with the problem of how to keep the bureaucracy loyal to itself.

Given the context, it was not surprising that the Socialist Education Movement quickly changed its target from corruption to ideological divergence, with the focus shifting from the basic levels to higher echelons. If in the early years the lack of a formal cadre corps was the problem for the CCP, the experience of having such a corps was not pleasant for the party.

Foreshadowed by the Socialist Education Movement, the Cultural Revolution began in mid-1966 and lasted for ten years. It was no less than a political chaos and it exhausted the nation. As many have pointed out (Tsou, 1986; Yan and Gao, 1988; White, 1989), the Cultural Revolution brought the nation to the verge of collapse. For the reasons given before, I will not elaborate on this period. However, a good comprehension of the CCP's modernization program in the post-Mao era must start with an analysis of the aftermath of the Cultural Revolution.

NOTES

1. "Intellectual party members" refer to the party members among doctors, professors, engineers, artists, and technicians.

2. See Teiwes (1979:121–123) for more explanations of these terms.

3. For example, the Report on Revising the Constitution of the CCP delivered by Deng Xiaoping at the Party's Eighth Congress of 1956 severely criticized the phenomenon of "departmentalism," referring to the phenomenon that many cadres always preferred to "do things according to their local needs."

4. For a fuller description and discussion of these measures, see Harding (1981:68–71).

5. Before 1954 Gao Gang was the party, government, and military head of the Northeast Region, and Rao Shushi served as the party secretary, government chairman, and political commissar of the East China Region. For Western analyses of the "Gao-Rao Affair," see Shurman (1968:498–517) and Teiwes (1979:160–210). For Chinese official explanations, see Mao (SW, 1977,5:161-167).

6. However, what the "important issues" would be was not specified and was left for the Central Committee to decide.

7. Between 1953 and 1957, center-controlled enterprises increased from 2,800 to 9,300. Materials subject to state distribution expanded from 227 types to 532 types. The central government controlled about 75 percent of national

financial resources (Xue, 1984:287–288).

8. The Soviet formula emphasized the role of technocrat bureaucrats, while denying the masses' participation in planning, research, and supervising.

9. The ratio of the highest-paid to lowest-paid cadres was 28:1 in 1956.

10. By 1979, 97 percent or 533,222 of the "rightists" had been rehabilitated, while about 5,000 cases were still under reexamination.

11. For minor party members as major victims of the antirightist campaign, see Teiwes (1979:304–305).

12. For the translations of this document and other important documents (to be discussed later), see Baum and Teiwes (1968:49–126).

13. Taoyuan was the place where Wang Guangmei, Liu Shaoqi's wife, did her "keypoint" investigations. After spending five months there under a pseudonym, Wang concluded in her report that 85 percent of the cadres in Taoyuan were corrupt, while the poor and lower-middle peasants were not reliable at all. For a full account of Wang Guangmei's "Taoyuan experience," see Baum (1975:83–89).

14. It was reported that Liu Shaoqi completely accepted his wife's conclusion, as he said that at the basic levels, 30 percent of cadres were corrupt, 40 percent were mediocre, and only 30 percent were good (Baum, 1975:91; Harding, 1981:208). Mao personally accepted this allegation. In August 1964, Mao repeated on several occasions that "we have been doing socialism for fifteen years thus far, but only control two-thirds of the land" (Chen Xuewei, 1989:153).

15. This meant that cadres and the masses should avoid "face-to-face" criticisms.

16. However, the document was only circulated within the party and made known to party members, not the general public.

17. The real shift of target toward higher-level "capitalist roaders" did not happen until the Cultural Revolution.

18. Official statistics for the Socialist Education Movement are still not available. The estimates were made by scholars in the West based on scattered Red Guard newspapers in the Cultural Revolution. See Oksenberg (1969:184), Baum (1975:103–104), Teiwes (1979:550).

19. The 4.5 percent rate referred to all the cadres who were accused of corruption. The number of cadres who actually received punishment was even lower.

Part III

TODAY

7

Modernization and Its Organizational Corollaries

The Cultural Revolution is the most tragic event in PRC history. The adverse effects of this decade on the country and on its people were beyond simple estimation. The exact figure of premature deaths is still unknown. But the losses and difficulties that the Cultural Revolution inflicted on the Chinese people could be felt everywhere in the years immediately following the "revolution."

By the time the Cultural Revolution ended, China's economy was near collapse. In 1976 while the output of industry and agriculture only increased by 1.7 percent over the previous year, the GNP decreased by 2.7 percent (Zhu, 1986:22). The average annual wage of city workers declined from 625 to 605 yuan between 1968 and 1976; the average income of peasants was only 62.8 yuan (Wang Hongmuo, 1989:14).

Yet, what the Cultural Revolution brought to China was more than a crumbling economy and worsening living conditions. A decadc of "power seizures" and inner party struggles crippled the state's capabilities for managing society. The political order of the whole country was thrown into chaos. As many as 2.9 million people were wrongly accused of "crimes against the party and socialism" during the Cultural Revolution (Wang Hongmuo, 1989). Many of them were arrested, imprisoned, or sent into internal exile. People were not only physically tortured but also psychologically humiliated. Some were killed, and others committed.suicide. Still others, though themselves not the targets of the Cultural Revolution, were victimized as they took part in the "great Revolution" with idealism and the spirit of adventure, but disillusioned and psychologically hurt by the destructive consequences of the movement.

Indeed, by the mid-1970s, dissatisfaction had prevailed among the Chinese people. In Harry Harding's (1987:37) description, "the intellectuals were angry at the persecution they had suffered at the hands of the radicals; young people resented Mao's betrayal of the Red Guard movement; workers were tired of stagnant levels of consumption and crowded living conditions. All were weary of continuous mass movements and ideological indoctrination." It was against this background that China began a new "Long March"—the reform.

THE MODERNIZATION PROGRAM

The Third Plenum of the Eleventh CCP Central Committee held in December, 1978 signaled another fundamental change of the CCP's general policy, as the party announced its decision to shift the emphasis of its work from class struggle to modernization.

The CCP's new program of modernization consisted of two equally important and closely related tasks: one was to restructure society by adopting development-oriented economic policies and the other to rebuild the state by establishing a rationally and legally oriented bureaucracy.

The economic reform was a painful but steadily evolving process. While, as many critics point out, there was no blueprint for the reform from its inception,[1] after more than a decade of reform has passed, one can discern some significant steps China has taken in reforming its economy.

From 1978 to October 1984, the institution of a household responsibility system to replace the commune was the main focus of the reform. Then, the period between October 1984 and September 1988 saw reform attempts in cities aimed at reducing procurement quotas and taxes on enterprises; loosing price controls on an increasingly larger number of products; enlarging managerial powers of enterprises regarding wages, employment, trade, and finance; and revitalizing private businesses. Finally, between late 1988 and 1991 there was a period of retrenchment and consolidation aimed at balancing the overheated economy. These policy innovations and experiments have pushed China increasingly toward a market-driven economy (see Perry and Wong, 1985; Riskin, 1987; Dorn & Wang, 1990; Chen, 1992). In fact, China's conceptualization of the economic reform has undergone important changes in order to keep up with the new developments

When the reform began in 1978, it was chiefly aimed at remedying the chronic ills of the existing central planning system. In the early years of the reform, China's reformers were hesitant (or not allowed) to talk about the functions of the market. The Third Plenum of the Twelfth Party Congress in 1984 proposed a conceptual innovation by using the term "socialist planned commodity economy" to characterize the Chinese economy. For the first time in post-1949 China, the leadership openly admitted the importance of commodity exchange under socialism. However, China did not formally endorse the concept of "market economy" as a characterization of reform until the Fourteenth Party Congress of October 1992 (RMRB, October 17, 1992). The Fourteenth Party Congress legitimized the concept of "China's socialist market economy" by admitting the use of markets as the primary resource allocator, as against planning, of the Chinese economy.

The twelve-year reforms were successful by most measures. The reforms have brought impressive changes to China's economy. Note, for example, the World Bank's (1990: xii) evaluation:

Over the last decade, China's GDP growth rate has averaged 9.5% per annum. Investment was high throughout (averaging 31% of GDP during the early 1980s and 38% of GDP since 1985) and was matched by a strong savings performance, which contained the need for external borrowing. Industrial modernization increased the competitiveness of China's manufactures in the international market and merchandise exports grew from $18.3 billion in 1980 to $52.5 billion in 1989. China's share of international trade rose from 0.97% to 1.7% during the same period. The average incomes for the 800 million rural population more than doubled and absolute poverty receded nationwide. In 1988, some 13% of rural households fell below the poverty line, compared with 17% in 1981. Infant and child mortality declined, the rate of population growth was slowed and universal education of five years was achieved.

NEW ORGANIZATIONAL POLICIES

The CCP's ambitious modernization program meanwhile requires changes in the party's organizational policy. The bureaucratic apparatus did not seem to accommodate to the reform, not only because of the damages caused by the Cultural Revolution. It also suffered some chronic problems.

China's vanguard-led revolution and centralized economic planning produced a highly hierarchical bureaucracy. The administrative organization of the country consisted of three levels: the central administration (*zhongyang zhengfu*), regional and local governments (*difang zhengfu*), and grass-roots working units (*jiceng danwei*). However, decisions made at the center were usually channeled down vertically through the so-called systems (*xitong*). Each system represented a distinct function or line of work, and was organized in a vertical order with institutions and personnel at each level of the administrative hierarchy performing assigned functions (Barnett, 1967:7). Responsibilities were centered in the national ministries, which gave instructions and directives downward and outward to localities.

While regional and local governments acted largely as the medium between the center and localities,[2] basic-level work units had almost no authority for themselves. The centralized control functioned through three main mechanisms: plans were made and resources distributed by the center; information continued to flow down through top-down channels; and more importantly, all areas were under the control of the party's visible hand through its local committees. According to Deng Xiaoping's (1984:316) own analysis,

The problems in our system of leadership . . . together with other factors . . . led to the decade of catastrophe known as the "Cultural Revolution." There is a most profound lesson to be learned from this. I do not mean that the individuals concerned should not bear their share of responsibility, but rather that the problems in the leadership and organizational systems are more fundamental, widespread and long-lasting, and that they have a greater effect on the overall interests of our country. This is a question that has a close bearing on whether our party and state will change political color and should therefore command the attention of the entire party.

Throughout most of the pre–Cultural Revolution period, the CCP's organizational policy had emphasized class background, revolutionary zeal, and loyalty to the party's cause. Though there were occasional debates on the "red" (*hong*) versus the "expert" (*zhuan*) and the party found some emerging bureaucratic tendencies as we illustrated before, the general configuration of the CCP's organization reflected its revolutionary nature. Many of the new recruits were political activists produced by political movements such as the Three and Five Anti's, the Antirightists Campaign, the Great Leap Forward, and the Socialist Education Movement. The same pattern continued during the Cultural Revolution on an even larger scale, when family backgrounds and loyalty to Mao's line became particular important.

Cadres recruited in this manner were ill-suited for the party's new course. Their education levels were too low to lead modernization. In 1979, for example, less than 10 percent of the cadre corps were college-educated, while more than 70 percent only had an education of high school or lower (Luo, 1987:101).

Another problem was the de facto lifelong tenure of the cadre corps. In pre-reform China, as in other political systems born of revolution, revolutionary seniority measured from the time the participant joined the revolution, decided a cadre's rank in the party and government. Only natural death and major political mistakes could induce changes. Although many veteran revolutionaries suffered persecution and demotion during the Cultural Revolution, a majority of them had been reassigned to jobs ranked equivalent to their former position by 1978 (Manion, 1992:3). As a result, when the party started the reform, it faced a shortage of younger, physical and mentally vigorous cadres it needed for the modernization program. In order to modernize the country, the cadre corps itself had first to be modernized.

Facing these problems and under the pressure of the economic reforms, the Chinese leadership cautiously embarked on institutional reform. Benjamin Ward (1990:119) rightly points out that organizational change had long been used as an important instrument of economic policy in China, in contrast to capitalist economies which preferred indirect instruments such as fiscal and monetary policy. Nevertheless, no one in China's top leadership has expected a comprehensive and rapid institutional reform which may go beyond the party's control and create troubles for itself. For the Chinese leaders, "the purpose of reforming the system of party and state is precisely to maintain and further strengthen party leadership and discipline, and not to weaken or relax them . . . . Without such a party, our country would split up and accomplish nothing" (Deng, 1984:324). Apparently, from the very beginning of the reform, the party has never had the intention to loosen its political control over society.

The organizational policies during the reform reflected the party's determination at economic modernization and its reservations about political reform. New organizational efforts were largely directed at those administrative matters that have significant impacts on economic development. They included institutional reorganization to reduce overlapping and inefficient decision making; the separation of power and function of the party and government to reduce power overconcentration; decentralization of economic managerial authority to allocate resources more rationally; and the reform of the cadre system to incorporate younger and better-educated people into the cadre ranks. All these were aimed more at efficient administration than at political democratization.

Institutional Differentiation

Since 1980, reformers have taken some important measures to differentiate inter-institutional relations by separating the authority and function of the party from those of government and separating government from the enterprise.

The 1982 constitution stated clearly that "all political parties . . . must abide by the Constitution and the law . . . . No organizations or individuals may enjoy the privilege of being above the Constitution and the law." Technically, this subjected the Chinese Communist Party to the law of the state. The constitutional limit of the power of the party was accompanied by some important organizational measures. The party gradually abolished within its organization those departments that duplicated government agencies. These departments had been established to supervise their counterparts in the government.[3] The party also reduced concurrent offices held by leading party cadres. For example, the first secretary of a party provincial committee was generally no longer the governor of that province. The power of party secretaries retreated as the Director Responsibility System (*shouzhang fuzhe zhi*) was introduced at the grass-roots level—an institutional arrangement of a powerful administrative directing system headed by the factory director (or manager) so as to ensure the coordinated and highly effective advance of the various tasks of enterprises (Jiang, 1982:6).

In factories, party committees gradually withdrew from the domain of daily administration, while managers assumed authority over plant production and operations. In rural areas, village and township governments were established to replace the people's communes which had combined all the activities of the party, administration, and production in the past.

More efforts have been made at separating government from enterprises. Enterprises in China had long been regarded as appendages to administrative organs and were deprived of independent decision-making power. The reform since 1978 has sought to "invigorate" enterprises by relieving them of their previously dependent status.

One important measure was to distinguish ownership (*suoyouquan*) from management (*jingyingquan*). The State Council's "Provisional Regulations on Further Extending the Decision-Making Power of State Industrial Enterprises" in 1984 set a series of new policies in this regard. Enterprises were owned by the state, but they enjoyed important operational rights, such as producing for the market after fulfilling their quotas; selling these products as well as overstocked items and goods rejected by state purchasing agencies; varying the price of marketed goods by up to 20 percent on either side of the state price or negotiating them with purchasers; and choosing their suppliers of state distributed materials. Other expanded powers involved the use of retained profits, and leasing and sale of surplus equipment, personal and wage matters, and the formation of joint ventures that cut across official administrative divisions.[4] These discretionary powers aimed at turning enterprises into "independent management units" (*duli jingyin danwei*), while the state still possessed the right to own the means of production.

Another measure was, as mentioned earlier, the establishment of the Director Responsibility System. Under the system, enterprise managers assumed all-round responsibility for factory production, operation, and administration, as they were empowered to determine long-term and annual plans, major technological improvements, administrative personnel, and employment.

The Director Responsibility System was further enhanced by the practice of industrial contracting which prevailed between 1984 and 1988. Under the contract system, the state contracted enterprises out to collectives or individuals, who undertook full responsibility for management and for any losses induced by mismanagement; in return, contractors were required to turn over to the state only a fixed proportion of their profits set by the contract and could retain the rest. By December 1988, more than 90 percent of state enterprises had to some extent implemented the contract system (WEH, December 19, 1988). Contracting, according to China's reformers, was a useful method that "could organizationally combine power, benefits, and responsibilities in an enterprise" (Liu, 1987: 152).

Finally, in recent years, the shareholding system emerged, representing a more thorough separation between the state administration and enterprises. The shareholding system was first initiated by local state-run and collective enterprises as a measure of fund raising. It began to prevail together with a dramatic growth of stock markets as CCP leadership tried to speed up the reform after Deng Xiaoping's southern tour of early 1992. Experimental Methods of Shareholding Enterprises, drafted by several governmental agencies and approved by the State Council in June 1992, rationalized the shareholding system as an effective way to alter state enterprises into fully autonomous ones with responsibilities for profits and losses.

Managerial Decentralization

Reforms since 1978 have significantly amplified local decision-making power through institutional decentralization. The most noticeable changes took place in the economic sphere, as the center relaxed its control over resource allocation, gave local authorities more autonomy to direct investment, and decentralized its managerial power over enterprises.

The center first decentralized its allocation power, as the planned allocation of resources by the center gradually declined after 1979. According to a recent *World Bank Report* (1990:60), the number of raw materials at the disposal of the center fell from 256 to 27, and the proportion of capital goods embraced by the state's mandatory plan declined from 80 percent to 20-30 percent from 1979 to 1989. Local governments undertook the major responsibility for material allocations in their own areas. They could also obtain resources and products through exchange and cooperative bargaining with their neighboring regions.

The center also decentralized another very important power, the investment power, to make local authorities more responsible for productive progress. Before 1984, all investment projects over 10 million *yuan* were subject to the center's approval. Starting from 1988, however, the State Planning Commission only reviewed those projects over 50 million. The rest were left under the jurisdiction of provincial authorities.[5] In addition, the local government's control over banks and local taxes also allowed them to intervene in investment activities.

Finally, the central government decentralized managerial power. As a matter of fact, as local governments became more articulated in resource distribution and investment, the center's ability to intervene in micro-economic management sharply declined. According to some statistics, of more than 400,000 industrial enterprises in the country, only some 190 were directly run by the central authorities by 1988 (Liu and Wang, 1988:44). These enterprises usually dealt with crucial sectors of the economy, such as military production, transportation, electric power, and post and telecommunications. A great majority of enterprises have come under the administrative control of local authorities, though the extent of administrative authority depends on the level of differentiation between the government and enterprises.

Cadre System Reforms

The cadre system has been one of the major reform targets since 1980. This reflected the CCP's intention to restructure the inefficient bureaucracy and accommodate it to the drive for economic modernization. The post-Mao reformers identified a number of problems associated with the party's personnel administration, such as life tenure employment, a low educational and professional level, overstaffing and inefficiency, and the lack of an administrative responsibility system. Since 1980, a series of countermeasures have been taken to cope with these problems.

As early as February 1982 the CCP Central Committee issued a "Decision on the Establishment of a Retirement System for Old Cadres" and called it "a system to ensure the normal and healthy development of the party and state's political life."[6] The document specified retirement ages for cadres: sixty-five for ministers and senior executives; sixty for other male cadres; and fifty-five for female cadres.[7] To please retired cadres, the party allowed them to keep some benefits and privileges associated with their previous positions,[8] such as automobile service, telephone, housing. Some of them were given pensions higher than their previous salaries. Others were invited to serve as consultants for government agencies or enterprises. The program of retiring old cadres was implemented rather smoothly. At the top level, the retiring of senior leaders was impressive. At the Fourth Plenum of the Twelfth CCP Central Committee held in September 1985, 131 senior leaders resigned from their posts in the central leading institutions—Party Central Committee, Central Advisory Commission, and Central Discipline Inspection Commission (Li and Luo, 1987:219). At the lower levels, by the end of 1986, about 1.37 million elder cadres who joined the revolution before 1949 had retired (RMRB, October 11, 1987). The most recent official statistics show that the total number of retired cadres reached 6.5 million in October 1992 (RMRB, October 16, 1992).

In the meantime, the party also made great efforts to recruit younger professionals into the cadre corps. To make sure that younger cadres would be promoted, the party center stipulated that the average age for ministers and governors should be around fifty to sixty, while bureau heads at both the central and local levels and major leading cadres of cities and prefectures should be around fifty, and county leaders around forty-five (Chao, 1985:231). The average age of cadres consequently declined. For example, the average age of the provincial leaders was reduced from 61.9 to 53.2 years between 1982 and 1985. By the end of 1991, 70 percent of the party and government cadres were under forty-five years old (RMRB, October 16, 1992). The educational level also became an important criterion for cadre selection. There was a rapid increase of college graduates among the administrative elite in the 1980s. According to the 1982 census, of 810,000 cadres holding leadership positions at the county level and above, only about 6 percent were college graduates; 22 percent had senior high school diploma and 72 percent had been educated at less than junior high school level. By mid-1991, after more than 15 million younger cadres were recruited, the proportion of college-educated cadres had reached 32 percent (RMRB, June 7, 1991).[9]

The reform of cadre system was accompanied by changes in government personnel management. These changes included rationalizing recruitment procedures, establishing performance evaluation systems, and reforming the civil service wage system. Reformers sought to rationalize cadre recruitment by introducing open competition into the previous allocation system.[10] Local authorities were allowed to make experiments with new recruitment methods aiming at open and objective cadre selection, such as publicly advertising vacancies, accepting self-recommendations, and holding competitive entry examinations.[11] Fixed-term contracts were then given to those candidates who demonstrated higher capabilities.[12] From October 1984 to mid-1991, the figure of contracted cadres increased from 60,000 to 3 million (RMRB, October 15, 1984; June 7, 1991).

Another change regarding personnel management was the establishment of cadre performance appraisal systems. To be "democratic, open, objective, and fair," evaluation methods included self-assessment, face-to-face interview, peer appraisal, public poll, and written examinations. Assessments were made in the following aspects: virtue (*de*), knowledge (*shi*), ability (*chai*), diligence (*qin*), and achievement (*ji*). However, in most cases, a cadre's work effectiveness reflected in his or her achievements outweighed other criteria. During the winter of 1986 and the spring of 1987, a massive evaluation process was under way for local cadres at and above county level. According to the report issued by the central organization ministry, in three provinces alone (Fujian, Guangdong, and Ganshu), about 130,000 people were involved in evaluations. In Hebei province, 10,183 cadres were evaluated. The result showed that 16 percent of those evaluated were ranked as "excellent," 78 percent as "qualified" or "generally qualified," and 6 percent as "not qualified." Cadres who failed evaluations were transferred to lower posts or nonleading posts (RMRB, July 11, 1987).

To accommodate other reforms of personnel management, the salary system of government officials was transformed from one based on grades (*jibie gongzizhi*) to a system based on responsibilities (*zhiwu gongzizhi*). As we mentioned in the last chapter, before the reform all state personnel were put on a thirty-grade wage scale, closely connected with their seniority in the cadre ranks. The problem with the system was that it offered little incentive for those who, though still young, had strong abilities and good work achievements. The new system adopted in July 1985 emphasized the level of responsibility. It had four components: (1) a basic living allowance; (2) a salary depending on the degree of responsibility and complexity of a particular job; and (3) a very small (maximum 20 yuan) tenure bonus to reward seniority.

THE PARTY'S OVERALL POLICY PATTERN

Indeed, the CCP leadership has taken a series of bold steps in liberalizing the economy and loosing the centrally controlled planning system. These include the introduction of "responsibility systems," the growth of a substantial private sector, decentralization of managerial power, and the recent introduction of stock markets.

However, entrenched party elites have proven highly resistant to any challenges to party monopoly and had no intention of accepting political pluralism. This in part explains why there were conservative setbacks in China's reform process from time to time (e.g., the campaigns against bourgeois liberalism in 1980–1982, against "spiritual pollution" in 1983–1984, against unhealthy tendencies in 1985, against bourgeois liberalism in 1987, against "peaceful evolution" in 1989). The CCP's reform policies imply the existence of a dominant conceptual apparatus composed of politically neo-authoratianism and economically developmentalism. It demonstrates the following policy pattern: (1) the maintenance of a strong state (controlled by the party) to secure the "right" (i.e., socialist) direction for the reform; (2) a mix of private (market) and public (planning) sector arrangements to push the economy toward a market-driven and plan-guided one; and (3) a streamlined and capable bureaucracy to provide institutional support for the drive toward modernization.

This policy pattern is based on the conviction that though China needs a market-driven economy, its backwardness requires "an authoritative top leadership group which can rally the social elite and the nation in this complicated environment to advance this historic reform firmly and rhythmically" (FBIS, April 2, 1992:15). In other words, the goal is not to relinquish the party's control but to make it more effective and efficient.

Such an arrangement represented a great leap forward from the pre-reform political and economic systems modeled on the Soviet Union. It brought new thinking to China's stagnant economy tied by state planning. But, as we will see in the following chapter, the new authoritarian policy pattern generated some consequences far beyond the party's expectation and control.

NOTES

1. Even the Chinese leaders themselves admitted that they were "wading through a river by grasping stone after stone for a solid footing on the river bed" (*moshi guohe*).

2. The central administration sometimes did rely on regions (*kuaikuai*) to implement its policies, such as in the early 1950s and during the Great Leap Forward. This, however, did not significantly change the hierarchical nature of China's administrative structure.

3. See Zhao Ziyang's speech on the Preliminary Meeting of the Seventh Plenary Session of the Twelfth Chinese Communist Party Central Committee (RMRB, November 11, 1987:1).

4. For details of these policies, see *The Selected Important Works Since the Third Plenary Session of the Eleventh Chinese Communist Party Central Committee* (Beijing: People's Publishing House, 1987), 207–210.

5. However, the trend has been partially reversed since early 1990: projects valued at more than 30 million yuan must have the approval of the State Council, except in a few industries such as chemicals (WorLd Bank, 1990:61).

6. For the details of the document, see the CCP Central Committee's Document Research Institute (1982:1086–1095).

7. Although there were no specific age limits for the state head and the premier, they were obliged to retire from office after a maximum of two terms.

8. According to some analyses, this was a concession by the reformers to the elderly cadres. See, for example, James Kuo-hsiung Lee (1987:21).

9. For a more detailed analysis of changes in elite background, see Li Cheng and Lynn White (1990).

10. The pre-reform allocation system worked in the following way: the state and local planning commissions collected information on actual and potential vacancies within the civil service based on development plans; the state and local education bureaus gathered information on graduates of institutions of higher education, senior high, or other specialized schools; and then authorities at different levels matched the "demand" with the "supply" and worked out hiring quotas for individual units.

11. From February 1989 to April 1990, 37 central governmental bodies and 27 provinces recruited about 20,000 state personnel through competitive examinations (RMRB, April 10, 1990).

12. Local governments even openly recruited bureau directors or heads of major factories. See *People's Daily* (February 2, 1985) for Shenyang and the *Organization and Personnel News* (February 5, 1986) for Ningbuo.

8

Corruption as Policy Consequence

Looking at China's reform process since 1978, one could indeed be amazed by its remarkable achievements, especially in the economic sphere. As an economist has observed, "so swift have been the economic reforms in China that not even the keenest observers could keep pace with what has been going on" (Ethridge, 1990:16). However, paradoxical results exist as well. Among the most obvious is the increasing visibility of transactions between power and personal gain. Notwithstanding the remarkable success, China's reform since 1978 has unfortunately generated some unintended consequences which make for more, different, and new corruption. This chapter looks at three paradoxical phenomena: (1) while the party had no intention of loosening its control over society, its allowance for subsystem autonomy nevertheless has provided opportunities for power abuses at subsystem levels; (2) while the reform tried to decentralize economic power and enhance the managerial capabilities of local authorities, the effort has nevertheless increased local patron-client networks; and (3) while the reformers intended to revitalize the economy by incorporating the market mechanisms into the economy, some of the reform measures have ironically invigorated the so-called official speculation.

"CELLULAR POLITY"

Contrary to the party's new authoritarianist devise, China's economic reform and administrative reorganization resulted in a diffusion of state power to local levels and facilitated the development of what David Lampton (1987:14-17) has called the "cellular polity."

The cellularization of the state organization was, first of all, characterized by proliferation of various institutions, their reluctance to share resources with each other, and, worse yet, the diversion of their interests from those of the center. The proliferation of governmental agencies was most obvious at the local levels. Though the state government made great efforts to streamline organizations, the "organizational simplification" campaigns usually had a lesser impact at the local levels than at the center.[1] The local governments were reluctant to cut down their administrative budgets. After the simplification campaigns, their agencies were always restored much faster than those at the center. According to some recent official statistics, most provincial governments had more than seventy departments and agencies, exceeding the authorized size by at least fifteen more agencies; altogether there were more than 30,000 government agencies at and above the county level in China in 1992 (LW, September 21, 1992:3). Institutional proliferation was accompanied by the drastic increase of personnel. As Table 8.1 shows, between 1978 and 1990 the total number of party and government officials climbed by 90.7 percent.[2] Administrative expenditures accordingly soared. The budget for administrative management increased by 474 percent from 6.7 billion to 31.7 billion during the decade 1980–1990 (RMRB, May 30, 1991).

Table 8.1
The Increase of State Personnel in China (in Selected Years)

Year	Number	Average Annual Increase
1978	18,000,000	—
1987	27,000,000	1,000,000
1989	30,000,000	1,500,000
1990	33,000,000	3,000,000

Source: Xinhua Agency (November 18, 1987), in FBIS, November 18, 1987, 17–18; RMRB, September 16, 1989 and June 7, 1991.

A second indication of the cellular polity was the dramatic increase of administrative corporations created by ministries, bureaus, and other administrative units which tried to diversify themselves, and various social and cultural associations established to protect and promote professional interests. These quasi-government institutions were even less controllable. As "economic entities" they enjoyed many administrative and economic prerogatives and therefore had their own economic interests to defend. Thus it was not surprising to find that many organizations and localities became more and more reluctant to share resources with each other. They resorted to various methods, legal and illegal, to protect their own markets. Manmade regulatory barriers included roadblocks, cargo seizures, and even direct highway robbery. "Although central authorities use the words 'independent kingdom' (*duli wangguo*) as a term of reproach, it is the sacred objective of every unit and territorial jurisdiction to achieve precisely this freedom of action" (Lampton, 1987:15).

More important, however, were the increasing power abuses at subsystem levels accompanying the cellularization of the political system. With subsystem autonomy granted, more opportunities became available for various organizational and territorial players to seek private gain. With the development of local interest, the necessity of using these opportunities also increased. One of the most obvious areas was misappropriation of public funds. In recent years, though the central government made numerous pleas to save money, energy, and other production materials, cases of misappropriation frequently occurred. Local governments continued to spend large sums in importing luxury automobiles although the country was in a shortage of foreign currency. Government officials often spent public funds in junkets in the name of inspection. As reported, for instance, a group of six officials went to six work units to examine product quality. Their one-month stay cost these units 55,400 yuan. One-fifth of the money was spent on fancy banquets. Apart from this, each member of the group received presents worth 1,100 yuan (JFRB, April 20, 1989). Holding banquets at public expense also became very common. It was reported that in 1988, 60–70 percent of the incomes of the large and medium sized restaurants throughout the country came from banquets held at public expense (FBIS, March 22, 1990:24–25). Here are just a few statistics: in about 50 days in early 1987 (around the New Year and the Chinese Spring Festival), 400 work units held banquets with public funds with a total cost of approximately 410,000 yuan at nine first-class restaurants in Shanghai (Su and Jia, 1990:110); according to a survey by Hunan Provincial Supervisory Department, in a half-month from December 1 to 15, 1989, 34 work units used public funds for banquets on 92 occasions (MB, March 22, 1990).

The central government was particularly upset by the practice of "small treasuries" (*xiaojinku*), referring to funds deposited by local units without the authorization of the superior government institutions. According to the official view, these "small treasuries" were sources of corruption where funds could either have come illegally or be spent improperly. But more important to the central government, these "small treasuries" caused a drain on state revenues and led to the expansion of consumption funds. As reported by the Xinhua News Agency (FBIS, November 29, 1989:30), the Kaili Typing and Printing House in Shanghai cheated the state out of more than 32,000 yuan by falsely reporting the number of staff members and workers. The money, deposited in a "small treasury" it set up, was used for drinking and dining. When it was discovered, there was only 1, 241 yuan left. In October 1989 the Petroleum and Natural Gas Corporation of China discovered that the "small treasuries" run by its subordinate units had taken 7,196 million yuan in deposits (ibid.).

Another common practice strongly condemned as corruption by the central government was the building of private houses with public welfare funds. Since 1986, 90 percent of the cities and counties throughout the country disclosed cases of this nature, involving 20,100 cadres. In order to build houses for themselves or for their children, some cadres took possession of public production bases; others took advantage of their power to get labor and materials without compensation; still others simply used public or collective funds to buy private houses. For example, Wang Qinghai, deputy chief of Shenyang Municipal Farm Machinery and Automobile Industrial Bureau, spent 56,000 yuan of public funds refurnishing his private house (RMRB, June 13, 1989). A vice-chairman of a county People's Congress Standing Committee in Guangdong built a house with twelve rooms and four sitting rooms for his family of four, with a per capita floor space of 106 square meters (FBIS, August 8, 1989: 22). In some counties, about 98 percent of cadres built apartments for themselves at public expense (ibid.). People called those places where cadres' private houses are located "cadres' special zone" (*ganbu tequ*) or "cadre street" (*ganbujie*), or "official residence street" (*guanfu jie*) (Hu, 1989:17-20).

All these activities were identified as corruption by the central government. In popular terms, however, it was usually said that "those above have their policies, those below have their countermeasures" (*shangyou zhengce, xiayou duice*). This well reflected what Stephen Ma (1990) called "negative adjustment," through which bureaucrats compensated for loss caused by new conditions, regardless of any consequences for society at large.

PATRIMONIAL RELATIONSHIP

The decentralization of the state power in the reform period did not increase the autonomy of society as much as it reduced the state's control over society. A "civil society" has not yet emerged in China.[3] Chinese society had limited autonomy not merely because there was a strong state. It was also because people were well organized into all-inclusive work units (*gongzuo danwei*), where the state penetrated society. The work-unit system subjected individuals to the indoctrination, surveillance, and administrative distribution of welfare of their own work units. To list a few examples, the approval of one's work unit was required to apply for party membership and for promotion, to get a marriage certificate, to rent an apartment, to divorce, to give birth, or to go abroad. This then created what Andrew Walder (1986:13) called "organized dependence": workers were economically, politically, and personally dependent on their work units and their supervisors.

Quite ironically, the center's decentralization policies enhanced rather than lessened people's dependence on their work units. The decentralization reforms reinforced the work-unit system and unintentionally the patrimonial relationship by granting local authorities more power. The center became more dependent on local cadres to implement its routine control, while the cadres became increasingly free from intervention, because government sanctions and institutionalized means of interest representation within the work units were not well developed. On many occasions, policy interpretation and enforcement fell entirely into the hands of individual cadres.

Jean Oi's account of clientalism in rural China describes the situation well. During the reform, the household responsibility system left the ultimate responsibility for production, sales, and consumption of grain with each individual household. However, rural cadres held crucial powers such as granting licenses, distributing scarce or rationed production materials, interpreting governmental policies, and securing loans. These powers enabled some rural cadres to "engage in activities ranging from illegally withholding a portion of peasant receipts from sales to the state, to imposing *ad hoc* surcharges, to extorting money from peasants at the purchasing station" (Oi, 1989b: 227). According to Ministry of Agriculture statistics, in recent years most farmers were asked to pay about 10 percent of their annual income to collectors of various funds in addition to taxes and dues. As a result, the State Council had to issue the Regulations on the Management and Supervision of Financial Levies and Labor Duties for Farmers in December 1991 to limit the amount of all fees a farmer pays to 5 percent of his/her annual income. Farmers in Sichuan province recently won the first court battle against local authorities and got back 50,000 yuan illegally charged money (CD, September 14, 1992).

In the urban areas, individual workers became more dependent on their work units, as the scope of resources and benefits at the latter's disposal expanded. The establishment of the "Director Responsibility System," which held individual cadres responsible for the making and execution of policies, at the same time increased the personal power of individual cadres. During the reform, the proportion of profits actually retained by enterprises increased steadily through three subsequent measures—profit retention (*lirun liucheng*), profit contract (*lirun chengbao*), and tax for profit (*ligaishui*).[4]

Profit retention allowed an enterprise to set up an "enterprise fund" by retaining 3-5 percent of its planned profit and 15-25 percent of its unplanned profit earned in excess of the planned target, after it had fulfilled state targets. The enterprise could produce and sell more to meet market demands and to accept processing jobs with materials supplied by clients. Enterprises could also retain the proportion of depreciation that had been remitted to the central government budget, and gradually increase depreciation rates if production grew. However, under the profit retention system, enterprise autonomy was very limited, for the rapid growth of the profit retention was not accompanied by independent economic accounting and increased responsibilities of enterprises. A new system was therefore developed to replace profit retention.

Under the system of profit contracts enterprises and their administrative superiors negotiated a "basic figure" of profit which enterprises would deliver to the state. Enterprises were then allowed to retain a very high proportion of profits above this basic figure, ranging from 20 to 100 percent, with the retention rates frequently increasing with the degree of overfulfillment. The "profit contract" epitomized what Kornai calls the "soft budget constraint" (Kornai, 1980; 1986). As Riskin observes, however, "because its terms depended upon the particular conditions facing individual enterprises—all of which were victimized in one way or another by the ineffective planning system—the plea of adverse conditions was almost always a convincing defence against high targets or penalties for non-fulfillment" (Riskin, 1987). Chinese reformers echoed this concern by replacing profit contracts with "tax for profit."

Tax for profit involved substituting a series of taxes, paid directly to state treasuries, for the previous system of profit deliveries channeled through an enterprise's administrative superior. Under this system, large and medium-sized state enterprises paid a 55 percent profit tax and small ones a progressive income tax. The government then claimed a share of after-tax profits. This system was intended to harden an enterprise's soft budget, improve its incentives, and simultaneously ensure that growing profits would be equitably shared by the state treasury and the enterprise (Riskin, 1987:346).

All these measures were intended to invigorate enterprises by the state's yielding a proportion of profits (*rang li*) to them. Nevertheless, as a great portion of the retained profits was used as bonuses by managers to reward workers, it could create patrimonial rulership based on material incentives and rewards (McCormick, 1990: 20), because to whom the bonuses go and how much are managerial decisions of factory leaders.[5] Factory managers could also use the retained profits to expand the work unit's residences, create jobs for children and relatives of their employees, or establish day-care centers.[6] Whether all these provided strong incentives for workers to work hard remains controversial. However, they did make workers more dependent on their work units for what they needed and thereby created a more paternalistic atmosphere.

Over time, all these tended to result in extensive patron-client networks: cadres exercised personalized authority as patrons obliged to give their clients favored treatments, whereas workers and peasants acted as clients who tried to maintain good relations with cadres in order to secure material benefits and personal favors. Patron-client ties also existed between cadres. Basic-level cadres often fell into the client role in relation to higher-level cadres. They needed to establish special connections (*guanxi*) in order to achieve favored treatment.[7] This, to some extent, explains why in recent years, gift giving and banqueting became common practices. According to a survey conducted by the *Sanyuefeng* (March Wind) magazine and China People's University in mid-1992 in China, the average amount of money per person spent on gift-giving was 118 yuan a year, approximately 11.8 percent of his or her annual income (CTW, September 27, 1992:70). This means that people had to use one month's salary to buy gifts for others. Here are some examples to illustrate how and why gift giving is necessary. It was reported that in Guangdong, in order to bribe concerned government officials so as to secure loans, two small companies had to spend more than 600,000 yuan (approximately 105,000 dollars) on gifts and banquets (Wang Jinye, 1989). Another example was that a district commissioner who came to inspect local business was offered nineteen banquets and twenty-five different gifts in a period of about two months, which cost 5,336 yuan of public funds (RMRB, June 2, 1989).

Worse yet, many officials acted not only as bribe takers but also as bribe seekers. This means that, instead of simply waiting for bribes, they extorted money, gifts, or other forms of returns from their clients. Li Qizhu, for instance, a former national model worker and the head of Tianjin Bicycle Factory, requested kickbacks of 55,526 yuan in cash from bicycle buyers within three years. He was later sentenced to seven years' imprisonment (BKWZ, July 4, 1989). Luo Guiyuan was another case in point. Taking advantage of his post as the warden of a jail in Hunan, Luo squeezed 140,000 yuan (about 24,500 dollars) out of a convict sentenced to death and helped him escape (RMRB, May 13, 1989).[8] More vulnerable victims of extortion, however, were private or collective enterprises. These businesses, usually small and weak, were often forced by corrupt officials to engage in bribery in order to stay in business. For example, as revealed by the *People's Daily* (June 22, 1988), Gao Yuncong, secretary of Jili District Party Committee of Luoyang City, Hunan, forced the Jili Chemical Factory to buy houses, cars, and color TV sets for him. When the factory refused, he instructed the local procuratorial organ to sue the factory for some simply nonexistent "problems." In the process, the procurator even summoned peasants taking part in construction of the factory and tortured them to extort confessions.

As a result of the prevalence of gift-giving, gift-taking, and gift-requesting practices, bribery was identified as the most popular form of corruption in China. According to the author's statistics, of the 132 major cases reported by the *People's Daily*, China's most authoritative newspaper, between July 1988 and June 1990, 47 percent were related to bribery (Table 8.2).

In addition to its prevalence, bribery usually involved huge sums. While in the early 1950s, embezzlement of a few hundreds yuan could induce imprisonment, the cases of graft involving hundreds of thousands of yuan were no longer rare in the 1980s. According to official statistics, the major cases of embezzlement and bribe taking involving more than 10,000 yuan[9] increased in recent years. In 1989, for example, the procuratorial organs at different levels investigated a total of 13,057 major cases, an increase of 3.4 times over the previous year. However, by the end of the first eight months of 1990, the number of major cases had reached the level of the entire previous year. The revenues obtained from fines and confiscated funds were about 634 million

Table 8.2
Major Forms of Corruption Reported by the *People's Daily*, June 1988–June 1990

Form	No. of Cases	%
Graft	62	47
Official Speculation	25	18.9
Embezzlement	21	15.9
Luxury living	11	8.3
Others[a]	13	9.8
Total	132	100%

Source: Compiled by the author.

[a]Others include nepotism and negligence of duty.

yuan, also a big increase over the year before (RMRB, October 13, 1990). In July 1989, Shanxi province reported the most serious embezzlement case in the province since 1949. Tan Zhengya, a purchasing agent, embezzled about 390,000 yuan (approximately 68,500 dollars) in one year. He was later sentenced to death. (RMRB, May 28, 1989). The sums of bribe taking also increased. Song Meiying, a policewoman in charge of household registration in Guangzhou, was sentenced to death for accepting more than 210,000 yuan in bribes from 1984 to April 1988 by allowing rural people to register illegally in the city (RMRB, August 14, 1989).

It is true that patron-client networks existed in the pre-reform period too. But the contextual meanings were different. Guenther Roth (1977:156–169) distinguishes two types of patrimonial relationships: one based on belief in the ruler's unique personal qualification, and the other on the temptation of material rewards.[10] What we have seen in the reform period was an intensification of the latter, as the material rewards at the disposal of local authorities increased. Now in many cases, individual cadres exercise personalized authority legitimated by the "director responsibility system" and the "contract system."[11]

OFFICIAL SPECULATION

As we pointed out earlier, since the reform the CCP has taken a series of measures to enliven the stagnant economy tied up by the rigid planning system, but it has never intended to totally give up the state planning system and reduce its reliance on the bureaucracy. There consequently surfaced the so-called dual-track phenomenon. Here are just a few examples:

1. In the same workshop, for the same job, operating the same kind of machine, there were two types of workers. One held the job for life under the state job assignment system; the other was a contract worker hired by the factory for a certain term and on different pay and benefit systems.
2. In the same steel plant, there were two prices—the state-set price and the above-quota market price—for the same product. The ratio between the two could be as high as 1:2.[12]
3. People started to develop dual-track vocations. During daytime they worked in factories. In the evenings they became vendors, bicycle repairmen, hairdressers, taxi drivers and so on. Sometimes about 50 percent of a person's income came from his or her "second vocation." There were also "Sunday engineers," who worked for their own factories or institutes on workdays and for some small collective enterprises during weekends.

4. Some cadres were appointed through traditional procedures, whereas others had to compete for government jobs through competitive examinations.
5. Students enrolled in the same universities were put under different systems. Those extra-quota enrolled students had to pay tuition and other expenses themselves or had them paid by their work units. Others enjoyed completely free education.[13]

Indeed, the dual-track systems created more opportunities for the Chinese people and revitalized Chinese society to a certain degree. However, chance usually favored party cadres and their networks. In recent years, tens of thousands of administrative corporations emerged to promote their business in the cracks between plan and market. The term "official speculation" (*guandao*) was thus developed to describe the buying and reselling practice conducted by these corporations—a novel but pervasive corruption practice in today's China.

It is perhaps nothing new in China for bureaucrats to engage in business. In traditional China, being an official and making a fortune were always linked together. In pre-reform years, government agencies directly managed enterprises by producing mandatory plans, controlling resources and supplies, setting prices, absorbing all revenues and costs, and regulating all labor. However, when everything was under strict state control, "transaction costs" (i.e., risks) for individual officials to directly engage in profiteering could be high.

Official speculation became one of the most salient forms of corruption under the shelter of two new conditions of the reform. One was the spread of administrative corporations and the other the dual-track price system.

There were two "corporation fads" during the reform.[14] The first one occurred in 1985 when the number of corporations of various types all over the country totaled about 320,000. Of these corporations, quite a few were speculative briefcase companies without funds, equipment, or even fixed addresses. Through screening and consolidation, the number was reduced to 180,000 in 1986 (RMRB, July 7, 1990). A second fad took place between 1987 and 1988 when the number of corporations reached about 477,000, with an average of more than 100,000 new corporations emerging each year (ibid.). These corporations altogether involved 40.88 million personnel. The corporations which emerged from the second "corporation fad" had several new characteristics: (1) Most of them were run directly by government agencies; for example, the central ministries and commissions under the State Council alone operated about 700 companies; (2) they engaged many state officials and even some high-ranking officials; according to statistics, about 47,900 cadres concurrently held positions in government agencies and corporations, and of them, 246 were cadres at ministerial or provincial level, 2,324 were bureau heads, and 8,193 were division cadres (RMRB, August 30,

1989); and (3) many of these corporations were run by retired cadres who held considerable "residual power" or children of high-ranking officials.[15] Making use of their political privileges and old connections, these people were able to gain access to scarce resources or cheaper materials so as to reap staggering profits.

Certain government policies contributed to the prevalence of administrative corporations. One was the policy of "creative earning" (*chuangshou*). In order to create a market-driven economy, the government urged all work units, especially those solely relying on government funds, to make money for themselves and thereby to reduce the government's financial burden. According to official rules, all the sideline earnings could be used by work units to develop themselves or promote the welfare of their employees. As a result, many government units engaged in profit-making activities by establishing corporations of their own. The government also encouraged corporations to reemploy personnel who had been laid off by streamlining institutions and old cadres who had reached retirement ages but still wanted to remain to "bring their residual heat into play" (*fahui yure*).

Another policy shelter for official speculation was the dual-track price system. Under the dual-track price system there was a mixture of several forms of prices—the state-set price, the floating price, and the market price. In theory, these prices were restricted to their respective spheres: state-set prices for the materials or products distributed or produced according to mandatory planning; floating prices for those under guidance planning; and market prices for the materials and products not subject to state control. Such an arrangement, indeed, injected momentum into the economy. From 1984 to 1987, for example, China's steel plants altogether raised 12.4 billion yuan in funds for reinvestment by selling extra-quota products at higher prices. However, the system also benefited those cadres who acted as go-betweens in market exchanges. These cadres connected suppliers and consumers and extracted high rents for themselves by acquiring items at state-set prices and reselling them at market prices.

Here is how speculative activities take place: Since administrative corporations were usually run by government cadres or their relatives, they were able to get state-controlled materials or products at cheaper (i.e., state-set) prices and then resell these goods to local or private enterprises at much higher (i.e., market) prices. A transaction like this usually brought these corporations or concerned individual cadres staggering profits. For example, a manager working for a trading center in Xuzhou city was able to make 14,000 yuan profit by reselling 18,000 tons of state-priced coal to local companies (RMRB, May 14, 1989). The Qingdao Wholesale Hardware Corporation got a total of more than 1.35 million yuan through buying and reselling some 23 million tons of state-planned products such as wire rods, round steel, and rolled plate (FBIS, October 28, 1988:49).

Official speculation often involved more than just one transaction. Also, in a chain of transactions there were usually more than just one profiteer. As each transaction drove up the price of a material a bit, the whole process could lead to a very high price for the material. For example, a steel pipe plant in Nanjing bought thousands of tons of steel plate through its "back door" connections at a cheaper price and then sold them to 31 small factories for a profit of 1.35 million yuan. Equally motivated by profit, these small factories resold the plate instead of using it for production. The same process went on until after 129 transactions, the price of the plate was raised from 1,750 to 4,600 yuan per ton (RMRB, July 21, 1989). It was not a surprise either that in 1988 the price for aluminum, originally priced at 6,000 per ton, finally reached over 14,000 yuan after many speculative transactions (RMRB, June 22, 1988).

Official speculation also took the form of selling "purchase quotas" or "approval notices" issued by the government to allow certain factories to purchase much-needed materials or products. These documents became saleable as they fell into the hands of administrative corporations. In 1988, for example, a corporation in Heyuan country made a profit of 560,000 yuan by selling 13 approval notices of purchasing a kind of imported plastic material (RMRB, November 22, 1988). Other documents such as employment quotas, production contracts, exit permits[16] also became saleable and therefore profitable. A cadre in the Labor Department of Huhehaote city was found to have received 33, 650 yuan by selling employment quotas (WHB, June 23, 1989). In numerous cases, construction companies profiteered from subcontracting construction projects to those who had offered bribes. In Shanghai, for example, a district official got more than 10,000 yuan bribes from those who were competing for contracting (WHB, November 13, 1988). On many occasions, indeed, official speculation did not need any financial investment. What profiteers had were power and connections. Sometimes a telephone call or a note could lead to a deal worth hundreds of thousands of yuan. In China the secret of business success has been summarized by many as "money (used for bribery) + face (human relationships and connections) + note (approval notices and documents)."

NOTES

1. See Hong Yung Lee (1992:56–60) for a discussion of the reasons.
2. Including those who work in party and government departments, in service units (*shiye dangwei*)—education, science and technology, and public health sectors, and in state enterprises.
3. See Thomas Gold (1990) and Dorothy Solinger (1992) for discussion of this concept and its relevance to China.

4. For details, see Wang Hongmuo (1989).

5. In China the wage bill consists of basic salary, bonuses, and other subsidies. The basic salary and subsidies are decided by the state, while the distribution of bonuses falls into the jurisdiction of factory managers. Based on China's official *Statistical Yearbook* (1989:133), since the reform the proportion of bonuses in one's wage bill has greatly increased from single-digit percent to about 30 percent. According to the interviews I conducted in summer 1990, in some "well-managed" factories, bonuses actually reached 50 percent of one's salary.

6. Some analyses consider it a mystery why Chinese managers are so anxious to keep their workers happy. A possible reason is, since the cadre system reform, the political "survival" of basic-level cadres (staying in power) not only relies on their loyalty to the center, but also (perhaps more importantly) depends on their job performance as decided by mass assessment and economic productivity of their work unit. For more, see Susan Shirk (1985: 202).

7. Jean Oi (1989a:128–130), has a good discussion of the patronage relationship between brigade leaders and team leaders in China's rural areas.

8. In some cases I give a dollar figure as a reference for those readers who are not familiar with the Chinese currency—RMB. Please bear in mind when reading these dollar figures that the per capital income in China is low (between $300 and $400 in the late 1980s and early 1990s) and some hundreds of dollars mean a lot to an average Chinese family.

9. A case involving 10,000 yuan or more is officially defined as a "major case."

10. Also quoted in Barrett L. McCormick (1990:20).

11. This is because both systems hold individual cadres responsible for the making and execution of enterprise policies.

12. For example, in 1987 the state price for a ton of thread-rolled steel was about 700 yuan, whereas the nonplanning price was 1,400 yuan. Of the 43.85 million tons of steel produced that year, 22.8 million tons (52 percent) were distributed at the state-fixed price; the prices of the rest were simply determined by the market (Yang, 1988:10).

13. Ibid.

14. As I write this book, another wave of creating corporations is under way. It was stimulated by Deng Xiaoping's much-publicized tour of the southern "special economic zones" in January and February 1992. The trip signaled Deng's determination to end the party's preoccupation with ideology in favor of a new emphasis on economic development. Soon after the tour, the party's Central Committee issued a statement promising to continue reform policy for 100 years. As the party leadership appeared more willing to accept those market mechanisms such as free price and private enterprise, more and more people began to practice "capitalism"—setting up private shops,

enterprises, and corporations. It was reported that in Beijing alone, more than 2,000 new businesses emerged each month in early 1992; by the end of July, the Beijing Bureau of Industry and Commerce had run out of business licenses (*Open Magazine*, August 1992:26). Unlike the previous "fads," however, this wave involves not only government cadres but also ordinary people. It is too early to judge the impact of this new development on China's economy. This book therefore does not include this one.

15. For example, Deng Xiaoping's son was once the chairman of the board of the Kang Hua Development General Corporation. The corporation had 171 subcompanies. Many of them were found engaging in illicit activities, such as tax evasion, speculation in scarce resources, and profiteering from importing limousines. The corporation was disbanded during the campaign of cleaning corporations in 1989 (RMRB, July 31 and August 1, 1989). It was reported that other party and state leaders such as former party general secretary Zhao Ziyang, former chairman of the National People's Congress Peng Zen, and former CCP Politburo member Hu Qiaomu, all had children engaged in business (ZM, No. 3, 1988).

16. As a special measure of control after the June 4th Incident, the Chinese people who were going abroad must apply to the government for an "exit permit."

9

Anti-Corruption in the Reform Context

Corruption is not a simple economic problem. It is a political matter concerning the public image and political legitimacy of the leading institution. A communist party like the CCP has claimed its legitimacy to rule on the basis of ideological infallibility and behavioral rectitude, the two putative attributes of a revolutionary vanguard (Chi, 1989:140). For a party which defeated rivals by its reputation for moral rectitude as well as its military power, it is certainly unbearable to be tarred with the same corrupt image as that of pre-1949 KMT.

THE BEGINNING OF A NEW ANTI-CORRUPTION CAMPAIGN

In the late 1980s, the public resentment against corruption reached a high point as reflected in several public opinion polls conducted then. In a survey by the Sociology Institute of the Chinese Academy of Social Science in 1987, 83.7 percent of 2,348 respondents from 30 cities identified corruption as the problem which disturbed them most (LW, May 23, 1988:27). According to another survey by the same institute the next year, among 12,000 people from 16 cities, "embezzlement and bribe taking" was believed the most prevailing social crime. As for the party's work style, 50.4 percent of the respondents described it as "not improved," 24.4 percent thought it "even worse," and only 22 percent of the respondents believed it "improved" (Zhu, 1989). Just before the student movement of 1989, a nationwide survey by an authoritative magazine, *Ban Yue Tan*, again confirmed people's resentment against corruption: respondents ranked corruption (78.15 percent) and inflation (65.4 percent) as the issues of most concern (*Ban Yue Tan*, May 11, 1989).

Facing the situation, the CCP Politburo for the first time put the problem of corruption on its agenda at a three days meeting in early June of 1988. The party leaders realized a twofold danger from rampant corruption: first, corruption was discrediting the party in popular eyes[1]; second, it had impeded the party's ability to control society because its policies were diluted to accord with local and individual interests. Thus, the leadership reached a conclusion that a new anti-corruption campaign was necessary as it was "concerned with the party and state's prestige and image among people, with the smooth implementation of party courses and policies, with the establishment of a clean and efficient government, and with the progress of reform and construction."[2] In the following days, the Party Central Committee circulated the Notice on Keeping Party and Government Apparatus Honest and Clean, calling on all state organs to give anti-corruption a high priority in their work. At the Third Plenum of the Thirteenth Party Congress held later in the year, the then party general secretary, Zhao Ziyang, pointed out,

> Keeping the party and state apparatus clean is an extremely important and urgent problem in the current stage of party construction . . . . Today, embezzlement, bribe taking, extortion, speculation, extravagance, and waste which occur among some party and state cadres are what people hate most . . . and hurt the image of the party and the government. If this problem is not resolved, we shall lose the support of the people. (FZRB, December 12, 1988).

After the party congress, the Secretariat of the Party Central Committee held a meeting exclusively focusing on the corruption issue. As reported, the meeting evaluated the situation of the cadre ranks and "found it necessary and urgent to give cleaning up the government high priority in the party's work" (Zhongguo Zhengfa Daxue, 1989:5).

However, behind the seeming consensus profound policy disputes existed, with respect to what had touched off corruption of such unprecedented severity and how to remedy corruption. Zhao Ziyang believed that corruption was an inevitable by-product of rapid social and economic change during the modernization process. With the reform moving ahead, especially with a further reduction of the state's monopolistic status, one could expect a breakdown of the transaction between official power and wealth. Proposing further reforms, Zhao Ziyang brought with him to the party's annual summer retreat at Beidaihe in 1988 a bold plan—the so-called "New Order for the Socialist Commodity Economy." The plan called for an ending of all state price controls in four to five years and great devaluation of currency to encourage exports. Li Peng and other party leaders,[3] on the other hand, advocated a retrenchment program, including postponing price reform, cutting down capital construction, strengthening ideological rectification, and recentralizing administration. It was reported that Deng Xiaoping distanced himself from the bold reform policy though he had given Zhao Ziyang full support before. As a result, Zhao was forced to make a self-criticism and openly express his support for the retrenchment plan. The retrenchment program, with anti-corruption as one of its major components, was thus formally adopted by the Party Central Committee in September 1988 in Beijing.

However, the high tide of the anti-corruption movement did not come until spring 1989, when the student demonstrations released the popular hatred against official corruption. As is well known, the corruption issue was an important catalyst of the 1989 movement. No matter whether or not it was a tactic on the students' part to legitimize their action or to secure popular support from the masses,[4] the fact was that the students's anti-corruption banner appealed strongly to the public. During the demonstrations, the most popular slogans were "Down With Venal Officials," "Opposing Official Speculation," and "Opposing Privileges." According to the *Boston Globe* of May 24, 1989, one worker from Beijing told a reporter that "the students have given all the people the courage to raise their voice." The following comments in the *Worker's Daily* reflected the public mood: "The people who should have got rich have not, but those who should not have lined their pockets" (*Worker's Daily*, May 5, 1989). Even Zhao Ziyang himself admitted when he met the representatives of the Asian Development Bank that "What the students resent most is corruption." It was reported that Zhao presented a four-point proposal to the party's Politburo Standing Committee in early May 1989, attempting to avoid the escalation of the student-government conflict. The proposal included some anti-corruption measures such as elimination of special privileges for senior party officials and investigation into corruption of high-level cadres and their relatives. But his proposal was outvoted 4 to 1, because other leaders regarded the student movement as "counterrevolutionary insurrection" rather than an anti-corruption oriented protest (MB, June 1, 1989:1). However, after the Tiananmen incident, even Deng Xiaoping himself had to admit the provocative function of the corruption issue in the event, as he told other party leaders that "the development this time from the student demonstrations to turmoil, and then to a counterrevolutionary rebellion, has an important reason. That is, rampant corruption has caused many people to lose confidence in the party and the government, and they believe that we are protecting corruption" (Wu, 1990:5). It was therefore not surprising to see that after the student demonstrations, the Chinese mass media dramatically increased the exposure of corruption cases to highlight the party's determination and efforts to repress corruption (Table 9.1).

In the meantime, China's procuratorial organs increased their acceptance, investigation, and prosecution of corruption cases (Table 9.2). In 1989, for example, China's procuratorial organs accepted a total of 116,763 cases of embezzlement and bribe taking. Of them, 58,926 were placed on file for investigation and prosecution. The cases accepted increased by 1.6 times and cases for investigation and prosecution increased by 1.8 times as against 1988.[5]

Table 9.1
Corruption-Related Reports by the *People's Daily*, July 1988–December 1989

Time	Number
July 1988	39
August 1988	33
September 1988	22
October 1988	36
November 1988	28
December 1988	33
January 1989	50
February 1989	24
March 1989	31
April 1989	18
May 1989	28
June 1989 (Tiananmen incident)	25
July 1989	66
August 1989	102
September 1989	30
October 1989	21
November 1989	14
December 1989	19

Source: Compiled by the author.

Table 9.2
The Growth of Cases of Embezzlement and Bribe Taking Handled by Procuratorial Organs, January 1988–December 1989

Period	No. of Cases Accepted	Monthly Average	No. of Cases Prosecuted	Monthly Average
1–12/88	45,700	3,808	21,045	2,047
1–9/89	64,842	7,204	36,408	4,045
10–12/89	51,921	17,307	22,518	7,506

Source: The statistics were compiled by the author based on RMRB, December 29, 1988; March 4, 29, 30, 1989; April 10, 1990.

In order to clear the party's image and raise popular confidence in the government, the CCP incorporated some new measures into its anti-corruption effort.

NEW RULES AND REGULATIONS

Same as in the previous campaigns, the anti-corruption campaign of this time was intended to curb divergent ideas and conduct of cadres and to unify the Chinese people around the party's cause. the campaign was, therefore, designed from above and implemented along hierarchical lines. In contrast to previous efforts, however, the campaign in the context of reform tried rational–legal methods. Having realized the problems associated with the legitimacy based on charismatic or traditional claims, the party now saw the necessity to rely on legal means to contain corruption and therefore the party's flagging legitimacy could be restored on a new and rational basis.

From January 1988 to march 1989, in about one and a quarter years, the party and the government issued about thirty documents to specify anti-corruption rules. These rules and regulations could be classified into three major categories:

1. Strengthening the centralized control over certain commodities and production materials. For example, according to a document issued in October 1988, a government unit must report its purchase of important commodities to its superior; the commodities subject to prepurchase approval increased from 19 to 29 kinds, including automobile, sofas, carpets, office furniture, blankets, washing machines, refrigerators, TV sets, vacuums, clocks worth over 50 yuan, lamps worth over 100 yuan, and imported liquor and cigarette. In late 1988 and early 1989, steel and chemical fertilizers were put under the monopoly of the central government.
2. Forbidding certain "unhealthy practices," such as gift giving in public affairs, squandering public funds, cadres' engagement in trade, excessive consumption of liquors and cigarettes in receptions.
3. Establishing rules and procedures to punish offenders. The Interim Provisions Governing Disciplinary Sanctions Against Corrupt Functionaries of State and Administrative Organs, for example, stipulated the following disciplinary penalties for embezzlement: (a) anyone who embezzled more than 5,000 yuan should be removed from office but the money he or she embezzled should be repaid in full plus interest; (b) anyone who embezzled 3,000–5,000 yuan or who embezzled money in order to make a profit, should have this serious offense put on record and receive a penalty up to removal from office, with the money being repaid; and (c) if everything is the same but the money he or she embezzled was less than 3,000 yuan, a person should have the offense put on record or receive a demotion penalty (RMRB, September 22, 1989).

CLEANING UP CORPORATIONS

Since the party perceived a close connection between the problem of official speculation and the proliferation of government corporations, it believed that a campaign to "clean up" corporations was necessary. The "clean-up" was implemented between October 1988 and December 1989. During the period, the party center and the State Council issued two importance documents. One was the Resolution to Clean Up Corporations issued in October 1988. It aimed at corporations run by government agencies, which, according to the central authority, should not engage in profit making. The document asked all government agencies to disconnect themselves from business corporations and it emphasized that no government agencies were allowed to take money out of their administrative budget or other government grants to invest in business. Later, in August 1989, another document was issued—the Resolution to Further Clean Up Corporations. The second document expanded the targets of the clean-up to include illegal or ill-managed non-government corporations, especially those involved in trading raw materials and key production goods. The document reaffirmed that the production and trade of raw materials and certain industrial goods remained under the jurisdiction of the central government.

The party leadership saw the following particular problems with the government corporations, in addition to the damage caused by their profiteering activities to the center's control over the means of production: they jeopardied the fairness of market competition, because they had monopoly power over important materials and products; their buying-selling-reselling activities caused drastic price increases; they also made raw materials stay in circulation, being sold and resold, without going into production; and finally, perhaps more importantly, they affected social morality and brought a bad image to the party and the government. As a result of the intensified clean-up efforts, by the end of April 1990, 88.8 percent of some 13,390 companies run by party or government agencies were abolished. The rest were transferred to economic sectors (RMRB, July 7, 1990). About 2,700 of them had been established by central ministries and other government bodies at the center (RMRB, January 20, 1990).

In addition to clamping down on illegal run or ill-managed corporations, the party center also banned its cadres from holding concurrent positions in corporations. On February 5, 1989, the Party Central Committee and the State Council circulated a notice requiring all the cadres who concurrently held positions in state apparatus and business corporations to quit their jobs in business. According to official statistics, one year after the decision was made, 96.4 percent of these cadres pulled themselves out of business (RMRB, July 7, 1990). The party center also publicized four "big cases" to show how some cadres had worked as go-betweens by means of their concurrent positions in government and in corporation to make profit. Ge Datong of *Economic Daily*, Chen Kaizhi of North China Industrial Corporation, Zhang Shuchun of Yanshan Chemical Corporation, and Xiang Yan of Jiangshu Zhenhua Chemical Industrial Corporation, were party cadres working for newly established government corporations. Taking advantage of their privileged access to important materials and products, they created great personal fortunes, ranging from several million to several hundred million yuan. They all received heavy sentences (GMRB, March 12, 1990).

The leadership paid particular attention to official speculation conducted by corporations. From October 1988 to June 1989, 25,884 cases of official speculation were investigated and handled, concerning 25,404 companies. Among them, 9,534 received economic sanctions, with 260 million yuan being recovered; 2,871 received the penalty of license suspension; 301 cadres were pursued on criminal charges for their illicit economic activities (RMRB, August 30, 1989). To highlight the top leadership's determination, the party center also publicized the cases of five high-profile corporations (China International Trust and Investment Corporation, Kang Hua Development Corporation, China Economic Development Corporation, and China Agricultural Trust and Trade Corporation.[6] The investigation results of the five corporations and their hundreds of subsidiaries showed that these "super" corporations had been engaged in illicit activities such as tax evasion, speculation in productive materials, and black market transaction in foreign currencies.[7] The Central Audit Bureau recovered a total of 5,133 million yuan (approximately 900 million dollars) from the five corporations (RMRB, August 17, 1989).

HIGH-LEVEL CADRES TAKING THE LEAD

Partially as a response to the skepticism about the top leaders' determination in tackling corruption of senior cadres and also as a measure to correct the party's image among the public, the party center requested all the high-ranking officials to take the lead in the anti-corruption campaign.

On July 1, 1989, the Politburo of the CCP Central Committee adopted a resolution, announcing that it had put seven issues of most concern to the masses on its immediate agenda. These issues included (1) further screening and consolidating corporations; (2) preventing children of senior officials from doing business; (3) ending "special supplies" of certain foods for leading cadres; (4) requiring the central authorities to use Chinese-model cars; (5) forbidding senior party and state cadres from excessively entertaining guests or presenting expensive gifts; (6) limiting leading cadres' overseas trips; and (7) seriously dealing with cases of bribe taking, graft, speculation, and so on (RMRB, August 11, 1989). Take leading cadres' overseas trips as an example. The central authority had very detailed restrictions on how many trips a cadre could have within a certain time and how long the trip could be. A document issued by the general office of the Party Central Committee in October 1989, stipulated that leading cadres could only go abroad once a year, with their stay in one country being limited to at most five days. It also specified the size allowance for a delegation accompanying leading cadres: a major party or government leader could have a delegation of 20 people with him or her; a leading cadre of central government agencies could bring 10 people; and a delegation accompanying local leaders could only have five people. In addition, permission was required when a leading cadre was going to take his wife with him (RMRB, October 8, 1989).

Urged by the central authority, provincial governments also took corresponding measures. Shanghai Party Committee stipulated that all public banquets should only be served with four courses and one type of soup, and leading cadres could only have one dish and one soup when treated by local basic-level work units (JFRB, September 11, 1988). Zhu Rongji, then the mayor of Shanghai, asked the procuratorial organs in the city to pay particular attention to Shanghai's 506 top cadres who served positions at and above the bureau level (JFRB, November 25, 1988). In Quizhou province, the party secretary ordered a "complete checkup" on the house-building record of provincial cadres since 1987 to see if there was any violation of public interests (RMRB, July 16, 1989). By early 1990, 12 provinces and municipal cities had adopted the so-called "avoidance system."[8] The system prohibited leading cadres from hiring their children and relatives in their subordinate units, involving any work related to their children and relatives, and serving any posts in their hometown (RMRB, October 10, 1989, and February 28, 1990).

The CCP also publicized a number of major corruption cases concerning high-ranking officials. Of the 132 cases reported in RMRB from July 1988 to June 1990, 53 percent involved high- and middle-ranking officials (29.5 and 23.5 percent respectively), but cadres at the sector (lower) level constituted the largest group (32.6 percent) (Table 9.3).

Table 9.3
Position-Level Distribution of Corruption Cases, July 1988–June 1990

Level	Frequency	Percentage
Ordinary cadre	19	14.4%
Sector head (lower level)	43	32.6
Division head (middle level)	31	23.5
Bureau head (higher level)	39	29.5
Total	132	100%

Source: Based on the 132 cases collected by the author from the reports in the *People's Daily* during the period.

In a well-publicized dismissal of high-level officials in 1990, Luo Yunguang, former vice-minister of railways, was accused of accepting bribes worth more than 5,000 yuan. The case involved eight other officials. They were all expelled from the party (RMRB, March 10, 1990). Other major dismissals involved Liang Xiang,[9] former Governor of Hainan province, and Qian Yongchang, former Minister of Transportation. They were both accused of taking advantage of their posts for personal gain (RMRB, September 15, 1990). In 1991 the central government publicized the cases of other two high–ranking cadres who later received the death penalty. Guan Zhicheng, the party secretary of the Capital Steel and Iron Corporation—one of China's giant corporations, reportedly embezzled 1.41 million yuan (about 240,000 dollars); Gao Shenxiang, the director of China Trust Bank in Shenzhen, had accepted bribes worth more than 1.8 million yuan (about 310,000 dollars) before his case was exposed.

CONFESSION AND ACCUSATION

"Confession and accusation" have been the party's anti-corruption measures since its early years. But this time they were applied on a much larger scale than that of the previous campaigns.

On August 15, 1989, the Supreme People's Court (SPC) and the Supreme People's Procuratorate (SPP) issued a public notice urging all those guilty of corruption to surrender themselves and confess their problems by October 31, 1989; otherwise, they would be severely punished. Then all kinds of propaganda machines were mobilized to keep up pressure on these people. During the 78 days from the notice to the deadline, 36,171 people throughout the country surrendered themselves, including 9,363 party members, 742 cadres at the division level and 40 at the bureau level. There was also a vice minster among them. The money involved exceeded 460 million yuan (roughly 80 million dollars) (RMRB, November 12, 1989).

At the same time, the party leadership encouraged the public to report corruption (*jubao*). The SPP and the Ministry of Supervision (MOS) established "corruption reporting centers" equipped with telephone hotlines in mid-1988. The SPP received and handles 3,000 cases in less than one month after its hotline was set up, while the MOS received 673 reports over its hotline within the first 13 days, averaging 44 telephone reports per day. Since then, these centers have each received tens of thousands of reports every year. In the first half of 1989, these reporting centers altogether had more than 172,000 reports, an increase of 16 percent over the previous six months. Shanghai's procuratorial organs in 1989 alone received 30,512 reports of accusation. Of them, 23,623 or 77 percent claimed that they were reporting corruption (JFRB, May 3, 1990). By early 1992, 3,100 "corruption reporting centers" had been established in China (RMRB, February 28, 1992).

However, there were some problems with public reporting. For one thing, though a great number of reports were received each year, only a small proportion of them actually resulted in legal action. For example, Shenzhen Reporting Center received about 1,020 reports in nine months of 1988. However, only about 210 of them were filed for prosecution (RMRB, January 17, 1989). This is because quite a few reports received through telephone hotlines were not related to corruption or only related to some minor problems. For instance, in the three months after the MOS set up its hotline, of 1,250 telephone reports it received, about 500 were to seek advice, 350 were related to other business, and only 400 reported corruption. Another problem was that many reports were in anonymity, which made further investigation difficult. In Tianjin, for example, from January to April 1989, 60 percent of reports were from anonymous letters (RMRB, June 21, 1989).

REMAINING PROBLEMS

Despite the party's determination to correct its image among the public and the severe measures it took to curb corruption, the anti-corruption campaign of 1988–1991 encountered some thorny problems with no easy solutions. First, the demarcation line between corruption and normal market activities is vague, because the party has continued to update reform policies to meet new conditions. For example, should all reselling activities be considered corruption? Do all kinds of transaction between power and wealth fall into the category of corruption? To what extent should an enterprise be allowed to pursue profits through nonofficial channels? There are no definite answers to these questions in China even today.

Second, different policies exist at different localities. Someone who is considered a "speculator" at one place may be regarded as a "reformer" at another. For example, a Shenzhen company resold forty cars in Shanghai and was praised for its successful trading activities, but its partners in Shanghai were punished because selling and reselling cars by individuals were not allowed there.

Third, many government corporations engage in selling and reselling commodities under the name of private business. Since China's reform policy gives private enterprises favorable terms, the corporations can use these special terms to cover their illegal activities.

Fourth, many corrupt activities, especially those of official speculation, are "collective actions." This means that they are results of collaboration of a number of government agencies and business corporations. A typical case was a speculation in 51,000 tons of chemical fertilizers, with 71 work unit, 5 party and government organs, and 22 leading cadres participating in the merry-go-round. Consequently, the procuratorial organ found it rather difficult to investigate the case (Lin, 1989).

Finally, many corrupt acts are backed from above. For example, some corporations had backstage supporters at high levels and, with official approval notices in hand, they could even defy investigations (BKWZ, July 18, 1989). Thus many people feel that during the campaign, high-ranking officials were spared and only "small fry" were punished (Tan, 1989:13).

Obviously, the emergence of the new patterns of corruption and the problems with anti-corruption are to some extent related to the reform context. However, it would be a mistake to blame the reform for corruption. Corruption in China is by no means confined to the reform period. Reform becomes the focus of this study not because it is particularly conducive to corruption, but because some of the CCP's policy initiatives and measures adopted for reform purpose have a close bearing on the patterns of corruption in the reform period. The development of corruption in China in recent years should not be attributed to too much reform; rather, as Jean Oi (1989b) correctly points out, it is a result of the incompleteness of the reform. The problem is not so much with the decentralization of power, but lies with the fact that while the central control over society is weakened, alternative checks on excessive subsystem autonomy have not been established; while economic reforms give cadres more power for policy innovation and implementation, the lack of political reform allows little chance to develop effective legal and institutional checks on them. Decentralization without democratization can only leave economic reform vulnerable to power abuse, therefore China needs a balanced reform agenda—bold economic innovations toward a market economy plus comprehensive political reform to install effective control over power holders.

NOTES

1. A vivid saying to describe cadre corruption at that time was that "a carton of cigarettes can knock down a government cadre."

2. See Li Peng's speech at the Party's Working Conference of the Central Government Organs (March 18, 1988), in Zhongguo Zhengfa Daxue, ed. *Selected Readings on Government Integrity* (1989:21).

3. They were reportedly supported by Chen Yun, China's senior economic planner since Mao's time.

4. For an analysis along this line, see Yan Sun (1991).

5. The figures for 1988 were 45,700 and 21,045, respectively.

6. Each of these corporations had among its senior staff influential persons including former ministers, vice-mayors, senior party secretaries, and relatives of Politburo members (Rosario, 1988:91)

7. China has had foreign currency control since 1949.

8. The system was first established and practiced in Hanan province, as the provincial authority found that nepotism had become a serious problem in government agencies. It was reported, for example, in a county public security bureau 60 percent of the employees had some kind of relationship with the bureau head, either as his relatives or as his good friends. Hanan's experiment with the "avoidance system" was highly praised by the party center (RMRB, May 10, 1989).

9. Some Hong Kong sources and Chinese dissidents overseas believed that the real reason for Liang's dismissal was his affiliation with Zhao Ziyang, who had been ousted from the party's leading position after the Tiananmen incident.

10

Conclusion

In the introductory chapter I stated that in order to avoid "empirical irrelevance," we must study the contextual origins, processes, and outcomes of corruption and then examine its relevance to and linkage with social science theory. This concluding chapter summarizes the main findings of this study, offers an evaluation of the significance of the policy outcomes perspective in interpreting China's corruption, and presents some theoretical reflections on corruption studies in general.

WHAT ACCOUNTS FOR CORRUPTION

The main argument of this study is that China's corruption represents the unintended consequences of the CCP's intended policies. To make the argument, the book has provided a detailed analysis of the CCP's general policy, organizational policy, and anti-corruption policy in the three periods of post-1949 China. It has also investigated the relationships between policy outcomes and the economic and political conditions shaping these outcomes. This study yields some important findings.

General Policy and Organizational Incompatibility

This study finds that the CCP has often been confronted with incompatibility between its general and organizational policies in its efforts to rule the country. In the first three years after the founding of the PRC, the CCP's major policy goal was to destroy old socioeconomic structures and prepare the nation for a new political and economic system. To reach the goal, the party overcame serious economic and financial difficulties to revitalize the nation's war-devastated economy; reorganized society to secure peace and order; and tightened control over actual and potential enemies[1] to eliminate any possible threats to the new regime. All these reflected the CCP's determination to transfer China from a semi-capitalist and semi-feudalist society to a socialist one, as the party itself claimed. However, these policy efforts put the CCP in an unexpected "contradiction between its ambitious goals and programs and its limited organizational capabilities" (Harding, 1981:62). It was unexpected because, having engaged in the wars (the Anti-Japanese War and the Civil War), the party had scarcely had a chance to train administrative experts of its own. Now, facing enormous tasks upon assuming power, the party suddenly found its administrative apparatus organizationally inefficient and politically unreliable: an effective administrative apparatus was far from ready for the task of transformation.

After spending three years in transformation and reorganization, the CCP shifted its core task from political transformation to economic development and organizational consolidation from 1954 onward. The organizational corollary of the shift was a rapid increase of state cadres and bureaucratic apparatus and significant entrenchment of their power. Drawing on the lesson of those early years, the party replaced the small, understaffed, and irregular governmental organizations with a strong, formal, and systematically structured bureaucracy, which was heavily loaded with political, economic, and administrative powers. The party also staffed its cadre ranks and state bureaucracies with more professional people. However, the party's paramount concern with the immediate task of social consolidation made it overlook a possible outcome of its policy, which soon became true. That is, while the party had to rely on a professional bureaucracy to manage the new society and to work as the administrative channel between the leadership and the masses, it also needed to keep the bureaucracy under control and to maintain its loyalty to the party center. To some extent, this reflects what Meaney (1988:5) terms "unique tensions" typical of a Leninist organization: the organization needs to prevent the dual danger of being assimilated into society so as to lose its identity and becoming so isolated from its power constituencies as to lose its authority.

Modernization since 1978 has been regarded as a third stage of the CCP's policy effort. After the catastrophe of the Cultural Revolution, the CCP attempted to revitalize society by decentralizing the economy and rationalizing the bureaucracy. To do so, it redefined its core task as the "four modernizations," opened the nation to the outside world, and carried out a series of economic and administrative reforms. Economically, the CCP partially dismantled the central planning system, reopened free markets, revitalized enterprise management, and replaced the people's commune with the rural household responsibility system. Administratively, the party reorganized its apparatus in order to eradicate overlapping institutions, especially at the upper levels. It also adopted a series of measures to professionalize governmental personnel and to rationalize cadre recruitment, promotion, and retirement systems. All these economic and administrative reforms successfully changed governmental and economic structures, but with the reform going on, other consequences became obvious as well, all beyond expectation: the weakening party control over society did not increase people's autonomy; decentralized economic structure further concentrated political power; and, finally, the revitalization of the economy stimulated the transaction between power and wealth.

Bureaucratic Corruption and Anti-Corruption Policy

This further leads to a second finding of the study: the incompatibility between the CCP's general policy and its organizational capacities affects the pattern of corruption in different periods.

During the period of transformation, the contradiction of the party's ambitious goals versus its low administrative capabilities underpinned what was considered corruption at that time. "The party's determination to carry out ambitious social and political reforms and to effect economic reconstruction even before its administrative apparatus was fully in place led inevitably to bureaucratism, waste, and commandism" (Harding, 1981:62–63). Besides, rapid recruitment of cadres to improve administrative strength tended to bring in those people who, as the party found, had little commitment to the party's political goals but were interested in sharing the fruits of its victory. Third, during those years, the party often had to give certain material incentives to those skilled personnel in exchange for their contribution to economic construction (Lowenthal, 1970); at the same time, however, the party found that, scared by communism and especially by the party's high ambition to dramatically transform society, capitalists and other small private entrepreneurs tried very hard to secure their privileges and rope in cadres in order to get political protection.

During the party's consolidation period, the increasing professionalization of the party and state apparatus upset the party, especially Mao who had an ideological aversion to the formal and hierarchical bureaucracy. The party leadership saw growing "unhealthy tendencies" among its local leaders. These tendencies, as defined by the internal party documents, included participation in "black market" and speculation; excessive eating and drinking; collusion between cadres and former landlords and rich peasants; and demoralization and lack of effective leadership (Teiwes, 1979:508–509).

Finally, the contradiction of concentrated political power versus decentralized economic/administrative structures underlay bureaucratic corruption during the modernization period since 1978. Because of structural decentralization, the party became more heavily dependent on local cadres to implement its policies and programs. With the exercise of authority becoming more and more localized, the degree of enforcement of power went further beyond the control of the center. Yet, on the other hand, structural decentralization did not reduce people's dependence on their immediate bureaucratic superiors. Most people were still employed by all-encompassing work units, which regulated and controlled many aspects of their lives. Presumably, the situation in rural areas might be better since the individual peasant household had replaced the collective as the unit of work and accounting and a freer market existed there. But the reforms did not take much power away from rural cadres either. Acting as intermediaries between the state and the peasants and as middlemen between state-planned distribution and market-directed production, cadres retained important powers. The standardization and rationalization of bureaucratic organizations did not reduce cadres' power so much as they changed power holders and modified the structures of power distribution. The reforms reshuffled the party and state apparatus. However, while the power holders changed, the magnitude of power was not reduced. Regardless of who was in power, the exercise of authority was personalized. Worse yet, on many occasions an emperor was replaced by a few emperors as a result of decentralized economic structures, while there were no checks over these power holders.[2] The entrenched bureaucratic power under the decentralized economic/administrative structures tended to breed more corruption, for fragmented management provided corrupters and the corrupted more opportunities to pursue their own interests in the name of local collectives.

In view of this analysis, it is not surprising to find that the three important policy periods of the CCP were each accompanied by a major anti-corruption campaign.

The Three and Five Anti's campaign during the transformation period was the earliest and perhaps most dramatic anti-corruption campaign in the history of the PRC. It started as a drive directed against embezzling public funds and accepting bribes among cadres. However, the focus of the campaign was more on capitalist entrepreneurs than on party cadres. Hundreds of thousands of private businesses were investigated, and many reportedly engaged in bribery, tax evasion, theft of state assets, cheating in labor or materials, and stealing of state economic intelligence.

The anti-corruption campaign accompanying the CCP's consolidation was the Socialist Education Movement. The movement once had anti-corruption as its central theme. The Four Clean-Ups originally referred to cleaning up economic accounting, public granaries, collective properties, and work point assessments. It was mainly directed at cadre corruption in these areas, which were believed to be the most important causes of peasant dissatisfaction. However, the content of "four clean-ups" soon changed. It became the clean-up of politics, economy, thought, and organization. The focus thus shifted from rural cadre corruption to nationwide "socialist education."

The economic rectification between 1988 and 1991 was the CCP's third prominent anti-corruption campaign. Beginning with the then party General Secretary Zhao Ziyang's statement that "in the process of reform and openness, the anti-corruption struggle is inevitable" (RMRB, October 25, 1987), continuing down to the Seventh Plenum of the CCP's Thirteenth Central Committee of 1991, the CCP gave wide publicity to the task of anti-corruption. From 1988 on, each year more than 100,000 party members were expelled from the party (Wu, 1989). A majority of them were charged with corruption-related wrongdoings. The number of corruption cases filed for investigation and prosecution also increased sharply. After the June 4th Incident, the new leadership became more vigorously determined to punish corruption officials severely in order to clean up the government's image (FBIS, October 19, 1989:13).[3]

Higher Political Goal

The aforementioned anti-corruption campaigns appeared to have had discernible targets, substantial implementation means, and follow-up disciplinary measures. However, they were, more importantly, integral parts of the CCP's general policy effort and served the party's "higher" political goals.

The Three and Five Anti's was one of the important vehicles to fulfill the party's overall project of transformation during the early years. It helped the CCP reorganize its organizational resources, strengthen administrative capabilities, and redistribute power, wealth, and status among various groups. This explains why the campaign not only involved cadres, but also quickly and stormily extended to the business circles.

However, the CCP's efforts to rebuild society caused problems for itself. After the party brought a large-scale party-state apparatus into existence in the 1950s, the bureaucratization of this apparatus increasingly upset the party leadership, especially Mao.[4] What worried them most was the perception that China was heading for "revisionism" of the Soviet type—a dictatorship of entrenched bureaucracies. The Four Clean-Ups campaign was therefore quickly switched to Socialist Education—a thought education movement directed at "capitalist roaders." Meisner (1977:288) describes the nature of the movement as "an attempt to counter the bureaucratization of Chinese political life, reverse socioeconomic policies that Maoists condemned as 'revisionist' and believed were creating new forms of capitalism, and revitalize a collectivistic spirit and consciousness both within the party and in society at large." Apparently, the anti-corruption campaign served as a handy tool in the CCP's class struggle, as it traced corruption to the collusion between party cadres and rich peasants and their joint exploitation of the masses. The Four

Clean-Ups was, thus, incorporated into the party's consolidation program.

The rectification between 1988 and 1991 was also more than an anti-corruption drive. It was an important part of the party's effort to rehabilitate itself while facing new social and economic crises. As many China watchers have observed, after having amazed the world by its achievements, China's reform bogged down after 1987. Partial deregulation of the price system and decentralization of government authority induced unexpected problems, such as increasing inflation and rampant corruption (Dittmer, 1990; Chan, 1990). However, the party was most concerned with people's declining confidence in the government. The "Circular of the CCP Central Committee on Keeping the Party and State Apparatus Upright" made it clear that "whether the party and state apparatus can avoid corruption is a problem concerning China's future and the party's fate" (RMRB, June 1, 1988). Therefore, underlying the CCP's interpretations of and countermeasures against corruption was a more important but familiar political agenda—to defend the party's legitimacy. That was why the CCP made great effort to associate corruption with "capitalist liberalism" while taking unprecedented measures to curb corruption to defend its legitimacy.

These findings reveal some derivative relationships between the party's policies and corruption from the incompatibility between the party's general and organizational policies to bureaucratic corruption and then to anti-corruption campaigns, which usually reflect the party's higher political goals. This suggests the cyclical nature of China's corruption problem (Figure 10.1): the general policies are often associated with organizational contradictions; these organizational problems further affect the patterns of corruption; the development of corruption then forces the party to wage anti-corruption campaigns; and finally, these campaigns are so designed as to serve the party's "higher" political goals.

In the final analysis, China's corruption problem is mingled with the CCP's policy efforts at social reconstruction. During the process, the party itself created a bureaucracy omnipotent yet contradicting with the party's own doctrine and socioeconomic basis. The CCP's revolutionary heritage and goals emphasize ideological zeal, mass line, and strict discipline. "This creates constant tension with poorly educated officials lacking a clear grasp of the ideological and policy goals of the party, others who fall into routinized bureaucratic patterns of behavior, and those who assume attitudes of superiority towards ordinary people and use their positions to seek special privileges" (Teiwes, 1979:8). The party consequently had to launch anti-corruption campaigns from time to time. However, these campaigns were at the same time deeply affected by the priorities of each stage of the CCP's social reconstruction. The problem identification, campaign targets, and disciplinary methods during these campaigns were limited by a number of other related yet higher objectives, such as consolidation and legitimation of

Figure 10.1
A Policy Outcomes Analysis of Corruption in China

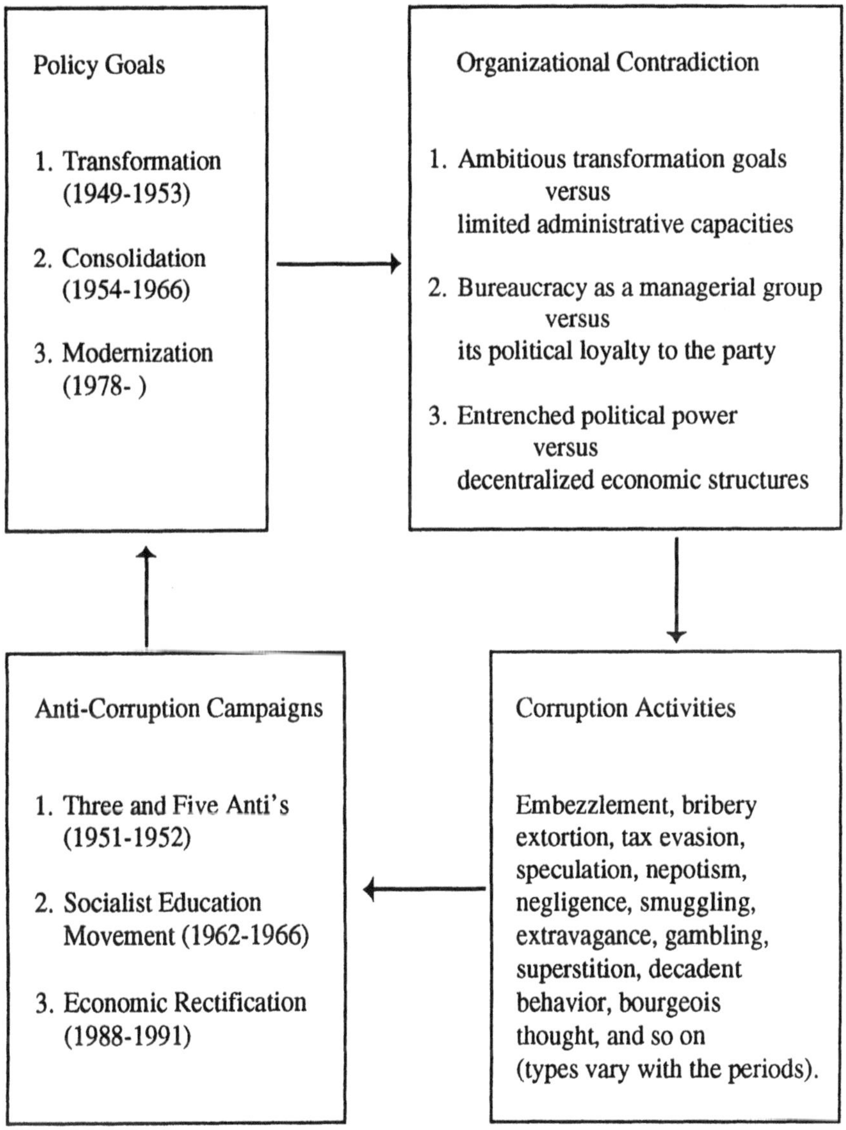

the CCP's leadership, redistribution of rules and resources among various social groups, and internalization of values promoted by the party. In short, the necessity of having a campaign against corruption was a policy outcome, but when and how to mount the campaign was largely a policy choice. The alternating campaigns and relaxations in post-1949 China mainly reflect which side of the contradiction was more acute—the need for political loyalty or the need for professional expertise.

THE SIGNIFICANCE OF THE POLICY OUTCOMES PERSPECTIVE

The foregoing findings are achieved based on the unique perspective of this study—the policy outcomes approach. In contrast to the tendency of universalization in conceptualizing and theorizing about corruption in the extant literature, the policy outcomes perspective offers a dynamic and dialectical way of understanding China's corruption.

The policy outcomes perspective is, first of all, dynamic. By suggesting that corruption results from unintended policy outcomes, the policy outcomes perspective rejects explanations that emphasize cultural, political, or socioeconomic exceptionalism. According to the policy outcomes perspective, social structures are producible and reformable rather than being given. The policy outcomes perspective focuses on the ways in which the structural properties of a given society are produced and reproduced as intended or unintended outcomes of human action.

To do so, the book first looked at the CCP's conscious dynamic role in transforming Chinese society. The party came to power with an explicit agenda to reconstruct society. It committed itself to subsequent programs of transformation, consolidation, and modernization. Hence the post-1949 history of the CCP was regarded as a policy process of three periods in which the party took the initiative. Such periodization in turn presents different definitions of and countermeasures against corruption under different political climates. As the findings of this study suggest, Mao demonstrated stronger anti-bureaucratic tendencies and had more anti-corruption zeal than the post-Mao leadership. This might be related to Mao's personal perceptions of bureaucracy, but it was also to a large extent due to the fact that during the early years of the People's Republic, the CCP, as a revolutionary vanguard party, remained ideologically zealous. It was hard for the party to tolerate corruption within its own ranks. Though it appears hasty to say that the CCP leadership in the reform period was less enthusiastic about anti-corruption than Mao, the party evidently did not effectively respond to the corruption issue until it threatened the party's own legitimacy.

This study then examined the congruence between policy motivations and policy outcomes in order to show how certain social conditions conducive to corruption have been produced in the CCP's policy process after 1949. The focus of the study is therefore corruption *as a product in a generative process* rather than *a legacy of certain cultures or social structures*. In this way, this study obtains a more dynamic approach to corruption than simply gauging the levels, forms, and mechanisms of corruption.

The policy outcomes perspective is also dialectical. While acknowledging that human actors are able to reflectively monitor their actions, it points out the limited knowledgeability of human beings: that is, human knowledgeability is always bounded by the unconscious or by unintended consequences of action. This study has investigated the contradictions involved in the CCP's purposive policy processes and explored how these contradictions contributed to the spread of corruption. It diagnoses corruption as a social disease, which has profound social content and tends to recur under certain conditions. However, these conditions are nothing but man's creation. In China's case, they are consequences of the party's own policies. By saying so, however, I do not mean that the CCP has intended to create corruption-conducive social relations. The fact is that, intentionally or unintentionally, the party's encounter with unprecedented social economic problems and its fashioned responses to these problems have brought such a reality: instead of being "mass-oriented," the party has increasingly relied on a large-scale bureaucracy to fulfill its political and economic goals; instead of being a cohesive organization, the party has faced increasing difficulties in effective control over its individual members; and instead of being self-restrained, individual party members have gradually institutionalized their privileges. This explains why the party frequently conducted self-rectification campaigns while engaging in social transformation and modernization, as seen in the fact that each of the CCP's general policies (transformation, consolidation, and modernization) was accompanied by a large-scale anti-corruption campaign (the Three and Five Anti's Campaign, the Socialist Education Movement, and the Economic Rectification). This study thus portrays a historical picture: while the CCP intends to establish effective control over society, it has to react at times to unintended consequences which have come along with its own policies. In other words, the CCP has often fought simultaneously on two fronts: one, daily problem solving to deal with chronic socioeconomic intricacies (bureaucratism, productivity, efficiency, and so on); and two, political campaigning to cope with new problems (corruption, political disloyalty, and the like) generated by its own problem-solving efforts.

This is further proven by the new anti-corruption attempt in China recently. While the party leadership has not quite finished its struggle with the nation's chaotic financial situation, it has to quickly respond to the rampant corruption of its cadre ranks. Beginning in July 1993 there has been a dramatic increase of articles (editorials or case reports) about corruption in Chinese newspapers. Later it was reported that the party leaders and the State Council had several close-door meetings in July and early August to discuss the corruption issue (LW, September 6, 1993). On August 20–25, the Discipline Inspection Commission of the CCP Central Committee held its second plenary session in Beijing. Jiang Zemin, the party's general secretary and the state president, addressed the meeting.[5] In his speech, Jiang expressed deep concerns about corruption, as he pointed out that corruption not only continued to exist within the party and government apparatus but was becoming more and more prevalent in some areas. He warned that corruption could cause so serious damage as to ruin the whole party and the regime as it did to many dynasties in Chinese history (RMRB, September 15, 1993). Following the speech, the Communique of the Discipline Inspection Commission's Plenary Session called on all the party members, government cadres, and the people in the country to "participate in the struggle against corruption" (RMRB, August 26, 1993). The State Council soon developed a plan of implementation requesting initial anti-corruption results to be seen by the end of the year. The State Council specified the following methods: (1) emphasizing the moral example of leading cadres in anti-corruption activities; (2) publicizing major corruption cases to warn the nation; and (3) clamping down on the "unhealthy tendencies" resented most by the public.

It may be too early to make any judgement or prediction about the party's new move, but some facts can be readily seen. In recent years, corruption has never ceased disturbing the country, even though a large-scale anti-corruption campaign was just over two years ago. A good example was entertainment with public funds. It has been one of the major targets in the previous anti-corruption campaigns, but the nation saw an ever-increasing public spending on eating and drinking. It was estimated that during the year of 1992, more than 80 billion yuan (about 14 billion dollars) public funds were spent on banquets (JFRB, June 26, 1993). However, more surprising to people was that all this took place under the central government's repeated injunctions against such practice.[6]

While old practices have continued, new forms of corruption began to prevail. This is why the party's Discipline Inspection Commission had to specifically ban certain practices (RMRB, August 26, 1993). According the Commission's regulation, leading cadres, namely those at and above the county level, are not allowed to accept any gifts in the form of cash, goods, or portfolio; nor should they engage in any stock exchange. This indicates that profiteering in the newly developed but highly restricted stock market has become a rather common practice among government cadres. However, this is to some extent made possible by the government's special policy about the stock market. As well known, after Deng's south tour in early 1992, there has been a dramatic growth of stock market in China as the party leadership's attitude toward the shareholding system changed from "acquiescing" to "encouraging."[7] Nevertheless, the scope of stock exchange is limited: it is only confined to certain enterprises in two major cities—Shanghai and Shenzhen. The access to the stock market therefore becomes a privilege and a means of profiteering for some people.[8]

Though the cause(s) and scope of the CCP's current anti-corruption move remain to be seen, it is clear that the effort takes place after a relatively short period of relaxation of the center's control over society in 1992 and early 1993 when the leadership tried a series of new reform policies to stimulate the economy and to revitalize the society. The relationship between the urgency of anti-corruption and these new policies merit a separate and detailed discussion.

BROADER IMPLICATIONS

Some broader implications follow the suggestion that corruption can be regarded as an unintended consequence of intended policy efforts. First, identifying corruption with policy outcomes makes it possible to talk about reducing corruption in practical terms. Some policy outcomes are unintentional but they are not unavoidable. As illustrated in Chapter 3, the policy outcomes perspective distinguishes a knowledge of outcomes from an intention of outcomes; the former may be present while the latter is absent.[9]

The CCP was not foolish in adopting these policies we discussed earlier. We must admit that given the circumstances and given the party's ultimate goals of social reconstruction, those policies were, in great measure, the party's rational choices. However, the problem for the Chinese leadership was that while pursuing other higher goals (e.g., social transformation and modernization), it did not have sufficient mechanisms to counteract unintended policy outcomes such as corruption, which had come along with its intentional policies. The party merely relied on ad-hoc campaign methods to contain corruption, while these campaigns only had a temporary effect on controlling corruption. What is worse, they often made cadres short-sighted and even more greedy in fear of losing power in the next political campaign. This has been proven by China's recurrent corruption problem.

The policy outcomes perspective sheds new light on the issue of corruption control. Since corruption results from political consequences, China should establish long-term institutional mechanisms within its society as well as the state to better detect and correct the unintended consequences of policy making. The CCP as the ruling party should take the responsibility for better policies in the first place. However, as a social and political agent with its own clear agenda to rule and restructure society, the party may not be able to (and sometimes not care to) contain the unintended consequences of its policies. Proposals to prevent corruption may be selected in terms of their impact on other policy goals. The job of curbing corruption is therefore left for other political institutions and social forces. China needs to develop independent social and political institutions to check the party power which, if left unmonitored, could easily become entrenched and all-encompassing.

Another important way of institutionalizing self-generative mechanisms to monitor the unintended consequences of policy making is for Chinese society to encourage a greater awareness of and responsibility for the issue of corruption from its grass-roots level. In China, in many circumstances, corruption is not an issue of high visibility and salience. The feeling of powerlessness leads the public to accept corruption as inevitable though not desirable. To change the situation, China should increase public scrutiny of political process, give the press more freedom, and, in the final analysis, democratize its political system to allow effective public participation and surveillance.

Regarding corruption as a policy outcome and therefore dissociating it from a certain type of political culture or political structures have another important implication. This "policy outcome" perspective denies the existence of the so-called socialist corruption. The similarities between China and the former Soviet Union in political structure and corruption patterns have been used as evidence of the existence of "socialist corruption." For example, Peter Harris (1986) points out six structural characteristics, such as hierarchy, oligarchy, closeness, all-embracing ideology, socialist planning and so on, which render communist systems unique in generating corruption. Peter Nan-Song Lee (1990:36–37) compares the similar patterns of corruption in China and in the former Soviet Union. He finds that in Soviet practice, *prinosheniye* ("bringing to") is equivalent to *songli* ("offering gift") in the Chinese context; and *krugavia poruka* (mutual guarantee) functioned in the Soviet Union in the same way as *baohusan* (protective umbrella) does in China to cover up wrongdoings. From the viewpoint of this study, however, the "socialist corruption" label is superficial and misleading.

The "socialist corruption" label neglects many important differences between China and the former Soviet Union. Lynn White III makes the following contrasts (1989:334):

> China's party has strained even more obviously against its limited resources than has the CPSU in Russia, at least since Stalin's time. China's revolution was less thorough in social terms than Russia's. The surviving prestige of non-Communist informal elites in China after Mao contrasts with the end of most non-party elites in Russia after Stalin. . . . The corps of professionals, which the Chinese government needed for modernization, has grown from both pre-1949 and post-1949 elites, despite all the political turmoil in the first quarter century of CCP rule. The relative uniformity of urban elites backgrounds in the USSR contrasts with the relative variation of those in China.

These comparisons indicate some significant historical differences underlying the seeming structural similarities between China and other communist countries such as the former Soviet Union. These differences have affected leadership perceptions of corruption as well as the actual patterns of corruption. One notable fact is that the communist party in the former Soviet Union apparently did not engage in so many anti-corruption campaigns as the CCP has done. Since this is not a comparative study, we are not going to make detailed comparisons here.

Clearly, the CCP has been caught in the dilemma of high political goals versus low administrative capabilities more than its former Soviet counterpart. Accordingly, as Lynn White (1989) correctly points out, the CCP's shortage of professionals made the pre-1966 Chinese leadership heavily reliant on class labels, patron-client networks, and political campaigns to fulfill its policy goals. The situation in the post–Cultural Revolution period has not changed much in this regard. Although the political campaign as a control method has to some extent lost its significance, clientalism still plays an important role in Chinese politics and society today (Oi, 1989a).

Another important factor, which was absent in the former Soviet Union, is Mao's egalitarian ideal. In China's context, egalitarianism represented an effort to break out of the ruling class–common people bifurcation (Fairbank, 1986). To the Chinese communists who had come to power through large-scale mass mobilization, it stood to reason that the new society should be mass-oriented. The contradiction between this egalitarian ideal and the bureaucratic reality made the "red versus expert" problem more acute in China than in the former Soviet Union. The CCP, especially Mao, was highly sensitive to and suspicious of increasing bureaucratic interests. This to some extent explains the frequent occurrence of patronage and campaigns—two alternative methods the party used to prevent its bureaucracy from divergence.

The differences in reform strategy between China and the former Soviet Union are also remarkable. As we have argued, entrenched political power and decentralized economic structure are among the most important factors leading to corruption in China's reform era. This contradiction was less notable in the former Soviet Union, however. Political democratization was the watchword of Gorbachev's reform. Confronted with bureaucratic resistance to reforms, Gorbachev was convinced that Soviet society needed radical democratization and the party needed thorough restructuring. His *glasnost* was a revolutionary change of orthodox belief that official corruption and the lack of discipline could be solved by administrative methods of the communist party itself. Gorbachev tried to tackle the problem by enlisting the support of the nonparty public, and ultimately by forming a "law-based society" in which the party would be subject to the law. *Glasnost* thus was envisaged as a form of supervision over the working of the state apparatus (Sakwa, 1991:72). In China, in contrast, while its economic structure was decentralized, political power remained concentrated in the hands of bureaucrats. The decentralized economic structures therefore provided individual cadres with more opportunities to profiteer for themselves or their individual work units.

The concept of "socialist corruption" is misleading as well. The concept makes the erroneous assumption that if the socialist system is changed, corruption will wither away. As a matter of fact, in today's world, neither socialism nor capitalism is free from the phenomenon of corruption. All in all, corruption has less to do with a particular system type than the concrete political and economic situation of a given country.

This study is open to a pessimistic and an optimistic reading. Some people may find it quite disappointing that despite endless anti-corruption campaigns, the corruption problem in today's China appears even more disturbing than before. They may even argue that too much effort at tackling corruption is not worthwhile, since neither socialism nor capitalism is immune from corruption. Other people may have a different view. They would emphasize the nature of corruption as a by-product of social transformation. Since China is involved in a reform process from a state-planned to a market-driven economy, corruption is mainly a transitional reflection of uncertainty and people's anxiety. According to this optimistic view, as the reform proceeds the corruption issue will become less prominent in China.

This study holds a mixed view. It believes that corruption can be prevented or at least reduced. But it does not think that corruption will wither away by itself in the modernization process. To contain corruption, China needs a balanced reform agenda. Decentralization without democratization can only leave the economic reforms vulnerable to power abuse. China needs not only bold economic innovations toward a market economy, but also comprehensive political reforms to install effective control over power holders.

NOTES

1. Such as former KMT officers, urban secret societies, rural bandits, and common criminals.

2. A comprehensive research project undertaken by the Research Institute of the Center for Rural Development under the State Council of the PRC in 1986 revealed the situation. It pointed out that after separation of powers (separating the party's functions from administrative ones and separating administrative from production functions of the commune), a party committee, an administrative organ, and an economic entity coexisted at the town level as leading institutions. This not only caused overlapping functions but also produced loopholes for power abuses (1988:27,225).

3. As reported, in 1989 the number of corruption cases handled by procuratorial organs all over the country was 116,763, an increase of 160 percent over the previous year (RMRB, March 6, 1990).

4. For a review of how China's leaders viewed bureaucracy in the late 1950s and early 1960s, see Martin King Whyte (1989:235–239).

5. It is usually a gesture to show the importance of the meeting.

6. The central government altogether issued thirty-six document against lavish eating and drinking, but was not able to contain the ever-prevailing practice. A newspaper editorial in Shanghai described this as "the failure of the government in managing the mouth" (JFRB, June 26, 1993). Another astonishing case was that a banquet of 50 people held by a company in Shenzhen cost 12 million yuan (roughly 175,000 dollars) of public funds (XMWB, July 2, 1993).

7. In August 1992, the total number of the shareholding enterprises in the country reached 3,683 (RMRB, August 11, 1992. In Shanghai alone, the volume of stock trade in the first half of 1992 reached 10.864 billion yuan (RMRB, August 5, 1992). About thirty types of stocks have been issued in Shenzhen and their value is over ten billion yuan (RMRB, May 9, 1992).

8. Other new forms of corruption have also developed and some are even very absurd. For example, a local party cadre in charge of recruiting members charged an applicant money for talking with the applicant about his application for party membership (BKWZ, August 30, 1993).

9. The author is indebted to Ira Cohen (1989) on this point.

References

Abbott, A. Kenneth. *Harmony and Individualism*. Taipei: Orient Culture Service, 1970.

Abram, Philip. *Historical Sociology*. Ithaca, N.Y.: Cornell University Press, 1982.

Agassi, J. "Methodological Individualism." *The British Journal of Sociology* 11 (1960): 244–270.

Alam, Shahid M. "Anatomy of Corruption: An Approach to the Political Economy of Underdevelopment." *American Journal of Economics and Sociology* 48 (1990): 441–455.

Alatas, S. H. *The Sociology of Corruption: the Nature, Function, Causes, and Prevention of Corruption*. Singapore: Times Books International, 1980.

Alexander, Herbert E., and Gerald E. Caiden, eds. *The Politics and Economics of Organized Crime*. Lexington, Mass.: Lexington Books, 1985.

Ali, Shaukat. *Corruption: A Third World Perspective*. Lahore, Pakistan: Aziz Publishers, 1985.

Amich, George. *The American Way of Graft*. Princeton, N.J.: Center for Analysis of Public Issues, 1976.

An Ziwen. "The Cadre Work in the First Three Years of the PRC." In *The Great Achievements in the First Three Years of the PRC* (in Chinese), edited by People's Publishing House. Beijing: People's Publishing House, 1952.

Appleby, Paul H. *Morality and Administration in Democratic Government*. Baton Rouge: Louisiana State University Press, 1952.

Bachman, David. *Bureaucracy, Economy, and Leadership in China: The Institutional Origins of the Great Leap Forward*. New York: Cambridge University Press, 1991.

Bailey, David. "The Effects of Corruption in a Developing Nation." In

Political Corruption: A Handbook, edited by Arnold J. Heidenheimer, Michael Johnston, and Victor T. LeVine. New Brunswick, N.J.: Transaction Publishers, 1989.

Bailey, Stephen. "Ethics and the Public Service." In *Public Administration and Democracy: Essays in Honor of Paul H. Appleby*, edited by Roscoe C. Martin. Syracuse, N.Y.,: Syracuse University Press, 1965.

Banfield, Edward C. *The Moral Basis of a Backward Society*. Chicago: The Free Press, 1958.

———. "Corruption as a Feature of Government Organization." *Journal of Law and Economics* 18 (1975): 587–605.

Barker, Ernest, ed. *The Politics of Aristotle*. Oxford: Clarendon Press, 1946.

Barnett, A. Doak. *Cadres, Bureaucracy, and Political Power in Communist China*. New York: Columbia University Press, 1967.

Baum, Richard. *Prelude to Revolution: Mao, the Party, and the Peasant Question*. New York: Columbia University Press, 1975.

———, ed. *Reform and Reaction in Post-Mao China: The Road to Tiananmen*. New York: Routledge, Chapman and Hall, Inc., 1991.

Baum, Richard, and Frederick C. Teiwes. *Ssu-Ch'ing: The Socialist Education Movement of 1962–1968*. Berkeley, Calif.: Center for Chinese Studies, 1968.

Beenstock, Michael. "Corruption and Development." *World Development* 7 (1979): 15–24.

Ben-Dor, Gabriel. "Corruption, Institutionalization, and Political Development: The Revisionist Theses Revisited." *Comparative Political Studies* 7 (1974): 63–83.

Benhardt, Kathryn. *The Ethics of Public Service: Resolving Moral Dilemmas in Public Organizations*. New York: Greenwood Press, 1988.

Benson, George C. S., and J. Baden. "The Political Economy of Government Corruption: The Logic of Underground Government." *Journal of Legal Studies* 14 (1985): 391–410.

Benson, George C. S., Steven A. Maaranene, and Alan Heslop. *Political Corruption in America*. Lexington, Mass.: D. C. Heath and Company, 1978.

Berg, Larry L., and Harlan Hahn. *Corruption in the American Political System*. Morristown, N.J.: General Learning Press, 1976.

Blankenburg, Erhar, Rainer Staudhamer, and Heinz Steinert. "Political Scandals and Corruption Issues in West Germany." In *Political Corruption: A Handbook*, edited by Arnold J. Heidenheimer, Michael Johnston, and Victor T. LeVine. New Brunswick, N.J.: Transaction Publishers, 1989.

Blau, Peter M., and Marshall W. Meyer. *Bureaucracy in Modern Society*. New York: Random House, 1987.

Bondadeo, Alfredo. *Corruption, Conflict, and Power in the Works and Times of Niccol'o Machiavelli*. Berkeley: University of California Press, 1973.

Brady, James P. *Justice and Politics in People's China: Legal Order or Continuing Revolution?* New York: Academic Press, 1982.

Brooks, Robert Clarkson. *Corruption in American Politics and Life*. New York: Arno Press, 1974.

Burns, John P. "Civil Service Reform in Contemporary China." *The Australian Journal of Chinese Affairs* 18 (1987): 47–83.

———. *The Chinese Communist Party's Nomenklatura System*. New York: M. E. Sharpe, Inc. 1989.

Butterfield, Fox. *China, Alive in the Bitter Sea*. New York: Times Books, 1982.

CCP Central Committee's Document Research Institute. *Selected Important Documents since the Third Plenary Session* (in Chinese). Beijing: People's Publishing House, 1982.

Caiden, Gerald E., and Naomi J. Caiden. "Administrative Corruption." *Public Administrative Review* 37 (1977): 301–308.

Caiden, Gerald E. "Comparative Administrative Corruption." *Hong Kong Journal of Public Administration* 3 (1981): 56–71.

———. "Toward a General Theory of Official Corruption." *The Asian Journal of Public Administration* 10 (1988): 2–26.

Carino, Ledivina V., ed. *Bureaucratic Corruption in Asia: Causes, Consequences and Controls*. Quezon City, The Philippines: JMC Press, 1986.

Cerny, Philip G. *The Changing Architecture of Politics: Structure, Agency, and the Future of the State*. Newbury Park, Calif.: Sage Publications, 1990.

Chamberlain, Heath B. "Party-Management Relations in Chinese Industries: Some Political Dimensions of Economic Reform." *China Quarterly* 112 (1987): 640–661.

Chan, Anita. "China's Long Winter." *Monthly Review* 41 (1990): 1–14.

Chao Zhi, ed. *An Outline of the Personnel System in the PRC* (in Chinese). Beijing: Beijing University Press, 1985.

Chang Chungli. "Merit and Money." In *The Chinese Civil Service: Career Open to Talent?*, edited by Johanna M. Menzel. Boston: D. C. Heath and Company, 1963.

Chen, C. S. *Rural People's Communes in Lien-Chiang: Documents Concerning Communes in Lien-Chiang County, Fukien Province, 1962–1963*. Stanford: Stanford University Press, 1969.

Chen Feng. "Ideology and Economic Pragmatism under State Socialism:Redefining the Ownership System in China, 1978–1991." Doctoral dissertation, Syracuse University, Syracuse, N.Y., 1992.

Chen Mingxian and Zhang Heng. *Studies on the New China at Forty* (in Chinese). Beijing: Beijing Polytechnic Press, 1989.

Chen Xuewei. "The Establishment of China's Party and State Leadership System, October 1949–September 1956" (in Chinese). *Fuyin Baokan Ziliao* 9 (1988): 35.

———. *Historical Enlightenment: A Study of the Ten-Year Construction Period, 1957–1966* (in Chinese). Beijing: Qiushi Press, 1989.

Chen Zhonghua. "On the Consistency between Opposing Bourgeois Liberation and Opposing Corruption" (in Chinese). *Guangming Ribao*, October 13, 1989.

Cheng Tianquan. "The Judicial Principles for Economic Crimes in Ancient China" (in Chinese). *Politics and Law* 3 (1983): 121–131.

Cheng Xuan, ed. *The History of Chinese Socialist Revolution and Construction, 1949–1985* (in Chinese). Haerbin: Heilongjian People's House, 1986.

Chesneaux, Jean. *China: The People's Republic, 1949–1976.* Translated by Paul Auster and Lydia Davis. New York: Pantheon Books, 1979.

Chi, Hsi-sheng. "Disciplinary Problems and the CCP's Rectification Campaign." In *Chinese Politics from Mao to Deng*, edited by Victor C. Falkenheim. New York: Paragon House, 1989.

Chow Ching-wen. *Ten Years of Storm.* New York: Holt, Rinehart & Winston, 1960.

Clapham, Christopher, ed. *Private Patronage and Public Power: Political Clientelism in the Modern State.* London: Frances Pinter, 1982.

Clark, Michael, ed. *Corruption: Causes, Consequences and Control.* New York: St. Martin's Press, 1983.

Clark, William A. *Crime and Punishment in Soviet Offialdom: Combating Corruption in the Political Elite, 1965–1990.* Armonk, N.Y.: M. E. Sharpe, inc., 1993.

Cohen, Ira. *Structuration Theory.* New York: St. Martin's Press, 1989.

Crozier, Michel. *Bureaucratic Phenomenon.* Chicago: University of Chicago Press, 1964.

Dai Qing. "Wang Shiwei and 'Wide Lilies'" (in Chinese). *Mingbao Yuekan* 5 (1988): 3–16.

DeLeon, Peter. "Public Policy Implications of Systemic Political Corruption." *Corruption and Reform* 4 (1989): 193–215.

———. *Thinking About Political Corruption.* Armonk, N.Y.: M. E. Sharpe, Inc., 1993.

Deng Xiaoping. *The Selected Works of Deng Xiaoping.* Beijing: Foreign Languages Press, 1984.

Deysine, Anne. "Political Corruption: A Review of the Literature." *European Journal of Political Research* 8 (1980): 447–462.

Dittmer, Lowell. *Liu Shaoqi and the Cultural Revolution.* Berkeley: University of California Press, 1974.

———. "China in 1989: the Crisis of Incomplete Reform." *Asian Survey* 30

(1990): 25–41.

Dittmer, Lowell and Samuel S. Kim, eds. *China's Quest for National Identity.* Ithaca, N.Y.: Cornell University Press, 1993.

Djilas, Milovan. *The New Class: An Analysis of the Communist System.* New York: Frederick A. Praeger, Inc. 1957.

Dobel, J. P. "Corruption of a State." *American Political Science Review* 72 (1978): 958–973.

Dorn James A. and Wang Xi. *Economic Reform in China: Problems and Prospects.* Chicago: University of Chicago Press, 1990.

Downs, Anthony. *Inside Bureaucracy.* Boston: Little, Brown and Co., 1967.

Dunn, William N. *Public Policy Analysis: An Introduction.* Englewood Cliffs, N.J.: Prentice Hall, 1981.

Durkheim, Emile. *The Rules of Sociological Method* [1895]. New York: The Free Press, 1982.

Eckstein, Alexander. *China's Economic Revolution.* London: Cambridge University Press, 1977.

———. *China's Economic Development, the Interplay of Scarcity and Ideology.* Ann Arbor: University of Michigan Press, 1975.

Ekpo, Monday U., ed. *Bureaucratic Corruption in Sub-Saharan Africa: Toward a Search for Causes and Consequences.* Washington, D.C.: University Press of America, 1979.

Ethridge, James M. *China's Unfinished Revolution: Problems and Prospects since Mao.* San Francisco: China Books and Periodicals, Inc. 1990.

Etzioni, Amitai. *Capital Corruption: The New Attack on American Democracy.* San Diego, Calif.: Harcourt Brace Jovanovich, 1984.

Fairbank, John King. *The Great Chinese Revolution, 1800–1985.* New York: Harper & Row, 1986.

Fan Shouxin. *The History of National Economic Recovery in the PRC, 1949–1952* (in Chinese). Beijing: Jiushi Press, 1989.

Feuer, Lewis S., ed. *Marx and Engels: Basic Writings on Politics and Philosophy.* New York: Doubleday, 1959.

Findlay, Mark, and Thomas Chiu Chor-Wing. "Sugar Coated Bullets: Corruption and the New Economic Order in China." *Contemporary Crises* 13 (1989): 145–161.

Fletcher, R. *The Making of Sociology.* New York: Charles Scribner's Sons, 1971.

Frederickson, George H. ed. *Ethics and Public Administration.* Armonk, N.Y.: M. E. Sharpe, Inc., 1993

Friedman, Edward. "Three Leninist Paths within a Socialist Conundrum." In *Three Visions of Chinese Socialism*, edited by Dorothy J. Solinger. Boulder, Colo.: Westview Press, 1984.

Friedrich, Carl. "Political Pathology." *Political Quarterly* 37 (1966): 70–83.

———. *The Pathology of Politics.* New York: Harper & Row, 1972.

Gao Shudong. "Changes in the Cadre System During the Early PRC" (in Chinese). *Tangshi Yanjiu* 6 (1987): 98–101, 167.

Gardiner, John. "Controlling Official Corruption and Fraud: Bureaucratic Incentives and Disincentives." *Corruption and Reform* 1 (1986): 33–60.

Gerth, H. H., and Wright Mills, eds. *From Max Weber: Essays in Sociology.* New York: Oxford University Press, 1958.

Gibbon, Kenneth M., and Donald C. Rowat, eds. *Political Corruption in Canada: Cases, Causes and Cures.* Toronto: The Canadian Publishers, 1976.

Giddens, Anthony. *The Constitution of Society: Introduction of the Theory of Structuration.* Berkeley: University of California Press, 1984.

Gold, Thomas B. "The Resurgence of Civil Society in China," *Journal of Democracy* 1 (Winter 1990): 18–31.

Goldman, Merle. *Literary Dissent in Communist China.* Cambridge, Mass.: Harvard University Press, 1967.

Gong Ting and Chen Feng. "Institutional reorganization and Its Impact on Decentralization." In *Changing Central-Local Relations in China: Reform and State Capacity*, edited by Jia Hao, Lin Zhimin, and James Chung. Boulder, Colo.: Westview Press, 1993.

Goodman S. David and Gerald Segal, eds. *China in the Nineties: Crisis Management and Beyond.* New York: Oxford University Press, 1993.

Gould, David J. *Bureaucratic Corruption and Underdevelopment in the Third World: The Case of Zaire.* New York: Pergamon Press, 1980.

Grossman, Gregory. "The Second Economy of the USSR." *Problems of Communism* 26 (1977): 25–41.

Gu, Zhibin. *China beyond Deng: Reform in the PRC.* Jefferson, N.C.: McFarland & Co. Publishers, 1991.

Guillermaz, Jacques. *The Chinese Communist Party in Power, 1949–1976.* Translated by Anne Destenay. Boulder, Colo.: Westview Press. 1976.

Haines, Valerie. "Social Network Analysis, Structuration Theory and the Holism-Individualism Debate." *Social Networks* 10 (1988): 157–182.

Halayya, M. *Corruption in India.* New Delhi: Affiliated East-West Press, 1985.

Hamilton, Edith. *The Echo of Greece.* New York: W. W. Norton & Co., 1957.

Harding, Harry. *Organizing China: The Problem of Bureaucracy, 1949–76.* Stanford, Calif.: Stanford University Press, 1981.

———. *China's Second Revolution: Reform after Mao.* Washington, D.C.: The Brookings Institution, 1987.

Harris, Peter. "Socialist Graft: The Soviet Union and the People's Republic of China—A Preliminary Survey." *Corruption and Reform* 1 (1986): 13–32.

Harrison, James P. *The Long March to Power: A History of the Chinese*

Communist Party, 1921–1972. New York: Praeger Publishers, 1972.

He Jiacheng. "Rectification and Economic Reform" (in Chinese). *Fazhan yu Gegai* 4 (1989): 18–25.

He Wei. "On 'Old Guards'" (in Chinese). *Zhishifenzi* 2 (1986): 32–37.

Hegedus, Andras. *Socialism and Bureaucracy*. New York: St. Martin's Press, 1976.

Heidenheimer, Arnold., ed. *Political Corruption: Readings in Comparative Analysis*. New York: Holt, Rinehart, and Winston, 1970.

Heidenheimer, Arnold J., Michael Johnston, and Victor T. LeVine, eds. *Political Corruption: A Handbook*. New Brunswick, N.J.: Transaction Publishers, 1989.

Hempel, Carl Gustav. *Philosophy of Natural Science*. Englewood Cliffs. N.J.: Prentice-Hall, 1966.

Hirszeowiz, Maria. *The Bureaucratic Leviathan: A Study in the Sociology of Communism*. New York: New York University Press, 1980.

Hodges, Donald C. *The Bureaucratization of Socialism*. Amherst: University of Massachusetts Press, 1981.

Holt, Robert. "A Proposed Structural-Functional Framework for Political Science." In *Functionalism in the Social Sciences*, edited by Don Martindale. Philadelphia: The American Academy of Political and Social Science, 1965.

Hope, Kempe R. "Political Bureaucratic Corruption and Maladministration in the Third World." *International Review of Administrative Science* 51 (1985): 1–8.

Hsiao, Kang-chun. *Rural China: Imperial Control in the Nineteenth Century*. Seattle: University of Washington Press, 1960.

Hsu, Immanuel C.Y. *The Rise of Modern China*. New York: Oxford University Press, 1975.

Hu Hua, ed. *Lectures on the History of the Chinese Revolution* (in Chinese). Beijing: People's Publishing House, 1962.

Hu Qili. "Creating a Democratic, Harmonic, and Mutual Trusting Environment" (in Chinese). *Liao Wang* 22 (1986): 4–6.

Hu Xiaohan. "An Examination of Private Houses" (in Chinese). *Raicanxuanbian* 254 (1989): 17–20.

Huntington, Samuel P. *Political Order in Changing Societies*. New Haven, Conn.: Yale University Press, 1968.

Jacoby, H. *The Bureaucratization of the World*. Berkeley: University of California Press, 1973.

Jiang Yiwei. ""Overall Reorganization is a Constructive Reorganization" (in Chinese). *Jingji Guanli*, 5 (1982): 6.

Jiangxi People's Government Office. "Building a Clean Government in Jiangxi" (in Chinese). *Zhongguo Xingzheng Guanli* 56 (1990): 19–20.

Jin Dexin, ed. *The History of the People's Republic of China* (in Chinese).

Henan: Kaifeng People's Publishing House, 1989.

Jin Guantao and Liu Gingfeng. *Prosperity and Crisis* (in Chinese). Changsha: Hunan People's Publishing House, 1983.

Jin Zitong. "Studies on Several Questions of Bribery Crime" (in Chinese). *Zhengzhi yu Falu* 2 (1982): 44–49.

Johnson, Chalmers. "What is Wrong with Chinese Political Studies?" *Asian Studies* 22 (1982): 919–932.

Johnston, Michael. "The Political Consequences of Corruption: A Reassessment." *Comparative Politics* 18 (1986): 459–477.

———. "Corruption, Inequality and Change." In *Corruption, Development and Inequality: Soft Touch or Hard Graft?*, edited by Peter M. Ward. London: Routledge, 1989.

Jowitt, Kenneth. "Study of Political Culture in Marxist–Leninist Systems." *American Political Science Review* 68 (1974): 1171–1191.

———. "Soviet Neo–Traditionalism: The Political Corruption of Leninist Regime." *Soviet Studies* 35 (1983): 275–297.

Kamenka, Eugene, and Martin Krygier. *Bureaucracy, the Career of a Concept*. New York: St. Martin's Press, 1979.

Kaw, Yinmaw. "Government Bureaucracy and Cadres in Urban China under Communist Rule, 1949–1965." Doctoral dissertation, Cornell University, Ithaca, N.Y., 1969.

———. "Patterns of Recruitment and Mobilizing of Urban Cadres." In *The City in Communist China*, edited by John W. Lewis. Stanford, Calif.: Stanford University Press, 1971.

Kincaid, Harold. "Reduction, Explanation, and Individualism." *Philosophy of Science* 53 (1985): 492-513.

Klavern, Jacob van. "The Concept of Corruption." In *Political Corruption: A Handbook*, edited by Arnold J. Heidenheimer, Michael Johnston, and Victor T. LeVine. New Brunswick, N.J.: Transaction Publishers, 1989.

Klitgaard, Robert E. *Controlling Corruption*. Berkeley: University of California Press, 1988.

Klugman, Jeffry. "The Psychology of Soviet Corruption, Indiscipline, and Resistance to Reform." *Political Psychology* 4 (1986): 67–82.

Knorr-Cetina, Karin and Aaron Cicourel, eds. *Advances in Social Theory: Toward an Integration of Micro and Macro Sociologies*. Boston: Routledge & Kegan Paul, 1981.

Kornai, Janos. *Contradictions and Dilemmas: Studies on the Socialist Economy and Society*. Cambridge, Mass.: MIT Press, 1986.

———. *The Socialist System: the Political Economy of Communism*. Princeton, N.J.: Princeton University Press, 1992.

Kramer, John M. "Political Corruption in the USSR." *Western Political Quarterly* 30 (1977): 213–224.

Kraus, Richard. "Culture: Cultural Politics and the Political Construction of

Audiences in China." In *Three Visions of Chinese Socialism*, edited by Dorothy J. Solinger. Boulder, Colo.: Westview Press, 1984.

Krislov, S. *Representative Bureaucracy*. Englewood Cliffs, N.J.: Prentice-Hall, 1974.

Krueger, Anne. "The Political Economy of Rent-Seeking Society." *American Economic Review* 64:3 (1974): 292–303.

Kuo, Ying-mao. "Patterns of Recruitment and Mobilizing of Urban Cadres." In *The City in Communist China*, edited by John W. Lewis. Stanford, Calif.: Stanford University Press, 1971.

Laaksonen, Oiva. *Management in China: During and after Mao*. Berlin: Walter de Gruyter & Co., 1988.

Lampert, Nickolas. *Whistleblowing in the Soviet Union: A Study of Complaints and Abuses under State Socialism*. New York: Schocken Books, 1985.

Lampton, David M., ed. *Policy Implementation in Post-Mao China*. Berkeley: University of California Press, 1987.

Lau, Chong-chor, and Rance P. L. Lee. "Bureaucratic Corruption and Political Instability in Nineteenth Century China." In *Corruption and Its Control in Hong Kong*, edited by Rance P. L. Lee. Hong Kong: The Chinese University Press, 1981.

Lee, Hong Yung. *From Revolutionary Cadres to Party Technocrats in Socialist China*. Berkeley: University of California Press, 1991.

Lee, James Kuo-hsiung. "An Assessment of Teng's Bureaucratic Reform, 1979–1984." *Issues and Studies* 23 (1987): 12–31.

Lee, Peter. "The Causes and Effects of Police Corruption." In *Corruption and Its Control in Hong Kong*, edited by Rance P. L. Lee. Hong Kong: The Chinese University Press, 1981.

Lee, Peter Nan-Song. "Bureaucratic Corruption during the Deng Xiao-ping Era." *Corruption and Reform* 5 (1990): 29–47.

Leff, Nathaniel H. "Economic Development through Bureaucratic Corruption." *American Behavioral Scientist* 8 (1964): 8–14.

Lenin, V. I. *Collected Works*. Moscow: Foreign Language Publishing House, 1963.

Lethbridge, H. J. *Hard Graft in Hong Kong: Scandal, Corruption, the ICAC*. Hong Kong: Oxford University Press, 1985.

LeVine, Victor T. *Political Corruption: The Ghana Case*. Stanford, Calif.: Hoover Institution Press, 1975.

Lewis, John. *Leadership in Communist China*. Ithaca, N.Y.: Cornell University Press, 1966.

Leys, Colin. "What is the Problem about Corruption?" *Journal of Modern African Studies* 3 (1965): 215–230.

Li Cheng and Lynn White. "Mainland China and Taiwan: Empirical Data and the Theory of Technocracy." *The China Quarterly* 121 (1990): 1–35.

Li Rui. *Lusan Conference* (in Chinese). Chunqiu Publisher, 1989.

Li Wenhai and Yang Gaimao. "The System of Shunning Nepotism among Government Officials during the Qing Dynasty." *RMRB*, January 16, 1989.

Li Yongchun and Luo Jian, eds. *The Chronicle of Political System Reform Since the Third Plenum of the Party Central Committee* (in Chinese). Beijing: Chunqiu Publisher, 1987.

Li Yue. "Cleaning the Government" (in Chinese). *Modern Wind* 10 (1989): 5.

Li Zhongying. "A Review of the Three Anti's Campaign" (in Chinese). *Tangshi Yanjiu* 5 (1984): 54–59, 71.

Lieberthal, Kenneth G., and David M. Lampton, eds. *Bureaucracy, Politics, and Decision Making in Post-Mao China*. Berkeley: University of California Press, 1992.

Lieberthal, Kenneth G. and Michel Oksenberg. *Policy Making in China: Leaders, Structures, and Processes.* Princeton, N.J.: Princeton University Press, 1998.

Lin Hai. "Corruption on Mainland Has Five Major Characteristics." *FBIS*, August 8, 1989, 22–23.

Liu, Adam Y. C. *Corruption in China during the Early Ch'ing Period, 1644–1660*. Hong Kong: Center of Asian Studies, University of Hong Kong, 1979.

Liu, Alan P. L. "The Politics of Corruption: The People's Republic of China." *American Political Science Review* 77 (1983): 602–623.

———. *How China is Ruled*. Englewood Cliffs, N.J.: Prentice–Hall, 1986.

Liu Boxun. "A Struggle with Enemies without Guns" (in Chinese). *Dangshi Wenhui* 27 (1989): 4–9.

Liu Cuiping. "On the Identity Between Opposing Bourgeois Liberation and Anticorruption" (in Chinese). *Guangming Ribao*, July 30, 1990.

Liu Guangdi. "On the Experiment of the CSIC" (in Chinese). In *The Central Party School and the State Commission of Economic System Reform*. Beijing: Economic Science Pres, 1987.

Liu Hongchao, ed. *Corruption and Anti-Corruption in Foreign Countries*. Beijing: Xinhua Publisher, 1989.

Liu Reizhong and Wang Chende. "Reasons of Growth of Economic Role of Local Governments at Present: An Analysis" (in Chinese). *Zhongguo: Fazhan yu Gaige* 1 (1988): 42–48.

Lo, Winston W. *An Introduction to the Civil Service of Sung China*. Honolulu: University of Hawaii Press, 1987.

Louthan, William C. *The Politics of Managerial Morality: A Value-Critical Approach to Political Corruption and Ethics Policy*. Washington, D.C.: University Press of America, 1981.

Lowenstein, Daniel H. "Political Bribery and the Intermediate Theory of Politics." *U.C.L.A. Law Review* 32 (1985): 784–851.

Lowenthal, Richard. "Development vs. Utopia in Communist Policy." In

Change in Communist Systems, edited by Chalmers Johnson. Stanford, Calif.: Stanford University Press, 1970.

Lukes, Steven. "Methodological Individualism Reconsidered." *British Journal of Sociology* 19 (1968): 119-129.

Luo Haigang. "Employ a New Generation of Cadre" (in Chinese). In *Theory and Practice of Political System Reform after the Third Plenum of the 11th CCP Central Committee*. Beijing: Chunqiu Press, 1987.

———. "A Probe into the Causes of Inner Party Corruption" (in Chinese). *RMRB*, June 17, 1989.

Luo Jingyi, ed. *Dictionary of the Party's Discipline* (in Chinese). Beijing: Workers' Press, 1989.

Luo Jingyi, Jiao Gengqiang, and Ye Xiaoling, eds. *An Anti-Corruption Dictionary* (in Chinese). Beijing: Xueyuan Publisher, 1989.

Ma Qibin. *The Chinese Communist Party at Forty, 1949–1989*. Beijing: The Press of the Chinese Communist Party Historical Documents, 1989.

Ma, Stephen K. "Chinese Bureaucracy and Post-Mao Reforms: Negative Adjustment." *Asian Survey* 30 (1990): 1038–1052.

Ma Yuping and Huang Yuchang. *China: Yesterday and Today* (in Chinese). Beijing: The Liberation Army's Publisher, 1989.

MacFarquhar, Roderick. *Contradictions Among the People, 1956–1957*. New York: Columbia University Press, 1974.

———. *The Great Leap Forward, 1958–1960*. New York: Columbia University Press, 1983.

MacRea, John. "Underdevelopment and the Economics of Corruption: A Game Theory Approach." *World Development* 10 (1982): 677–687.

McCormick, Barrett L. *Political Reform in Post-Mao China: Democracy and Bureaucracy in a Leninist State*. Berkeley: University of California Press, 1990.

McMullan, M. "A Theory of Corruption." *The Sociology Review* 9 (1961): 196.

Manion, Melanie. "Politics and Policy in Post-Mao Cadre Retirement." *China Quarterly* 129 (1992): 1–25.

Mao Zedong. *Selected Works*. Beijing: Foreign Languages Press, 1961–1965.

March, James G., and Herbert A. Simon. *Organization*. New York: John Wiley & Sons, 1958.

Markovits, Andrei S., and Mark Silverstein. *The Politics of Scandal: Power and Process in Liberal Democracies*. New York: Holmes & Meier Publishers, 1988.

Martin, Robert. *Party Recruitment in China: Patterns and Prospects: A Study of the Recruitment Campaign of 1954–56 and its Impact on Party Expansion through 1980*. New York: Occasional Papers of the East Asian Institute, Columbia University, 1981.

Meaney, Constance Squires. *Stability and the Industrial Elite in China and the*

Soviet Union. Berkeley: Institute of East Asian Studies, University of California, 1988.

———. "Market Reform in a Leninist System: Some Trends in the Distribution of Power, Status, and Money in the Urban China." *Studies in Comparative Communism* 22 (1989): 203–220.

Medard, J.F. "Public Corruption in Africa: A Comparative Perspective. *Corruption and Reform* 1 (1986): 115–132.

Meisner, Maurice. *Mao's China, a History of the People's Republic*. New York: The Free Press, 1977.

Merton, Robert K.. "The Unanticipated Consequences of Purposive Social Action." American Sociological Review 1 (1936): 894–904.

Miliband, R. *The State in Capitalist Society*. London: Weidenfeld & Nicolson, 1969.

Moodie, G. C. "On Political Scandals and Corruption." *Government and Opposition* 15 (1980): 208–222.

Mouzelis, Nicos. "Restructuring Structuration Theory." *Sociological review* 37 (1989): 613–635.

Mouzelis, Nicos P. *Organization and Bureaucracy*. Chicago: Aldine Publishing Co., 1967.

Myers, James. "China: the 'Germs' of Modernization." *Asian Survey* 25 (1985): 981–987.

———. "Another Look at Corruption." *Issues and Studies* 23 (1987): 28–49.

Myrdal, Gunnar. "A Call for Reform." *Development Digest* 6 (1968): 99–105.

Nagle, John D. *Introduction to Comparative Politics: Political System Performance in Three Worlds*. 2nd ed. Chicago: Nelson-Hall Publishers, 1989.

Nan Bo. *The Chinese in the Business Fad* (in Chinese). Chengdu: Chengdu Science and Technology University Press, 1993.

Nas, Terifik, Albert Price, and Charles Weber. "A Policy Oriented Theory of Corruption." *American Political Science Review* 80 (1986): 107–119.

Nathan, Andrew. *Chinese Democracy*. New York: Random House, 1985.

———. *China's Crisis: Dilemmas of Reform and Prospects for Democracy*. New York: Columbia University Press, 1990.

Naughton, Barry. "False Start and Second Wind: Financial Reforms in China Industrial System." In *The Political Economy of Reform in Post-Mao China*, edited by Elizabeth J. Perry and Christine Wong. Cambridge: Harvard University Press, 1985.

Niebuhr, Reinhold. *The Children of Light and the Children of Darkness*. New York: Scribner's, 1944.

Nye, Joseph S. "Corruption and Political Development: A Cost-Benefit Analysis." *American Political Science Review* 61 (1967): 417–427.

Oi, Jean. *State and Peasant in Contemporary China: The Political Economy of Village Government*. Berkeley, Calif.: University of California Press, 1989.(a)

———. "Market Reforms and Corruption in Rural China." *Studies in Comparative Communism* 22 (1989): 221-233.(b)

Oksenberg, Michael. "Local Leaders in Rural China, 1962–1965: Individual Attitudes, Bureaucratic Position, and Political Recruitment." In *Chinese Communist Party in Action*, edited by A. Doak Barnett. Seattle: University of Washington Press, 1969.

O'Neil, John, ed. *Modes of Individualism and Collectivism*. New York: St. Martin's, 1973.

Ostergaard, Clemens Stubbe. "Explaining China's Recent Political Corruption: Patterns, Remedies, and Counter Strategies at the Local Level." *Corruption and Reform* 1 (1986): 209–234.

Ostergaard, Clemens Stubbe and Christina Peterson. "Official Profiteering and the Tiananmen Square Demonstrations in China." *Corruption and Reform* 6 (1981): 87-107.

Palmier, Leslie. *The Control of Bureaucratic Corruption: Case Studies in Asia*. New Delhi: Allied Publishers, 1985.

Pang Shong, and Han Guang. "A Historical Review of Changes in the Party and Government Leadership System in China" (in Chinese). *Fuyin Baokan Ziliao*, 1 (1988): 13–32.

Parsons, Talcott. *Essays in Sociological Theory*. New York: The Free Press, 1954.

People's Handbook (in Chinese). Beijing: People's Publishing House, 1952.

Perez-Diaz, V. M. *State, Bureaucracy and Civil Society: A Critical Discussion of the Political Economy of Karl Marx*. London: Macmillan, 1978.

Perry, Elizabeth J., and Christine Wong, eds. *The Political Economy of Reform in Post-Mao China*. Cambridge, Mass.: Harvard University Press, 1985.

Peters, John G., and Susan Welch. "Politics, Corruption, and Political Culture." *American Politics Quarterly* 6 (1978): 345–356.

———. "Political Corruption in America: A Search for Definitions and Theory, or if Political Corruption is the Maintenance of American Politics." *American Political Science Review* 72 (1978): 974–984.

Popper, K. R. *The Open Society and Its Enemies*. London: Routledge & Kegan Paul, 1966.

Price, Jane L. *Cadres, Commanders, and Commissars: The Training of the Chinese Communist Leadership, 1920–45*. Boulder, Colo.: Westview Press, 1976.

Price, Robert M. *Society and Bureaucracy in Contemporary Ghana*. Berkeley: University of California Press, 1975.

Pye, Lucian. *Mandarin and the Cadre: China's Political Cultures*. Ann Arbor, Mich.: Center for Chinese Studies, the University of Michigan, 1988.

Qi Long. "The Hard Evidences of Bourgeois Savage Attack" (in Chinese). *Xinhua Yuebao* 2 (1952): 23–29.

Qian Qizhi. "Reflections on the Authorized Sizes of Local Agencies" (in Chinese). *Zhongguo Xingzheng Guanli* 51 (1989): 1–3.

Ren, Xiao. "The Dynamics and Process of Administrative Reforms in China, 1982–1988" (in chinese). *Zhengzhixue Yanjiu* 6 (1989): 8–28.

Research Institute of the Center for Rural Development. *Reforms Facing Institutional Innovations* (in Chinese). Shanghai: Sanlian Press, 1988.

Richman, B. A. *Industrial Society in Communist China*. New York: Random House, 1969.

Riskin, Carl. *China's Political Economy: The Quest for Development since 1949*. New York: Oxford University Press, 1987.

Robinson, James Harvey. *The Human Comedy*. London: The Bodley Head, 1937.

Rodzinski, Witold. *The People's Republic of China, A Concise Political History*. New York: The Free Press, 1988.

Rosario, Louise do. "Big Four, Less One." *Far Eastern Economic Review*, November 17, 1988, 91–92.

———. "Eternal Mandarins." *Far Eastern Economic Review*. November 9, 1989, 33–34.

Rose-Ackerman, Susan. "The Economics of Corruption." *Journal of Public Economics* 4 (1975): 187–203.

———. *Corruption: A Study in Political Economy*. New York: Academic Press, 1978.

Roth, Guenther. "Personal Rulership, Patromonialism, and Empire Building." In *Scholarship and Partisanship*, edited by R. Bendix and G. Roth. Berkeley and Los Angeles: University of California Press, 1971.

Rundquist, Barry S., Gerald Strom, and John Peter. "Corrupt Politicians and Their Electoral Support: Some Experimental Observations." *American Political Science Review* 71 (1979): 954–963.

Sakwa, Richard. *Gorbachev and His Reform, 1985–1990*. Englewood Cliffs, N.J.: Prentice-Hall, 1991.

Sands, Barbara N. "Decentralizing an Economy: The Role of Bureaucratic Corruption in China's Economic Reforms." *Public Choice* 65 (1990): 85–91.

Schaffer, B. "Access: A Theory of Corruption and Bureaucracy." *Public Administration and Development* 6 (1986): 357–376.

Schrecker, John E. *The Chinese Revolution in Historical Perspective*. New York: Greenwood Press, 1991.

Schurman, Franz. *Ideology and Organization in Communist China*. Berkeley: University of California Press, 1968.

Schwartz, C. A. "Corruption and Political Development in the USSR." *Comparative Politics* 11 (1979): 425–444.

Scott, James C. "The Analysis of Corruption in Developing Nations." *Comparative Studies in Society and History* 11 (1969): 325–341.

———. *Comparative Political Corruption.* Englewood Cliffs, N.J.: Prentice-Hall, 1972.

Selden, Mark. *The Yenan Way in Revolutionary China.* Cambridge, Mass.: Harvard University Press, 1971.

———. *The Political Economy of Chinese Development.* Armonk, N.Y.: M. E. Sharpe, Inc., 1993.

Senturia, Joseph J. "Corruption, Political." *Encyclopedia of the Social Sciences*, vol. 4. New York: Crowell-Collier-MacMillan, 1931.

Seshadri, K. "Bureaucracy: A Marxist Interpretation," *Administrative Change* 4 (1982): 175–203.

Shao Deman. *The History of Chinese Modern Political Thoughts.* Beijing: Law Publishing House, 1983.

Shils, Edward. *Political Development in the New States.* 's–Gravenhage: Mouton, 1962.

Shirk, Susan. "The Politics of Industrial Reform." In *The Political Economy of Reform in Post-Mao China*, edited by Elizabeth J. Perry and Christine Wong. Cambridge, Mass.: Harvard University Press, 1985.

———. *The Political Logic of Economic Reform in China.* Berkeley, Calif.: University of California Press, 1993.

Shumer, S. M. "Machiavelli: Republic Politics and Its Corruption." *Political Theory* 7 (1979): 5-34.

Sivalingam, S. "Bureaucratic Corruption in Malaysia: The Incongruence Between Social and Legal Norma." *Philippine Journal of Public Administration* 27 (1983): 418–435.

Smis, Konstantin M. *USSR—The Corrupt Society.* New York: Simon and Schuster, 1982.

Smith, Brain C. *Bureaucracy and Political Power.* Sussex: Wheatsheaf Books Ltd., 1988.

Smith, Charles W. "A Case Study of Structuration: the Pure-Bred Business," *Journal for the Theory of Social Behavior* 13,1 (March 1983): 3–17.

Solinger, Dorothy J. "Urban Entrepreneurs and the State: The Merger of State and Society." In *State and Society in China: the Consequences of Reform*, edited by Arthur Lewis Rosenbaum. Boulder, Colo.: Westview Press, 1992.

———. *China's Transition from Socialism: Statist Legacies and Market Reforms, 1980–1990.* Armonk, N.Y.: M. E. Sharpe, Inc., 1993.

Song Bincheng and Lei Xueya. "The Basic Situations of Institutional Changes and Reforms in the PRC" (in Chinese). *Fuyin Baokan Zhiliao*, May 1988, 23–24.

Spence, Jonathan. *The Search for Modern China.* New York: W. W. Norton & Company, 1990.

Staats, A. W. *Social Behaviorism*. Homewood, Ill: Dorsy Press, 1975.

Staats, S. J. "Corruption in the Soviet System," *Problems of Communism* 21 (1972): 40–47.

Stavis, Benedict. *China's Political Reforms: An Interim Report*. New York: Praeger, 1988.

Su Shangrao. "Institutional Changes of the Central Government" (in Chinese). *Chinese Administrative Management* 5 (1987): 27–32.

Su Ya and Jia Lusheng. *Who Is Able to Contract*? (in Chinese). Guangdong: Huacheng Press, 1990.

Sun, Yan. "The Chinese Protests of 1989: The Issue of Corruption." *Asian Survey*, 31 (1991): 762–783.

Sztompka, Piotr. *Sociological Dilemmas: Toward a Dialectic Paradigm*. New York: Academic Press, 1979.

Takahara, Alio. *Politics of Wage Policy in Post-Revolutionary China*. London: MacMillan Press Ltd., 1992.

Tan, Tammy. "Skepticism Greets Deng's Anticorruption Vow." *FBIS*, October 19, 1989, 13.

Teiwes, Frederich. *Politics and Purges in China*. New York: M. E. Sharpe, Inc., 1979.

———. *Politics at Mao's Court: Gao Gang and Party Factionalism in the Early 1950s*. Armonk, N. Y.: M. E. Sharpe, Inc., 1990.

Theobald, Robin. *Corruption, Development and Underdevelopment*. London: MacMillan Press Ltd., 1990.

Tilman, Robert O. "Emergence of Black-Market Bureaucracy: Administration, Development, and Corruption in the New States." *Public Administration Review* 28 (1968): 437–444.

Tong Zhimin. *The Reform of Cadre Management System in Socialist Countries* (in Chinese). Beijing: Guangming Ribao Press, 1987.

Tsou, Tang. *The Cultural Revolution and Post-Mao Reform: A Historical Perspective*. Chicago: University of Chicago Press, 1986.

Tucher, Robert C. *The Marx-Engels Reader*. New York: W. W. Norton & Company, 1978.

Tullock, Gordon. *The Economics of Special Privilege and Rent Seeking*. Boston: Kluwer Academic Publishers, 1989.

Unger, Jonathan. "The Struggle to Dictate China's Administration: The Conflict of Branches vs. Area vs. Reform." *The Australian Journal of Chinese Affairs* 18 (1987): 15–45.

Walder, Andrew G. *Communist Neo-Traditionalism: Work and Authority in Chinese Industry*. Berkeley: University of California Press, 1986.

Waley, Arthur. *The Analects of Confucius*. New York: The MacMillan Company, 1989.

Wang Hongmuo. *The Process of Reform and Openness* (in Chinese). Hunan: Hunan Publishing House, 1989.

Wang Jinye. "China's Loudou Phenomenon" (in Chinese). *Liao Wang* 36 (1989): 6–7.

Wang Huning. "The Changing Central-Local Relationship in China: Its Political Implications" (in Chinese). *Fudan Xuebao* 5 (1988): 1–8, 30.

———. *Anti-corruption, China's Experiment* (in Chinese). Haiko: Sanhuan Publisher, 1990.

Wang, James. *Contemporary Chinese Politics: An Introduction*. 2d ed. Englewood Cliffs, N.J.: Prentice-Hall, 1991.

Wang Yanan. *A Study of Chinese Bureaucratic Politics* (in Chinese). Beijing: Chinese Social Sciences Press, 1987.

Ward, Benjamin. "Forty Years of Chinese Socialism." In *Building a Nation-State: China after Forty*, edited by Joyce K. Kallgren. Berkeley, Calif.: Institute of East Asian Studies, 1990.

Waterbury, J. "Corruption, Political Stability and Development: Comparative Evidence from Egypt and Morocco." *Government and Opposition* 11 (1976): 426–445.

Watkins, J. W. N. "Ideal Types and Historical Explanations." In *Modes of Individualism and Collectivism*, edited by John O'Neil. London: Heinemann, 1973.

Weber, Max. "Bureaucracy." In *From Max Weber: Essays in Sociology*, edited by H. H. Gerth and C. Wright Mills. New York: Oxford University Press, 1958.

———. *Economy and Society*. Berkeley and Los Angeles: University of California Press, 1971.

Welch, Susan, and John G. Peter. "Attitudes of U.S. State Legislators Toward Political Corruption: Some Preliminary Findings." *Legislative Studies Quarterly* 2 (1977): 445–463.

Wen Yu. *China's Leftist Disaster* (in Chinese). Beijing: Chaohua Publisher, 1993.

Wendt, Alexander E. "The Agent-Structure Problem in International Relations Theory." *International Organization* 41 (1987): 335–370.

Werner, Simcha. "New Directions in the Study of Administrative Corruption." *Public Administration Review* 43 (1983): 146–154.

White, Gordon. "The Postrevolutionary Chinese State." In *State and Society in Contemporary China*, edited by Victor Nee and David Mozingo. Ithaca, N.Y.: Cornell University Press, 1983.

White, Lynn T. III. "Changing Concepts of Corruption in Communist China: Early 1950s vs. Early 1980s." *Issues and Studies* 24 (1988): 49–95.

———. *Policies of Chaos: The Organizational Causes of Violence in China's Cultural Revolution*. Princeton, N.J.: Princeton University Press, 1989.

Whyte, Martin King. "Who Hates Bureaucracy? A Chinese Puzzle." In *Remaking the Economic Institutions of Socialism: China and Eastern Europe*, edited by Victor Nee, David Stark, and Mark Selden. Stanford,

Calif.: Stanford University Press, 1989.

Williams, Robert. *Political Corruption in Africa*. Aldershot: Gower, 1987.

Wilson, James Q. and Richard J. Herrnstein. *Crime and Human Nature*. New York: Simon and Schuster, 1985.

World Bank. *China: Between Plan and Market*. Washington DC: The World Bank, 1990.

Wraith, Ronald, and Edgar Simpkins. *Corruption in Developing Countries*. London: Allen and Unwin, 1963.

Wu Haimin. *The Republic Gave An Ultimatum: How 50,000 Corrupt Officials Turned Themselves In* (in Chinese). Beijing: Xueyang Publisher, 1990.

Wu Hongwei. "Our Party is the Leading Force in Combating Corruption" (in Chinese). *RMRB*, July 31, 1989.

Xie Baogui. "The Function of the Chinese Procuratorial Organ in the Combat against Corruption." *Asian Journal of Public Administration* 10 (1988): 71–79.

Xie Yong. *The Chinese Communist Party's Discipline Handbook* (in Chinese). Beijing: China Prospect Publisher, 1987.

Xue Muqiao. *China's Socialist Economy*. Beijing: Foreign Language Press, 1981.

———. *Talk on the Reform of Economic System*. Beijing: Economic Management Press, 1984.

Yan Jiaqi and Gao Gao. *The Ten-Year History of the Cultural Revolution*. Tianjin: Tianjin People's Publishing House, 1988.

Yan Yan, "Resolutely Stopping the Unhealthy Tendency of Building Private Houses among Leading Cadres" (in Chinese). *Liao Wang* 18 (1990): 17–18.

Yang, Lien-sheng. "The Concept of 'Pao' as a Basis for Social Relations in China." In *Chinese Thought and Institution*, edited by John K. Fairbank. Chicago: The University of Chicago Press, 1957.

Yang, Mayfair Mei-Hui. "The Gift Economy and State Power in China." *Comparative Studies in Society and History* 31 (1989): 25–54.

Yang Jisheng. "The Dual-Track Phenomenon" (in Chinese). *Liao Wang* 37 (1988): 10–12.

Yao Hen and Luo Zhongmin. "The CCP's Anti-Corruption Struggle during the Japanese War" (in Chinese). *Digest of the Party History* 3 (1989): 58–59.

Yeh, Miton. "Modernization and Corruption in Mainland China." *Issues and Studies* 23 (1987): 11–27.

Yu Guangyuan. "Resist the Attacks of the Bourgeois Class, Determinedly Uphold the Leadership of the Working Class." In *The People's Republic of China, 1949–1979, A Documentary Survey*, vol. 1, edited by Harold C. Hinton. Delaware: Scholarly Resources, Inc. 1980.

Zhang Fuling. "The Establishment of State Apparatus During the Early PRC and Its Characteristics" (in Chinese). *Fuyin Baokan ZiliaoZhongguo Xiandaishi*, October 1989, 159–163.

Zheng Derong and Zhunang, eds. *Teaching the History of the Chinese Communist Party* (in Chinese). Jiling: Jiling People's Publishing House, 1980.

Zhongguo Zhengfa Daxue, ed. *Selected Readings on Government Integrity* (in Chinese). Beijing: Zhongguo Zhengfa Daxue, 1989.

Zhu Jiaming. "The Cultural Revolution: Its Economic Roots and Effects" (in Chinese). *Zhishifenzi* 2 (1986): 22–27.

Zhu Jianhua and Zhu Yang, eds., *The History of the People's Republic of China* (in Chinese). Haerbin: Heilongjian People's Publishing House, 1989.

Zhu Qinfang. "The State of Mind of Urban Workers" (in Chinese). *Liao Wang* 2 (1989): 8–10.

Index

About the Author

TING GONG is an Assistant Professor of Political Science at Ramapo College of New Jersey. She holds advanced degrees from Fudan University in China and Syracuse University.

www.ingramcontent.com/pod-product-compliance
Ingram Content Group UK Ltd.
Pitfield, Milton Keynes, MK11 3LW, UK
UKHW041637031026
15587UKWH00001B/351